Task Force Patriot and the End of Combat Operations in Iraq

Pat Proctor

GOVERNMENT INSTITUTES
An imprint of
THE SCARECROW PRESS, INC.
Lanham • Toronto • Plymouth, UK
2012

 **Government Institutes**

Published by Government Institutes
An imprint of The Scarecrow Press, Inc.
A wholly owned subsidary of The Rowman & Littlefield Publishing Group, Inc.
4501 Forbes Boulevard, Suite 200, Lanham, Maryland 20706
http://www.govinstpress.com

Estover Road, Plymouth PL6 7PY, United Kingdom

British Library Cataloguing in Publication Information Available

Library of Congress Cataloging-in-Publication Data
Proctor, Pat, 1971–
    Task Force Patriot and the end of combat operations in Iraq / Pat Proctor.
        p. cm.
    Includes index.
    ISBN 978-1-60590-777-2 (cloth : alk. paper) — ISBN 978-1-60590-778-9 (e-book)
    1. Proctor, Pat, 1971– 2. United States. Army. Task Force Patriot. 3. Iraq War,
2003—Personal narratives, American. I. Title.
    DS79.766.P76A3 2012
    956.7044'342—dc23   2011036285

™
∞   The paper used in this publication meets the minimum requirements of American
National Standard for Information Sciences—Permanence of Paper for Printed Library
Materials, ANSI/NISO Z39.48-1992.

Printed in the United States of America

To my best friend, Aree

Contents

Acknowledgments   vii

Introduction   1

Chapter 1   Ad Dawr   9

Chapter 2   Corporal Carrasco   39

Chapter 3   Lt. Col. Ahmed al Fahal   63

Chapter 4   The Jadir Brothers   81

Chapter 5   Sheikh Sabah al Shimiri   119

Chapter 6   Task Force Wolfhounds   163

Epilogue   199

Index   205

About the Author   217

Acknowledgments

*F*irst, I would like to thank all of the men and women who have stood shoulder to shoulder with me through two tours in Iraq, and especially all of the Proud Americans of Task Force Patriot. Special thanks go to Lt. Col. Robert "Bubba" Cain for teaching me everything I will ever know about commanding a battalion and Maj. Tim Blackwell and Maj. Matt Payne for teaching me everything I will ever know about running one. Thank you, also, to Mike Samander; with your wise council over evening cigars and your keen negotiating skills, you, as much as any soldier in the task force, contributed to our success. I apologize to all of the civilians and soldiers in Task Force Patriot that I was not able to mention in this book. Please know that I will forever be in awe of the sacrifices you have made for your country.

Second, I would like to thank my agent, Grace Freedson, for believing in me and my work way past the point where it made logical sense. Your passion was a huge inspiration to me in completing this book.

I would also like to thank Mr. James Hill and all of the hardworking folks at the Department of the Army's Office of the Chief of Public Affairs.

Thank you to my lovely wife, Aree, and my children, Amy and Jonathan, for their heroic patience with all of the rigors of being an Army family. Thank you, as well, to my mom and dad, Patricia and Ronald, for all of their help holding down the fort each day I was gone.

And, above all, I thank God, through whom all things are made possible.

The views expressed in this book are those of the author and do not reflect the official policy or position of the Department of the Army, Department of Defense, or the U.S. government.

Introduction

 $\mathcal{T}$ he US Army that went to war in Iraq in March 2003 was the US Army that the Vietnam War built. That is not to say that the Army was the same Army that fought in Vietnam. In fact, it was anything but. Rather, the US Army that crossed the border from Kuwait into Iraq on 21 March 2003 was profoundly changed by the US Army's experience in Vietnam—or rather the American military's interpretation of that experience. While some of these changes were for the better, others created unintended consequences when the US Army was faced with yet another grueling insurgency, this time in Iraq.

In the early 1980s, when the US defense establishment finally began to grapple with the implications of the Vietnam War that had ended a decade before, they sought a clear guide for policy makers in deciding when and where to use military force (and, more importantly, when and where not to use military force). Their goal was to prevent the US military from becoming mired in similar wars in the future. President Ronald Reagan's secretary of defense, Caspar Weinberger, was the first to enunciate a clear policy. It was later amended by Chairman of the Joint Chiefs of Staff, Gen. Colin Powell. The policy recommendations, which have since become known as the Powell Doctrine, advocated the use of overwhelming force in conflicts with clear objectives and definable exit strategies. The American security establishment's answer to the Vietnam War, then, was to not fight another Vietnam War.

The logical conclusion of the Powell Doctrine was Air-Land Battle. This military doctrine reached its zenith during the 1990 Gulf War—an aerial campaign of massive, precision firepower followed by a brutally effective lightning invasion that swept aside the world's fourth-largest military and restored Kuwaiti sovereignty. But, most importantly, within a matter of months, the US military returned to the United States to fanfare and parades.

It was not until thirteen years later, when the US military found itself embroiled in a guerilla war against a variety of enemy factions in a hostile land full of hostile people, that the US Army realized its folly; it had deluded itself into believing that it could simply choose not to fight wars it was not good at fighting. Yet, in the finest American tradition, the officers of the US military rolled up their sleeves and started trying to figure out the problem.

The first tool they turned to was actually an offshoot of Air-Land Battle: Effects-Based Operations. The doctrine advocated analyzing the environment as a system of systems and trying to identify key nodes in that system that, if acted upon, would produce the desired effect. Unfortunately, the theory was a victim of its origins; it was designed by airpower theorists to select targets for bombing, where the effects of actions could be accurately predicted. Such was not the case when your nodes were people rather than power plants and your action was building schools instead of dropping bombs.

As Effects-Based Operations fell, counterinsurgency rose. Gen. David Petraeus and a corps of civilian and military intellectuals began an insurgency of their own, inside the US military; they revived a doctrine that had lain dormant since the age of post–World War II anticolonialism and had briefly found favor in the latter days of the Vietnam War, before being rejected by the 1980s revisionists within the US Army. The US military insurgents were successful, enshrining their doctrine in Field Manual (FM) 3-24, *Counterinsurgency*. US Army and coalition forces must, this doctrine demanded, isolate the insurgents by living among the populace, protecting them from the insurgents, and addressing their grievances. The populace would then, this doctrine promised, turn away from the insurgents and toward the government of their country. Gen. Petraeus briefly took command of the Combined Arms Center, in charge of all of the Army's combat training centers and the Army's premier midgrade educational institution, the US Army Command and General Staff College at Fort Leavenworth, Kansas. Once counterinsurgency was firmly entrenched as the new paradigm for US Army operations, Gen.

Petraeus went forward to take command of all coalition forces in Iraq in 2007 and put counterinsurgency into practice.

Another change the Vietnam War wrought on the US Army was its view of the media in warfare. The "credibility gap" created during the Johnson years, in the view of 1980s military revisionists, had created a hostile public that refused to believe US military claims and turned against the war. The military solution was simple: never lie to the press. The post-1980s Army struggled, however, to put this solution into practice. Small, short wars like Panama, Grenada, and even the Gulf War allowed the US military to tightly control access to the battlefield and shape what the press saw or did not see. It was not until press coverage of the disastrous military operation in Mogadishu, Somalia (immortalized in the book and movie *Blackhawk Down*), that the US military began to appreciate that it had wished away the problem of media coverage.

The solution the US military arrived at on the eve of the Iraq war was, at the time, radical: absolute disclosure. International media would be "embedded" with US and coalition forces and would accompany them during the invasion, with unfettered access to the battlefield and no censorship of the stories they sent back to their respective countries. The program was wildly successful during the invasion, when the war was going swimmingly for the coalition. But once the invasion gave way to arduous guerilla warfare, the media picture became a liability to the war effort. It is an American media axiom that "if it bleeds, it leads"; every night the US and international press served up a steady diet of car bombs, suicide vests, and improvised explosive devices (IEDs), and the American public began to sour on the war. The US Army began to sour on the media, too, becoming increasingly insular and hostile to press coverage of their operations.

Gen. Petraeus' arrival and the strategy the president had sent him to implement—the Iraq "surge"—finally stopped the bleeding. At the same time that he changed the focus to protecting the populace and addressing their grievances, Petraeus threw open the shutters of Multi-National Force–Iraq (MNF-I, the senior military headquarters in Iraq), opening it to press scrutiny. He candidly admitted how bad the situation was and allowed the press renewed access to every corner of the war. This effort, combined with the success of Petraeus' new counterinsurgency strategy, "reset" the media's preconceptions about the war and created a new narrative of returning from the brink. US public opinion followed, and within two years, the American public could once again see the proverbial light at the end of the tunnel.

This turnaround in public opinion finally gave President George W. Bush the political and strategic freedom to chart a course for America's exit from Iraq. In late 2008, the United States and Iraq settled on a security agreement that had US forces leaving Iraqi cities by June 2009, ending combat operations by August 2010, and leaving Iraq by December 2011.

A final change the Vietnam War wrought on the US Army in the Iraq war was the practice of one-year unit rotations. During the Vietnam War, each soldier would rotate into South Vietnam to complete an individual one-year tour. The practice created a host of problems. It was difficult to create cohesive units because of the massive personnel turnover that was constantly taking place. The unit was constantly faced with the imperative of training new soldiers for the rigors of the dangerous combat environment before they were hurt or killed by those dangers. For married soldiers, their families had to carry on alone, without the support of other unit families.

Once it was clear that the US Army was not going to be able to simply declare victory and leave Iraq, the Army leadership, wary of the Vietnam example, decided to rotate entire combat brigades into and out of theater. This solved the problem of training new soldiers; they would all train together—first at their home station and then in Iraq, under the guidance of the departing unit—before being fully exposed to the dangers of combat. Each brigade's families, supported by a military rear detachment, could lean on one another for support while their soldiers were deployed.

Yet this practice also created problems that the US Army was never able to solve throughout the Iraq war. On the eve of the War on Terrorism, the US military had conceived and implemented a process called Army Force Generation (ARFORGEN) in which units would go through a "life cycle" of resetting, training, and becoming available for deployment. The massive demand on the small, all-volunteer Army for personnel in Iraq turned this cycle—which began to be sarcastically referred to as Iraq-FORGEN—into a brutal merry-go-round of training, deployment, and redeployment that wreaked havoc on soldiers and their families. Moreover, the complex environment of Iraq, simply put, took more than a year to effectively understand. Every year US forces switched out, but Iraqi politicians, security leaders, sheikhs, and of course insurgents never left. No matter how good the transfer of information from old unit to new, each new force that arrived in Iraq had to contend with a three- to four-month "memory gap" in which all of these Iraqi stakeholders were able to exploit American ignorance to advance their own interests.

Six years of war in Iraq had profoundly transformed the US Army as well. The Americans who entered Iraq in March 2003 led with heavily armored M1 Abrams main battle tanks and M2 Bradley infantry fighting vehicles, but trailed with unarmored, thin-skinned trucks and high-mobility multiwheeled vehicles (HMMWVs, pronounced "hum-vees"). The soldiers mostly wore woodland-patterned camouflage and nothing for protection but a Kevlar helmet. If they were lucky, they had desert camouflage and a flak vest. They fought with the massive firepower and lightning speed of Air-Land Battle, with little consideration for security in rear areas. The Iraqi populace was an obstacle to be bypassed on the way to finding and killing massed formations of Iraqi soldiers.

The US Army that had emerged by mid-2009 would have been unrecognizable to the same soldiers six years before. The Americans had parked their tanks or shipped them back to the United States. In their place, heavily armored HMMWVs and mine-resistant armored personnel vehicles (MRAPs, a sort of huge, armored bus) now lumbered about the battlefield, seldom slowing or stopping on their way from place to place. When they did stop, heavily armored soldiers, with high-tech digital camouflage, state-of-the-art body armor, and precision optics atop M4 carbines, stepped out onto a complex battlefield, equally prepared to close with and destroy the enemy, engage in politics with local sheikhs and imams, or plan projects to rebuild infrastructure. This was the military force that US Marine general Charles Krulak had envisioned in the 1990s when he predicted his "three-block war" (in which forces would be fighting, doing peacekeeping, and engaging in humanitarian assistance, all "within the space of three contiguous city blocks"). This was the counterinsurgency US Army.

The Dragon Brigade (4th Brigade, 1st Infantry Division) was conceived in the darkest days of the Iraq war. In 2004, as the demand for personnel in Iraq was becoming acute, the US Army began an effort it called "growing the Army," in which it created additional brigade combat teams (self-contained, multifunctional Army units of around 3,000 soldiers that could deploy as independent, modular units, without their parent headquarters). The Dragon Brigade, established in January 2006 at Fort Riley, Kansas, was an incremental step in this effort.

The brigade was created from scratch, with personnel and equipment flowing into the unit throughout 2006. The brigade was not scheduled to deploy until 2008, but the demand of the Iraq surge, combined with the campaigning of the brigade's first commander, Col. Ricky Gibbs, convinced the Army to rush them into the fight. They were still receiving equipment even after they arrived in the toughest areas of Baghdad in February 2007. The unit's deployment was extended to fifteen months, and it saw some of the toughest fighting of the surge, losing nearly one hundred soldiers during its deployment. In the process, it also established itself as one of the toughest light infantry brigades in the conventional Army.

Due to the desperate demand for ground troops during the surge, the Dragon Brigade's field artillery battalion, Task Force Patriot (2nd Battalion, 32nd Field Artillery), parked its towed howitzers and joined the other combat arms battalions of the brigade as a ground maneuver force. The battalion was stationed in the Mansour district of Baghdad, just across Route Irish from its sister battalion, Task Force Black Lions (1st Battalion, 28th Infantry). (Route Irish was the road from the coalition's fortified "Green Zone" to the Baghdad International Airport—BIAP—often referred to at the time as the deadliest road on earth due to the constant threat of IEDs.) The battalion was split from the Dragon Brigade and attached to the Strike Brigade (2nd Brigade, 101st Airborne Division).

Task Force Patriot got its name from its battalion crest (an insignia worn on the beret and dress uniform of every soldier in the battalion), which bore the words "Proud Americans," a moniker also frequently used to identify the battalion. This battalion had last seen combat in South Vietnam, including participation in the incursion into Cambodia in 1970, before being deactivated in the mid-1970s. Now it was back in the thick of the fight, but without its big guns.

While the rest of the Dragon Brigade saw heavy casualties, Task Force Patriot had no soldiers killed, though tragically its commander was gravely wounded. Lt. Col. Greg Gadson, Patriot 6, was traveling to a sister battalion to attend a memorial for fallen soldiers when his up-armored HMMWV was struck by an explosively formed projectile (EFP, a particularly lethal form of IED). Lt. Col. Gadson was evacuated from Iraq and lost both legs. He was replaced by Lt. Col. Mike Lawson, who commanded Task Force Patriot for the remainder of its deployment.

As soon as the Dragon Brigade returned from Iraq, it was back on the Iraq-FORGEN treadmill. Over the next year, from summer 2008 to summer 2009, the vast majority of its personnel changed, including all of its battalion commanders and the brigade commander. Its equipment was refurbished and reissued, and it hurriedly prepared for its next deployment. While the Dragon Brigade was slated for deployment to Iraq, there were strong indications that it might be diverted to Afghanistan. As a result, the brigade spent considerable energy preparing for that war; the Proud Americans fired over 10,000 artillery rounds, training to provide artillery fires, rather than maneuver forces, in Afghanistan. Throughout the brigade's training, personnel and equipment continued to arrive and be hastily integrated into the unit.

It was not until just before the brigade's capstone training event, its mission readiness exercise (MRX) at the National Training Center (NTC) at Fort Irwin, California, that the Dragon Brigade staff finally concluded that the brigade would indeed go to Iraq and that the Proud Americans battalion would indeed be a maneuver unit. With only three months left until deployment, Task Force Patriot had to hastily reorganize and retrain, a process its sister infantry battalions had had a year to complete.

It was at this time that I joined Task Force Patriot as its S3 (operations officer). I was a relatively senior major to be beginning the job because of the strange course my Army career had taken to that point.

I had been an observer/controller (O/C, a kind of coach/grader) at the NTC at Fort Irwin when the Iraq war began. Back then, the training center was still training Army forces to fight Air-Land Battle, to face off against Soviets in the plains of West Germany, despite the fact that the Soviet Union had collapsed over a decade before.

We O/Cs were out in the Mojave Desert, training the first Stryker brigade (a highly digitized, networked, interconnected, motorized light infantry brigade), when the Marines pulled down the statue of Saddam Hussein in Baghdad. We grumbled, sure we were going to miss the whole war. However, once it became clear that the US Army was in for a long, grueling conflict, NTC began a startling transformation into a guerilla warfare laboratory. This was the front line of the Army's journey from Air-Land Battle to Effects-Based Operations to counterinsurgency. None of that made us feel any better about being trapped there for three-year tours while our peers went off to fight the war.

I finally made my escape by going to the yearlong US Army Command and General Staff College (CGSC) in its first winter class since

World War II (a side effect of the sudden demand for majors in the war). During the course, I became fascinated with the changing face of war and decided to take a detour from the normal Army officer path of progression. I applied for the US Army School of Advanced Military Studies (SAMS), both an educational institution and a think tank for emerging doctrinal concepts and military theory. I was accepted but would not be able to begin for seven months after the end of CGSC.

I finally saw my chance to deploy and finagled a short, six-month tour in Iraq. It was a three-way "drug deal" between the Center for Army Lessons Learned (CALL, which wanted to capture lessons from the senior headquarters in Iraq); SAMS (which wanted me to do research for my projected monograph, a requirement of the course); and MNF-I (which was happy to have free labor). I was told before I arrived that I would work in the information operations (IO) cell, which was related to my proposed monograph topic. When I arrived, I discovered that they wanted me to help create an IO cell—Gen. George Casey Jr., then commander of MNF-I, had abolished his, and his staff wanted to build a new one before Gen. David Petraeus arrived. After spending the first three months of 2007 standing up the IO cell, I snuck my way onto the Joint Strategic Assessment Team, a cast of luminaries (including legends like Col. H. R. McMaster and Ambassador Robert Ford) assembled by Gen. Petraeus and Ambassador Crocker to create a plan for implementing the surge in Iraq.

After Iraq, it was back to Fort Leavenworth, Kansas, for SAMS. The emerging concept that was being incubated within its walls was "operational design," a postcounterinsurgency method for understanding, identifying, and solving problems on a complex, ever-changing battlefield. It rejected the certitude and mechanical planning of conventional military operations and instead advocated a sort of iterative experimentation to achieve success in an environment of ill-defined problems. It is difficult to overstate what a departure this thinking was from the traditional planning paradigm that had informed military planning since the age of Napoleon. For a military culture that rewards decisive, even audacious action, deliberation and "looking before you leap" was revolutionary.

Nor can I overstate the profound effect this new way of thinking had on me when, following SAMS and a mercifully short obligatory stint as a division planner, I was let out of purgatory to join the Proud Americans. I was a bit long in the tooth for a battalion S3, but no less eager to rejoin the fight. I arrived just in time to travel with the battalion to NTC and then deploy Task Force Patriot to Iraq.

• 1 •

Ad Dawr

*T*he weeks before Task Force Patriot (2nd Battalion, 32nd Field Artillery) deployed to Iraq were a flurry of activity. After the battalion returned from the National Training Center (NTC) at Fort Irwin, California, an inevitable engine groaned to life, pulling us through the myriad of activities that had to be completed to move our 350-man organization from Fort Riley, Kansas, to Camp Buehring, Kuwait, and then on to northern Iraq. After four years of deploying brigades to Iraq and Afghanistan, this engine had not exactly become a well-oiled machine, but it did move soldiers from here to there. There were records to update and inoculations to receive. There was last-minute equipment and personnel to receive. There were connexes (large metal shipping containers) to load and move to the rail yard, and barracks and headquarters buildings to close.

But, for the staff of Task Force Patriot, the most important task was planning what the battalion would do once it arrived in Iraq, how it would fight its little corner of the war. The first challenge was figuring out exactly what corner of Iraq that would be. The Dragon Brigade (4th Brigade, 1st Infantry Division) had known for a year (rumors of an Afghanistan diversion aside) what brigade it would replace in Iraq; it would go to the Salah ad Din province to replace the Bronco Brigade (3rd Brigade, 25th Infantry Division)—like the Dragon Brigade, a light infantry brigade—from Schofield Barracks, Hawaii. A short survey of the Secret Internet Protocol Router Network (SIPRNet, a sort of secret version of the World Wide Web only accessible by the US government and select allies) quickly identified that the Bronco Brigade's field artillery battalion, Task Force Steel (3rd Battalion, 7th Field Artillery), was operating as a motorized infantry battalion in the Tikrit *qa'da* (district). The Task Force Patriot staff made the logical assumption that the battalion would replace this like-sized unit and assume a similar mission.

The staff began its mission analysis, the process of identifying all of the facts about Tikrit qa'da, our projected area of operations (AO). Using the SIPRNet, we were able to identify names, faces, and parties for the political leaders in the provincial government. We identified several of the key US military facilities in the area, and the key Iraqi police and army units with which the battalion might be working. The goal of this search was to identify questions that Task Force Patriot's commander, Lt. Col. Cain, could carry forward when he went with the Dragon Brigade commander, Col. Henry "Hank" Arnold III, and the other battalion commanders to Iraq for a predeployment site survey (PDSS) of the brigade's anticipated area of operations.

Lt. Col. Robert "Bubba" Cain was older than most brand-new battalion commanders—in his mid-forties—because he had served as an enlisted soldier before becoming an officer. Before enlisting he had been a rebellious youth in small-town Alabama and then starting quarterback at Troy State University. He was thin and weathered and fought hard to hide a weariness that occasionally overtook him. But he was passionate about his profession and genuinely loved every soldier he commanded. Combined with his easygoing nature and his personable southern manner, he engendered fierce loyalty in everyone who served under him. He also had the solid competence of a very experienced combat veteran; this would be his third deployment to Iraq since the beginning of the war.

Lt. Col. Bubba Cain took command of the Proud Americans just a week before I arrived at the unit, and just a few weeks before the battalion departed for NTC. We were lucky. A few officers showed up after our culminating training event, just in time to say good-bye to their families and get on the plane. It was Iraq-FORGEN logic at work. As long as a unit had all of its people and all of its equipment before it departed, everything would turn out fine. It completely disregarded the need to train soldiers before they deployed and get their families settled and integrated into the family readiness group (FRG, a support group run by the spouses of soldiers in each unit to provide support for families while the unit's soldiers were deployed). This kind of "just-in-time manning" had become the norm in an Army stressed to rebuild and deploy units in rapid succession.

"Patriot 6," Lt. Col. Bubba Cain, the commander of Task Force Patriot, returned from his PDSS with news that threw the staff into yet another iteration of mission analysis. He had completed his entire PDSS believing that we would assume responsibility for the Tikrit qa'da. However, just as he returned, he was told we would take Tuz qa'da, a small qa'da in the extreme southeast of the Salah ad Din province.

After a few weeks of planning for this new area, the Dragon Brigade staff finally settled on an arrangement of its battalions. We would be replacing both Task Force Steel in the Tikrit qa'da and elements of Task Force Cacti (2nd Battalion, 35th Infantry) in the ad Dawr qa'da. The staff conducted additional mission analysis to capture what information it could about the unfamiliar ad Dawr qa'da. We were also now able, because of the contacts Lt. Col. Cain had made during the PDSS, to make contact with the units we would replace and get much more current information about both qa'das.

When we were satisfied we had gathered as much data as we could, we departed from the normal, analytical methods of military planning and paused to better educate ourselves about our projected area and what we were being asked to do. We divided the staff into four two-man working groups—studying the strategic context for our mission, each of the two qa'das, and the history of the region—with a time and date to report to the whole group. In these group sessions, we discussed the ideas each working group provided and consolidated them into a shared understanding.

As we brought all of these perspectives together, a picture began to emerge of our area and what we should be doing there. Salah ad Din province was the home province of Saddam Hussein and the center of power under his regime. Even after the fall of the regime, the province remained the most important in Sunni Arab Iraq, its cultural, intellectual, and economic center. Since the beginning of the war, the battalion's area of operations, the Tikrit and ad Dawr qa'das, had become a study in contrasts. The Tikrit qa'da contained the provincial capital and many of the most powerful provincial leaders. However, just downstream on the Tigris River in the ad Dawr qa'da, the people had no political power at all; in the early 2009 provincial elections, the qa'da did not win a single provincial council seat. The upcoming national elections, scheduled for early 2010, would select new parliamentarians for the Council of Representatives in Baghdad but would not remedy the disenfranchisement of ad Dawr within Salah ad Din province.

In the midst of this disenfranchisement was a huge pool of soon-to-be-unemployed, military-aged males—the Sons of Iraq. This hodgepodge military force, stood up by Sunni sheikhs as part of the al Sawah ("the Awakening" movement) to defeat al Qaeda in Iraq, was now in a state of limbo. The central government in Baghdad didn't want them but continued to pay them—reluctantly and often late—for fear they would drift into the ranks of insurgent groups. In our area, there were over 1,500 Sons of Iraq, an appealing prize for our dominant insurgent group, Jaysh Rijal al Tariqa al Naqshabandiyah (JRTN, literally "Army of the Men of the Order of Naqshabandi," the armed wing of the New Ba'ath Party).

The brigade had directed the Proud Americans to advise and assist Iraqi police and army units in AO Proud Americans. Yet all of the reports from the units the battalion would replace and the military transition team (MiTT) in the area uniformly praised the quality of both the Iraqi police and army. Advising and assisting the Iraqi security forces would require very little effort.

Another factor that loomed large over our impending deployment was the transition that would soon take place in Iraq. President Obama had already announced that he would reduce US forces in Iraq to 50,000 by August 2010 (this policy was actually a fulfillment of the security agreement between the United States and Iraq made by the Bush administration in mid-2008). Indications were that the brigade would begin some dramatic transition around March 2010. It was unclear whether that meant redeployment (returning to the United States) or expansion to a much larger area of operations, but it was clear that the Patriot battalion was under a time crunch, with only about six months—from October 2009 to March 2010—to concentrate on the Tikrit and ad Dawr qa'das. We had to be realistic about what we could accomplish in that short time.

The staff pulled all of these elements together to form our campaign plan. We believed that if we did nothing, ad Dawr's disenfranchisement would worsen, and the Sons of Iraq would be fired and sent back into their communities unemployed. This would leave the ad Dawr qa'da with 500 military-aged males, many former insurgents, available for recruitment by the dominant insurgent group in our area, JRTN. Our goal was that the Sons of Iraq find gainful employment and ad Dawr find a legitimate, nonviolent voice in the politics of Salah ad Din province. Task Force Patriot, then, had three problems:

1. We only had six months to affect the situation in our AO. After that, qa'da governments and security forces would be on their own.
2. There was a sizable force of Sons of Iraq that the government was reluctant to pay. JRTN was already actively recruiting them, and these were all potential insurgents if the situation deteriorated after we departed.
3. Ad Dawr qa'da had no political representation in the Salah ad Din provincial government. When coalition money departed, reconstruction projects in the qa'da (which provided both employment and an influx of cash into the local economy) would dry up, fomenting discontent in the rural populace (which contained a large number of former Sons of Iraq).

Our plan to solve these problems was to try to find alternate employment for the Sons of Iraq and to create a relationship between the ad Dawr qa'da government and the Salah ad Din provincial government that would endure after US forces departed. In addition, of course, as directed by Col. Arnold, we would partner with Iraqi security forces in our area of operations. This formed the foundation of the campaign plan that the task force carried forward into Iraq.

We put together our plan and briefed the battalion's battery and company commanders only days before we began loading planes and departing for Kuwait, en route to Iraq. I deployed with the battalion commander and the bulk of the battalion, but a few officers deployed early to prepare the way for Task Force Patriot's arrival in Kuwait. This advance party was led by the battalion executive officer (XO), Maj. Tim Blackwell. While the rest of the battalion spent a mercifully short time at Camp Buehring, the hot, sandy training way station for units awaiting aircraft to enter Iraq, Maj. Blackwell was not so lucky. He ended up spending nearly six weeks in Buehring because, after the battalion moved forward, the brigade tasked him to remain and take charge of the trail personnel who were the last to travel to Iraq. When he finally arrived in Iraq, he joked that he had been there long enough to legitimately begin wearing the combat patch indicating he had served a combat tour with US Army Central Command (ARCENT), the unit responsible for Kuwait.

Maj. Tim Blackwell had preceded me as the battalion S3 (operations officer) before becoming the XO, second in command of the battalion. Blackwell was a second-generation soldier, a graduate of Cameron University in Lawton, Oklahoma (just outside the gates of Fort Sill, Oklahoma, spiritual home of the US Army field artillery branch). He had previously deployed to Iraq as part of a MiTT and was severely wounded by an improvised explosive device (IED), leaving him permanently unable to join the younger soldiers in the daily ritual run for physical training. He instead maintained his physical fitness by lifting weights. As a result, he was a big, imposing African American. The Proud Americans' junior officers often jokingly compared him to Debo, the bullying antagonist in the movie *Fridays*. He was firm but fair, and he was deeply conscientious about his duty to keep the battalion—and the battalion commander—out of trouble.

While Maj. Blackwell was enjoying sunny Camp Buehring, Kuwait, Lt. Col. Cain and I traveled to Taji, along with the other commanders and S3s of the Dragon Brigade, to attend the Counterinsurgency–Stability Operations Course (COIN-SOC). This weeklong course, a requirement for every brigade combat team entering Iraq, was developed in the early days of the counterinsurgency revolution that swept the US Army to promulgate the new doctrine across the force. Now that the US Army had internalized the doctrine, the role of the course had changed. While there were still a few classes, a great deal of the course was now consumed by visits from the brigade's higher commanders—Maj. Gen. Caslen of Multi-National Division–North (MND-North, the 25th Infantry Division from Hawaii); Lt. Gen. Jacoby of Multi-National Corps–Iraq (MNC-I, I Corps from Fort Lewis, Washington); and Gen. Odierno of Multi-National Force-Iraq (MNF-I, the highest coalition headquarters in Iraq). Each shared his understanding of Iraq and the Dragon Brigade's future AO.

COIN-SOC also presented us with an opportunity to meet some of the current military commanders in our future area of operations as well as a few of the key Iraqi political and military leaders. The most important of these sessions was presented by Col. Walter Piatt, commander of the Bronco Brigade that our Dragon Brigade would replace. With him he brought two Iraqi-American interpreters, one an attractive but barely

competent young woman called Rasha, the other an Iraqi man. Both
wore Iraqi-made imitation army combat uniforms (ACUs). Col. Piatt also
brought three leaders from Salah ad Din—Maj. Gen. Hamed (the provincial director of police, PDOP); Maj. Gen. Salah (the Kurdish commander
of the 4th Iraqi Army Division); and Brig. Gen. (ret.) Abdullah Jebarra
(provincial council member and former deputy governor).

The afternoon was stolen by Brig. Gen. (ret.) Abdullah. He spoke
Arabic for a few minutes, until it was clear that Col. Piatt's female inter-
preter, Rasha, was unable to keep up, and then began speaking English.
He stood up and walked to a Salah ad Din map projected on a screen
at the front of the classroom and began describing a massive scheme to
divert irrigation water from the Tigris into the deepest reaches of the al
Jazeera al Tikrit (literally "the desert west of Tikrit") and the al Jalaam al
Tikrit (literally "the desert east of Tikrit").

The audience, the leaders of the Dragon Brigade, watched in rapt
attention. Breaking the spell, Col. Piatt asked Brig. Gen. (ret.) Abdullah
Hussein al Jebarra al Jibouri how much his scheme would cost. Without
hesitating, Brig. Gen. (ret.) Abdullah responded, "Forty-five million dollars" (well beyond the total resources a brigade would get for an entire year
for Commander's Emergency Response Program funds, and ninety times
the amount a brigade could get approved for a single project). Even Brig.
Gen. (ret.) Abdullah laughed.

Reconstruction money was another of the many ways in which the Iraq
war had been transformed beyond all recognition by 2009.

In the early days of the war, the US Army grappled with how to stem
the tide of a growing insurgency and quell the anger of an increasingly
restless Iraqi population. The solution seemed relatively simple. It was not
hard to understand why Iraqis wading hip deep through raw sewage, surrounded by garbage that was not being picked up, drinking filthy water,
and living in homes with no electricity in the 120-degree summer were
angry. This was a problem America could solve. All the US Army needed
was money.

At first the US Army used captured former-regime funds, often
found stashed in hidden coffers in Ba'ath Party leaders' homes, to meet
these needs. The program was quickly formalized by Paul L. Bremer and
the Coalition Provisional Authority and dubbed the Commander's Emergency Response Program (CERP). But former regime money soon began

to run dry in a country with so many needs that was no longer generating revenue. The US Congress was initially skeptical about using American dollars to fill the gap, so the Department of Defense sent a series of recently returned combat commanders before Congress to describe the good the CERP money had done in repairing damaged infrastructure, putting unemployed military-aged males to work, and, most importantly, quelling the seething anger of the Iraqi population. The campaign paid off; Congress first authorized $180 million and then raised that limit to $500 million. By 2009, billions of dollars had been spent on CERP.

However, CERP had a number of unintended consequences that no one had anticipated back in 2003. US military commanders, consumed with the immediate demand to address the grievances of angry Iraqis, made CERP, after oil, the dominant economic engine in Iraq. As a result, an entire industry grew across Iraq, a network of patronage in which Iraqi political, police, and army leaders got close to US commanders and then parlayed that closeness into CERP contracts for their cronies. An entire social class—the CERP contractors—emerged. They spoke fluent English, were masters of the intricacies of this Iraqi patronage network, and were well versed in the byzantine process by which CERP funds were coaxed from the American military bureaucracy.

US military commanders were not work-site foremen, city planners, or civil engineers. They didn't know how much it cost to build a sewage system or renovate a school. All they knew was they wanted the people in their area to like them more and shoot at them less. They didn't care how much that cost, as long as it fit inside prescribed spending limits that allowed them to gain quick approval for the projects they needed. CERP contractors quickly learned to exploit this weakness in the CERP process. Suddenly, every small project cost $49,999 (the limit for battalion commander approval), and every big project cost $499,999 (the limit for brigade commander approval). By filling this lucrative new niche in the Iraqi economy, CERP contractors became fabulously wealthy.

There was also a darker side to the CERP monster the United States had created. Many of the sheikhs and political and security force leaders at the top of the patronage pyramid also had ties to the insurgent networks that were fighting against US forces. In its most benign manifestation, these links created a kind of protection racket. When projects continued to flow into a neighborhood, the insurgency was quiet, but as soon as the CERP spigot was turned off, insurgent attacks increased until the money began to flow again. However, in the worst cases, American forces actually found themselves funding the insurgency they were trying to destroy.

Americans in general, and the US military in particular, had a violent cultural aversion to corruption. The more cronyism crept into the CERP process, the more Americans tried to regulate and reform the process. In 2009, this reform effort had generated a tome ironically called *Money as a Weapon System* (*MAAWS*), a collection of pseudo-regulatory standard operating procedures that strictly dictated spending limits, acceptable CERP projects, and the mountain of paperwork required to get approval for a project.

By establishing a bureaucracy around CERP, the US military sought to combat Iraqi corruption. In practice, however, these new constraints also worked against the original purpose of CERP, to allow the ground commander to quickly address the grievances of the population in his area. Ironically, the byzantine *MAAWS* rules actually caused military commanders to enter into an unholy alliance with the CERP contractors, to work the system together to milk money out of the US military bureaucracy. The US commanders had the best of intentions—addressing humanitarian needs, quelling anger in their area, and reducing attacks against US troops—but the *MAAWS*, rather than reducing Iraqi corruption, had unintentionally created US military corruption.

Another unintended consequence of *MAAWS* was to give provincial reconstruction teams (PRTs) a vote in the expenditure of CERP funds.

PRTs were another way in which the Iraq war had transformed beyond all recognition since 2003. In the darkest days of the insurgency, when the US Army was grappling with how to fight this seemingly new form of warfare, there was a faction that contended that the Army was having trouble because it was not supposed to be doing what it was being asked to do. For those who subscribed to this argument, the purpose of the military was, as conservative firebrand Rush Limbaugh once said, "to kill people and break things." Nation building and reconstruction, this faction contended, was a job for the State Department.

This view was, of course, completely ahistorical. The US Army had fought many more "small wars," heavy on reconstruction and garrison duties and light on direct combat, than it had major conflagrations. For every American Civil War or World War I or II, the US Army had spent decades in ignominious small wars. The Army fought to quell the Native Americans' insurgency as Americans expanded west in the nineteenth century. In the twentieth century the US Army spent a decade in the Philippines and many more years in the "banana republics" of Central America fighting insurgencies. Even the United States' biggest war, World War II, had been followed by long periods of reconstruction and rebuilding in Japan and Germany that were driven not by the US State Department but by the US military. When Gen. Douglas MacArthur wrote the constitution for post–World War II Japan, the country didn't even have a US ambassador.

For those who believed that the US Army shouldn't be doing small wars, the mantra was "interagency," a euphemism for putting the State Department in charge of Iraq so the US Army could leave. For these adherents, the first step in that direction was the PRT. These teams, a tiny collection of a dozen or so civilians—State Department employees, US Agency for International Development (USAID) and US Department of Agriculture (USDA) representatives, and augmentee contractors—began in Afghanistan as a supporting cast to US Army brigades in charge of provinces. In this role, they were fairly effective, providing ground commanders with additional expertise and access to other sources of funds, like USAID funds, to address the grievances of Afghan populations. The program soon migrated, in a limited fashion, to Iraq.

When President George W. Bush announced the Iraq surge, he also began a surge of PRTs across Iraq. The State Department was reluctant to acquiesce. Many had philosophical disagreements with the entire war. Others believed the country was beyond saving. Yet others simply didn't want to go to Iraq. The State Department finally met the demand through the hiring of contractors. Many of these contractors had valuable skills, like former city planners or military officers. Others, however, like dieticians or criminal justice majors or librarians, had absolutely no business being in Iraq.

PRTs would have just been an ineffective curiosity had it not been for the US-Iraqi security agreement, signed in 2008. Under this agreement, all US military forces would leave Iraqi cities in June 2009, and "combat operations" would end in August 2010. The military response to this requirement, driven by the interagency clique, was to make the period between June 2009 and August 2010 a period of transition from US military primacy to US State Department primacy in Iraq. On the ground, in each province, this would mean handing the reins for the war in Iraq over to the PRT, with US military forces in support.

Military veterans of the wars in Afghanistan and Iraq had no illusions about the PRTs' ability to take over operations in each province. Each US Army brigade commander and staff developed their own coping mechanism for meeting this unrealistic requirement. The Arrowhead Brigade (3rd Brigade, 2nd Infantry Division) in Diyala (southeast of Salah ad Din) implemented a strategy of support and ignore; they gave their entire field artillery battalion, the Red Lion Battalion (1st Battalion, 37th Field Artillery), the mission to work at the behest of the PRT, providing mobility, security, additional staff, and manpower to the organization, but otherwise ignored their activities. The Bronco Brigade, the brigade our Dragon Brigade would replace in Salah ad Din province, pursued a strategy of staff and humor; they augmented the PRT headquarters with military officers from their brigade and sat in on all of the PRT's meetings and briefings, but otherwise did whatever they needed to do to win the war in their province, regardless of the PRT's wishes or desires. There were many other strategies across Iraq for coping with the unrealistic expectation of putting the PRT in charge of the war in each province, but they all amounted to paying lip service to the Army's State Department counterparts.

In keeping with the US military leadership's stubborn determination to turn the war over to the State Department, the Salah ad Din PRT joined the Dragon Brigade at COIN-SOC at Camp Taji for the entire week, sitting in on all of the classes and briefings and offering their own insights and perspective on how we should view Iraq, our new AO, and Iraqi leadership.

During several of the breaks, I got a chance to meet members of the Salah ad Din PRT. The first I met was Barbara Yoder, the PRT governance chief. She was a short, stout woman with gray black hair and a round, aged but cherubic face. She had a tentative, diplomatic manner, a kind of impatient politeness that intended to take you somewhere but refused to insist. She immediately volunteered that we would not be receiving a "satellite PRT," a civilian representative to carry out the policy of PRT leadership in each qa'da. I hoped to coax from her some insights on ad Dawr; there was so little information about the area in any of our secret or unclassified sources. I was only able to elicit that, at one point, the Salah ad Din PRT had established regular meetings between the ad Dawr qa'da council and the provincial council but that, for some reason, the meetings had died out. She would not provide more information.

The team leader for the PRT, David Stewart, was not much more forthcoming. He was a tall, thin man with a broad, full, graying moustache and bushy salt-and-pepper hair that made him stand out in the room full of Army officers with closely cropped haircuts and no facial hair. He provided a quick primer on the structure of Iraqi governance from the qa'da to the national level and a firm reminder that the PRT was now in the lead in Salah ad Din. On the topic of CERP, he carried the common theme that had permeated every briefing during COIN-SOC: CERP should be used as a tool to teach the Iraqi government to manage budgets and projects. In other words, CERP was a tool for PRT to train the Iraqi government; US military commanders just signed the checks. He then, finally, began to discuss each qa'da in slightly more detail. I took particular note of his observations on ad Dawr. "Ad Dawr is the last kinetic [combat] fight in Iraq." He added, "US forces and PRT don't go there."

We also learned from Stewart's briefing that there was a power struggle under way in Salah ad Din province between the provincial council and the provincial governor, Mutashar Hussein al Aliwi. The provincial council appointed the governor just after the provincial elections in early 2009. However, for reasons that David Stewart did not explain, the provincial council had, as was their prerogative under Iraqi law, voted to remove him from office. The governor refused to recognize the vote without an order from Baghdad, and a stalemate ensued.

Col. Hank Arnold closed the conference by talking alone with his officers, the last time we would all be together before we departed to our separate areas of Salah ad Din province. He began by asking who had read David Kilcullen's *Accidental Guerilla*. The book had been required reading for the brigade, but few in the room had read it because so many had arrived just before our mission readiness exercise (MRX) at NTC. Undeterred, he talked about a passage in the book in which US forces in Afghanistan found a project, a road, that had everyone's support, from the local, provincial, and national Afghan government to the farmers and informal family and tribal leaders in the region. He dismissed the talk we had heard all week in COIN-SOC about using CERP to enable the PRT to train the Iraqi government. Instead, he told us, we should look for our own "Afghan road," that project that would meet the interests of all of the different actors we must influence in our individual areas of operation.

From Camp Taji, it was on to Contingency Operating Base (COB) Speicher, our home for the next year. Before the Iraq war, COB Speicher was al Sahra (literally "the Desert") Airbase. Since late 2005, it had been the home of the series of US Army divisions that had held the role of MND-North, the brigades that had had responsibility for Salah ad Din province, and the battalions that had had responsibility for Tikrit qa'da. It was named after Cpt. Scott Speicher, an American naval aviator shot down over Iraq on the first night of Operation Desert Storm. The base sat along Highway 1 (the main artery through northern Iraq that US forces called Main Supply Route, MSR, Tampa) about twelve kilometers north of Tikrit. At the entrance to the base was a small collection of old, Saddam-era buildings that had served as Iraqi air force offices and quarters. Beyond that to the west was a massive airstrip, capable of supporting any aircraft in the US military inventory. While the claim may have been spurious, the staff of the aviation brigade with responsibility for the airfield claimed that COB Speicher was the sixth busiest airport on earth. Beyond the airstrip were miles and miles of miles and miles, the trackless expanse of the al Jazeera al Tikrit.

The complex of US bases across Iraq were yet another example of the ways in which the war had transformed since 2003. In the early days of the occupation, US bases were entirely under the control of the forces responsible for each area. Bureaucracy was at a minimum, and the few rules that were in place at the bases were focused on maintaining order and discipline and facilitating the fighting of the war. However, as the infrastructure and civilian contractor population of the bases grew, running and securing them became too cumbersome for the tenant units. To solve this problem, US Central Command (CENTCOM) contracted security companies—chiefly Triple Canopy, which hired mercenaries from Nigeria and other countries to man the towers and gates of facilities across Iraq—and began to tap US Army National Guard units whose only duty was to run the administration of each base. Bureaucracy grew exponentially. By 2009, simply getting Iraqis in the front gate of COB Speicher for meetings was a multi-day ordeal, filled with red tape and ever-changing regulations. Hooking up a computer to the secret or unclassified network required an even more byzantine list of steps and procedures. The garrison army had come to Iraq.

However, the first challenge Task Force Patriot faced when it arrived in Tikrit was not the insurgency or the garrison army, but "Steel 6," Lt.

Col. Glenn Waters, the commander of Task Force Steel. Lt. Col. Waters was a force of nature, headstrong, full of energy, and always on the move. One of the first stories the officers of Task Force Patriot heard when they hit the ground was the story of how Steel 6 had been shot a few months earlier. Steel 6 had had a contract disagreement with Mullah Jummah, a religious leader from the Khadasia neighborhood of north Tikrit, over a CERP project. According to most accounts, Lt. Col. Waters decided to take an armed, ten-vehicle patrol to await Mullah Jummah at the steps of the Khadasia mosque on Friday (the Islamic Sabbath) after weekly prayers. Mullah Jummah finally emerged after waiting for two hours to see if the Americans would go away. When Steel 6 stormed toward the mosque to meet him, an unseen assailant shot him in the right buttock. Two days later, a video of the shooting was up on the Internet as JRTN propaganda. While the injury had permanently reduced his gait to a hurried waddle that appeared tortured under his short but sturdy muscular frame, the incident had otherwise done little to slow him down.

Our first morning on COB Speicher began with an operations and intelligence (O&I) brief from the leadership of Task Force Steel, chaired by their commander, Steel 6, Lt. Col. Glenn Waters. The staff officers and the company and battery commanders from each battalion—Task Force Steel and Task Force Patriot—were packed into a small conference room inside a plywood building in Task Force Steel's life support area (LSA) on COB Speicher.

This, as it turned out, was the last time we were able to assemble this whole group in a formal briefing to pass knowledge to us for the remainder of the relief in place (RIP). From the time this briefing ended until the transfer of partnership (TOP, hastily renamed from the traditional "transfer of authority" to convey that the Iraqis now ran Iraq), the RIP between Task Force Steel and Task Force Patriot was a flurry of chaotic activity—commanders and leaders all over the AO meeting key Iraqis, equipment being transferred from old unit to new, and soldiers redeploying to the United States faster than we could sap them of their knowledge. Complicating the problem, Steel 6 would frequently disappear into Tikrit, taking Patriot 6, Lt. Col. Bubba Cain, with him for days at a time. It made it impossible to plan his schedule, let alone organize briefings to transfer knowledge in an orderly manner.

Despite the difficulties, the Task Force Patriot staff did begin to develop a clearer picture of AO Proud Americans than it had before it arrived in Iraq. A pattern emerged as we began to meet key leaders in our area of operations. All of the power brokers, the key provincial council members, key police officials, and key bureaucrats, were from one city in the AO, al Alam, across the Tigris River from Tikrit. Moreover, they were all from the same tribe, the al Jibouris.

The affluent town of al Alam sat north of the Tikrit–Kirkuk road (what US forces called Alternate Supply Route, ASR, Clemson) just after the bridge across the Tigris. Small groves, orchards, and farms sat along the river's edge, sloping gradually upward to the east, toward Highway 2 (what US forces called ASR Dover). At the top of the slope, above the flood-plain, large, ornate homes—often protected within walled compounds or surrounded by multiple substructures—were packed tightly together along narrow, winding roads. It was immediately clear from the conditions of the homes that this was among the wealthiest areas in Salah ad Din.

One was immediately struck when traveling through al Alam at just how different it was from the rest of Iraq. Thriving markets, restaurants, and pool halls dotted the town. Large office buildings lined Highway 2 through al Alam. When Americans traveled through the town, children still played in the streets and waved enthusiastically to the passing vehicles. Americans could safely take off their body armor and walk around the town without fearing for their safety. It was an island of normalcy in a vast ocean of violence and animosity.

It was a measure of the importance of this town that, in addition to being a thriving village, it was also the seat of the al Alam *nahiya* (subdistrict). While in theory the al Alam nahiya was subordinate to the Tikrit qa'da in which it lay, in reality, the qa'da had no power over the nahiya. The nahiya could go directly to the provincial council, bypassing the qa'da, in order to secure services or money. Whenever a town had problems wresting money or resources from its qa'da (nearly always the situation in every qa'da), its leaders petitioned for (but were normally denied) the right to form their own nahiya. The fact that al Alam was able to achieve this status spoke volumes about its power in the Salah ad Din province.

This village had a few prosperous farms, but its biggest industry was the provincial government and security forces; since the beginning of the Iraq war, the most important leaders in Salah ad Din province—the government, police, and army—all came from al Alam. This is not to say that the village made its money directly from government or police or army pay. Rather, the leaders in the city parlayed these positions into patronage networks for which they petitioned US forces for CERP projects. An entire subindustry, CERP contracting, had grown up in the village to generate ready-made proposals, complete with three bids ostensibly from separate contractors, and scopes of work perfectly calibrated to be rapidly approved by MND-North. And, of course, the government and security leaders in the city, with access to US forces to solicit this business, received a generous share of the proceeds.

The favorite CERP project for any CERP contractor was a school. Schools were cheap to build or renovate (providing the biggest profit margins) and appealed to the altruistic intentions of US forces (making them more likely to be approved). As a result, clean, freshly painted schools dotted al Alam. In fact, al Alam almost certainly had more schools per capita than any other town in Salah ad Din. Al Alam's contractors didn't just work in al Alam, however. On the contrary, if a project was taking place anywhere in Tikrit qa'da (where the vast majority of projects in Salah ad Din province were executed), it was a safe bet that it was being built by a contractor from al Alam. They had, simply put, cornered the market.

It was no accident that al Alam was the postwar center of power in Salah ad Din province. Al Alam was an al Jibouri city. The al Jibouris were one of the largest tribal confederations across Sunni Arab Iraq. The al Jibouris' head sheikh lived near Kirkuk, but important subtribe sheikhs lived throughout the so-called Sunni Triangle. The tribe was not universally pro United States. In fact, in many areas, especially in Kirkuk province, the al Jibouris were the dominant tribe in the Sunni separatist insurgency, JRTN.

However, the al Jibouris in al Alam and Tikrit were among the most pro-US Iraqis in Sunni Arab Iraq. This alignment was entirely due to Sheikh Naji Hussein al Jebarra al Jibouri, head sheikh of the al Alam al Jibouris at the beginning of the war. He was the first to realize the economic and political benefits of siding with the Americans when no other Sunnis would. As a result, his tribe took over many of the key government, police, and army positions in Salah ad Din when the United States was establishing Iraqi civil governance and security forces in the region. Sheikh Naji's first brother, Brig. Gen. (ret.) Abdullah Hussein al Jebarra al Jibouri, was appointed deputy governor of the province. His second brother, Jassem Hussein al Jebarra al Jibouri, became the chief of the

Salah ad Din branch of the Iraqi National Security Agency. Likewise, the al Jibouris got in on the ground floor of what would become the CERP contract industry in Salah ad Din. Being the first tribe to align with the Americans had made them fabulously wealthy.

Sheikh Naji Hussein al Jebarra al Jibouri was kidnapped by al Qaeda in Iraq near Samarra on 9 January 2007. He was never seen again, presumably beheaded. His first son, Sheikh Muawiya Naji al Jebarra al Jibouri, took over as sheikh of the al Alam al Jibouris and established the first al Sawah council to organize resistance to al Qaeda. He was killed by an IED in October 2007. The title of sheikh of the tribe then fell to Sheikh Naji's second son, Sheikh Khemis Naji Hussein al Jebarra al Jibouri.

As successive elections formalized power in Salah ad Din, Brig. Gen. (ret.) Abdullah Jebarra's nominal position slipped from deputy governor of security to deputy chairman of the provincial council to simply provincial council member for al Alam. But the key political and security positions held by his tribe made him easily the most powerful man in Salah ad Din province and, by virtue of the Salah ad Din's importance, one of the most powerful men in Sunni Arab Iraq.

Brig. Gen. (ret.) Abdullah Jebarra had a more refined appearance than most Iraqis. While, as brother of the slain Sheikh Naji Hussein al Jebarra al Jibouri, he was technically a sheikh himself, he eschewed the traditional white *dishdasha* (robe) and *shemagh* and *agal* (headdress) of other sheiks for a business suit or, at home, a long, dark, formal-looking, high-collared, button-down robe. His steel-gray hair was neatly manicured into a tight, businesslike haircut. His darker gray moustache was exactingly trimmed as well. He spoke both Arabic and passable English through a broad, narrow mouth that concealed yellowed, smallish, square teeth. He was gracious, but not in the exaggerated, theatrical way of other Arab tribal leaders. He was soft-spoken but decisive and forthright. While many of the most powerful men in Salah ad Din would remain in the background and speak through subordinates, he was easily accessible and seemed to always appear at the key point on the battlefield to ensure that the people of Salah ad Din knew where credit should be placed for the benefits befalling them. He was, in the American model, a politician.

Just as all of the provincial leaders seemed to come from the al Alam al Jibouris, all of the key leaders we met in the ad Dawr qa'da government were from the city of ad Dawr and the al Duri tribe. The city of ad Dawr ("ad doo-er," literally "the Houses") was a residential area of about 25,000 people on the east bank of the Tigris River, halfway between Tikrit (to the north on the opposite side of the river) and Samarra (to the south on the east side of the river, just as ad Dawr). The town was also across the river (but slightly downstream) from Owja, Saddam Hussein's home village. Ad Dawr was bisected by Highway 2 and featured a traffic circle at its center. The town was dominated, however, by the al Duri mosque and a number of large houses built along the riverbank in the extreme west of the city. In the extreme northwest of the city was the small Khadasia neighborhood of ad Dawr with about one hundred large homes.

A bypass (which US forces referred to as the "military bypass") ran around the town to the east and featured a number of checkpoints alternately manned by "concerned local citizens" (CLCs, analogous to, but conspicuously differently named than, the Sons of Iraq) and local Iraqi police. Overlooking the bypass was a man-made hilltop, perhaps twenty meters high, continuously manned by ad Dawr local police, allowing them to watch over all approaches to the city. While the bypass was easily accessible from the south, to get on the bypass from the north (from the direction of al Alam) one had to drive into the northern outskirts of the city, turn sharply left, pass a technical college which had had its second floor toppled by a bomb, and then turn sharply right onto the bypass. In the process, one had to pass through a number of checkpoints. While the bypass was generally several hundred meters outside of town, at its closest point it was only about twenty meters from the cinder-block homes on the southeastern outskirts of ad Dawr. It was at this point that US force patrols frequently received small arms fire or were attacked by IEDs or homemade grenades.

If one continued east out of the city, one would pass ad Dawr University, a tight, walled collection of buildings with lush green trees that contrasted it from its surroundings. Beyond the university another kilometer and set yet further off the road was the small village of abu Dalef. This planned community of perhaps a hundred homes was itself dominated by two prominent buildings: the dusty green abu Dalef mosque and the home of ad Dawr's favorite son, Izzat Ibrahim al Duri, former vice president of Iraq and the highest-ranking member of the former Ba'ath regime still at large. Beyond that lay the vast al Jalaam ad Dawr (literally "the desert east of ad Dawr").

When the day finally arrived to go to ad Dawr, we could not help but be anxious. We had been focused on this town since before we arrived. We had heard all of the stories about ad Dawr, the violence and the casualties. Task Force Steel had had ad Dawr within their area of responsibility for the first several months of their tour before it was handed over to Task Force Cacti. Now, riding through the town in Lt. Col. Glenn Waters' convoy, we were retracing every spot in the city where his soldiers had been attacked. "Next to that light post over there is where we got attacked with a homemade grenade. . . . We took small arms fire right here." Driving brazenly through the middle of town with Waters and his personal security detachment (PSD), we could not help but conclude that he was taking one last victory lap through the city to prove to them (and himself) that they had not beaten him.

Our next stop in the tour was through the housing complex called Mujamma (literally "factory"), a few miles south of ad Dawr. The housing complex was built by Hyundai in 1980 to house workers at the Salah ad Din Company factory across the street, a facility now occupied by coalition forces as Patrol Base (PB) Woodcock. When the factory was open, the complex had drawn Sunni Arabs from across Iraq. Now that the factory was closed, these employees had been joined by squatters, often insurgents or criminals hiding from prosecution in their home provinces. In its day, the complex had probably been glistening and modern. Now, I thought to myself, after six years of war, the village looked like hell's housing projects.

As we drove through the city, the glares were even more piercing than those we had drawn in ad Dawr. A boy emerged from a crowd of young men standing on one corner and shot out his middle finger at us as we approached. Lt. Col. Glenn Waters, embarrassed by the challenge during his victory tour, ordered a mounted pursuit, but the crowd quickly dispersed beyond the reach of our mine-resistant armored personnel vehicles (MRAPs).

As we drove through the last street before leaving Mujamma, I noticed a satellite dish sitting low, mounted to a balcony ledge rather than off the roof like other satellite dishes in the neighborhood. The dish was painted with a prewar Iraqi flag (still bearing the three stars of the Ba'ath party). It flashed by so fast I thought nothing of it. But, a few days later, US Special Forces, along with their Iraqi emergency response battalion (ERB) partners, launched a raid in exactly the same spot. Their supporting aircraft took laser hits (in an attempt by the insurgents to blind the pilot) and ground fire, but the ground team managed to capture key members of a JRTN media cell that was producing propaganda videos and uploading them to the Internet through a satellite uplink.

When we finally arrived at PB Woodcock, we were greeted by the Task Force Cacti's Bravo Company commander, Bayonet 6, who treated us to more stories of attacks. He told us that his force had quit going to ad Dawr. He had been attacked on eleven of his thirteen patrols in the city, usually by homemade grenades tossed over walls at him. Full of counterinsurgency doctrine and too quick to second-guess this infantry company commander, my immediate reaction was that he had "let the enemy win" and force him out of his town. My own reaction should have served as a warning, but it didn't. I would recall the reaction with regret a few months later.

After our briefing with Bayonet 6, Lt. Col. Sam Whitehurst, Cacti 6, commander of Task Force Cacti, arrived from Forward Operating Base (FOB) Brassfield-Mora, south of Samarra on the other side of the Tigris, and we were on our way to ad Dawr. As the Bravo Company commander had recommended, we parked our MRAPs in the cemetery on the southwest edge of town and began the short walk toward the ad Dawr qa'da chairman's office. Despite the MRAPs on the other side of the wall, the short walk along the high wall surrounding the cemetery was nerve wracking after hearing the accounts of homemade grenades being lobbed at Bravo Company's patrols. I was glad to be turning north onto a more open street. As we walked, small clusters of residents surveyed us. The disdain was palpable. Unlike in most Iraqi towns, children did not approach us, an unmistakable sign that they were not hearing nice things about us at home.

Tension lowered a bit as we entered the qa'da council compound and the rickety sheet-metal gate was rolled closed behind us. On our left as we entered was the cinder-block skeleton of the new joint coordination center (JCC) being built with CERP dollars. Across the gravel drive was a rare spot of lush green grass. As we walked through a narrow iron gate, we stepped into a cool green courtyard, shaded with a few modest but green trees. We were guided to an open office door, and we finally took off our oppressively hot, heavy body armor and helmets and stepped into the office.

This was the office of Sheikh Mahsood Shahab Ahmed al Duri, chairman of the ad Dawr qa'da council. That Mahsood ran ad Dawr was immediately clear when one entered his office. His clean, flowing white *dishdasha* and his *shemagh* and *agal* were a stark contrast to the shabby, war-torn appearance of the city he led. A massive wooden desk dominated his polished, ornate office. Atop the desk sat two prewar Iraqi flags (still bearing the Ba'ath party's three stars). Mayor Uthman al Duri, the nominal leader of the city, sat on a small stool at a corner of Sheikh Mahsood's desk, grunting affirmations and nodding supportively as Sheikh Mahsood spoke.

When we arrived in his office, along with Lt. Col. Sam Whitehurst and Lt. Col. Glenn Waters, Sheikh Mahsood graciously greeted us and offered us a rare luxury, ice-cold Dan colas. Talk gradually turned to business. Lt. Col. Bubba Cain, commander of the incoming Task Force Patriot, told Sheikh Mahsood, "Projects are tied to security. No security, no projects."

Mahsood simply grunted and nodded his halfhearted agreement.

Lt. Col. Cain asked him, "What can US forces do to help the people of ad Dawr?"

Mahsood immediately responded, "We need a new qa'da council building with air conditioning and new furniture. And I need a new office."

Sheikh Mahsood had made a critical error. The extreme self-interest of the response, when contrasted with the dire conditions in the rest of the city that Lt. Col. Cain had just seen on the short walk to Sheikh Mahsood's office, made an irrevocable first impression on the leaders of Task Force Patriot that Sheikh Mahsood would never shake.

When we returned to PB Woodcock from our trip to ad Dawr to see Sheikh Mahsood, we were greeted by Sheikh Ali Nwaf Diab al Shimiri, the deputy chairman of the qa'da council. Sheikh Ali had brought us a "small" lunch. His sons spread out tacky plastic tablecloths over the long conference table and began to carry in a meal of roasted chicken on beds of rice, ten times more food than our small group could consume. All the while, he apologized for the meager meal and implored us to come see him at his home, where he could show us true hospitality. After we were finished, he insisted that the food be taken out to our soldiers so that they could eat as well.

Sheikh Ali was a smaller, attractive, if slightly overweight man. He was ornately adorned in a clean white *dishdasha* with a sheer, gold-rimmed *abaya* (cloak). His long *shemagh* and crisp tight *agal* were of the traditional Arab style but seemed somehow more formal than those of the other

"sheikhs" we met around Iraq. His facial hair was cut into a finely manicured moustache and "soul patch" on his chin. He was sweetly perfumed,
and his soft, almost musical voice exuded refinement.

Armed with a more detailed picture of AO Proud Americans, the Task
Force Patriot staff reassembled and discussed what it had learned. As the
discussion progressed, we began to suspect that the cause of disenfranchisement in the ad Dawr district was not political but tribal. We decided
we needed to reframe the problem. The staff began to mine all of the
secret and unclassified sources available for the history of the al Jibouri
and al Duri tribes. After a few days of investigation, we believed we had
found an answer.

When Vice President Saddam Hussein had executed his coup and
deposed President Ahmad Hassan al Bakr to become president of Iraq, he
did so with the help of tribes from his home province, the al Jibouris and
the al Duris. Both tribes shared in the spoils of his victory; the al Jibouris
took many of the top positions in the Iraqi army, especially the Republican
Guard, while the al Duris took many of the key political positions, including the vice presidency. After the Gulf War, however, the al Jibouris decided they had had enough and hatched a succession of plots to overthrow
Saddam Hussein. Saddam's reprisals were ruthless. Hundreds of senior al
Jibouris were killed. Only the fact that Saddam needed them to run his
army saved the tribe from extinction.

The al Duris had remained loyal throughout this episode, so perhaps
the al Jibouris resented that the al Duris had not joined them when they
turned on Saddam. Perhaps some al Duris even participated in Saddam's
purges of the al Jibouris. The Task Force Patriot staff believed it had
discovered a tribal feud and that ad Dawr's lack of representation in civil
government was only the political manifestation of this deeper problem.

Based on this insight, we changed our approach. Instead of only
working on the political problem (the lack of political representation for
ad Dawr in the provincial government), we would work on the "social-
political" problem (which also encompassed the possible dispute between
the powerful al Jibouri tribe and the weaker al Duri tribe). We would
continue to foster communication between the district and provincial
governments (in the political realm), but we would also find the key tribal
leaders in each tribe and foster a reconciliation, a *sulh*, between the two
tribes (in the social realm).

We were also beginning to understand that enfranchising ad Dawr or bringing the al Duris back into favor with the more powerful tribes was going to be a hard sell, not just with the al Jibouris, but also with our higher headquarters. In a briefing to the assistant division commander for operations (ADC-O) for MND-North, the general with direct responsibility for the region of northern Iraq that included Salah ad Din, he shared his view of ad Dawr. He believed coalition forces should simply post warning signs at intervals around the city, warning all to stay away, and leave ad Dawr to its own devices. Ad Dawr, he believed, would never join the new Iraq. Our own brigade commander, Col. Hank Arnold, no doubt held a similar view after his convoy was attacked by a homemade explosive while passing the city, the first attack on Dragon Brigade soldiers since we had arrived in Iraq.

The Task Force Patriot staff, conditioned by years of counterinsurgency indoctrination, was undeterred. All we needed to do, we believed, was isolate the population from the insurgents by constant presence in the city and begin to address the grievances of the ad Dawr populace, their political disenfranchisement. If we did that, counterinsurgency theory held, the populace would turn on the insurgents and defeat them themselves.

As the TOP ceremony approached, there were still many tasks left to do. Chief among them were meeting the remaining key leaders in AO Proud Americans and convincing the leadership of the Bronco and Dragon brigades that Task Force Patriot was ready to take the fight. To further both goals, on the evening of 21 September, I traveled with Patriot 6 and Steel 6 to Tikrit.

The city of Tikrit was the capital of both the Salah ad Din province and the Tikrit qa'da. It was not, contrary to popular belief, the hometown of Saddam Hussein. Saddam was actually from the village of Owja, immediately south of Tikrit. However, once Saddam became president, he claimed Tikrit as his own. He exchanged his tribal affiliation, albu Nasiri, for the moniker of al Tikriti (literally "of Tikrit") and used the designation as a tool to draw together all of the various tribes of the Tikrit qa'da into one coalition under his leadership.

Tikrit definitely benefited from his patronage. In a few short years, Tikrit went from a sleepy backwater suburb of Samarra, the previous capital of the province (and once the principal city of Sunni Arab Iraq), to a bustling,

Mahmoon Palace in northwest Tikrit, the site of the Tikrit joint coordination center (JCC).

affluent power center. Opulent palaces sprang up across the city. Tikrit University (immediately north of the city and southeast of COB Speicher) was constructed and quickly became one of the largest universities in Iraq. The massive Saddam Mosque in the middle of the city, a monument to the man who made Tikrit, still defied attempts to rename it.

This night, Steel 6's PSD brought us to the Tikrit JCC in the ornate Mahmoon ("Birthday") Palace on Saddam Boulevard in northwest Tikrit for our "M-14" (meaning mission assumption minus fourteen days) brief to Bronco 6, Col. Walter Piatt, commander of the Bronco Brigade. Mahmoon Palace, looking out away from Tikrit toward the northwest and the al Jazeera al Tikrit, had been a place for Saddam to publically demonstrate his power. The palace was built as a massive, multistory parade-reviewing stand. Iraqi army or police forces would march southwest, down Saddam Boulevard, divert left through the middle of the palace grounds, and then, after passing the massive palace topped with its beautiful marble stair steps that had once held lush theaterlike seating, they could turn right back onto Saddam Boulevard and march southwest away from the palace. In fact, the famous photograph of Saddam Hussein in a business suit, wearing a fedora and firing a hunting rifle into the air was taken while he stood atop Mahmoon Palace reviewing passing troops.

Postinvasion, the palace grounds had been walled in with the ubiquitous "T-walls" (four-meter-high, poured-concrete, interlocking movable wall sections that could be arranged by crane into any barrier configuration required). The compound had, over time, housed various US and Iraqi army forces. By late summer 2009, Mahmoon Palace had become the Tikrit JCC. It was manned by a small contingent of fewer than twenty American soldiers. Security was provided by Emergency Response Unit (ERU) 2, a special police battalion headquartered across Saddam Boulevard and slightly further down the street. A team of Tikrit *shurta* (policemen) continuously manned a small operations center side by side with American counterparts to allow the two forces to share information and coordinate their activities.

The M-14 brief was a quick status update on the situation in AO Proud Americans and our progress in the transfer of partnership from Task Force Steel to Task Force Patriot. After the formal portion of the briefing was over, the various police leaders, including S.Lt. Col. Khalil, commander of ERU 3, and the other ERU commanders who had gathered outside, were brought into the conference room for dinner and refreshments. It was then that we met one of the most colorful characters in Sunni Arab Iraq, Lt. Col. Ahmed Subhi al Fahal al Jibouri.

Lt. Col. Ahmed was a large man, with a broad face dominated by a huge, white-toothed smile that exuded confidence and pride. His great hands and wide fingers seemed designed for beating men into submission. His snug-fitting police uniform, decorated with the obligatory menagerie of patches and emblems, stretched tightly across his broad shoulders and barrel chest, creating an aura of strength and power even when he stood motionless, which was seldom. On his left breast, he wore a name tape that bore the initials *ISOF*, presumably standing for "Iraqi Special Operations Forces," which of course he was not.

He spoke a bit of English. His voice was growling, and his words invariably came out with the tone of commands, even when he tried noticeably to soften them. One imagined that he spoke the same way in Arabic. His words seemed to have a compulsory power that forced others to obey, even when they were not technically his subordinates.

His background was legend, and he was such a talked-about figure that one never knew what was truth and what was myth. He was rumored to have been a major in the Iraqi intelligence forces. One could easily imagine him torturing or beating dissidents into admitting the secret animus they held in their hearts against their revered leader, Saddam Hussein. Whether this was true or not, it added to the mystique and fear that swirled around him.

One also often heard stories of his postinvasion exploits. Some were charming, but with a moral. As one such story went, while patrolling the streets of Tikrit, a young boy stopped him and, in play, demanded that he surrender and submit to a search. Ahmed, according to the story, allowed the boy to search him and then gave the boy his "bribe" in order to allow Lt. Col. Ahmed to go on his way; the story both painted Ahmed as the benevolent tyrant who would humor a child and also subtly underlined the requirement that bribes be paid to the police.

Other stories were less subtle. As one tale went, Lt. Col. Ahmed al Fahal found an insurgent setting an IED along Highway 1. Ahmed set fire to the man in his own car, leaving a sign on the charred hulk, warning, "This is what happens to terrorists in Tikrit." The moral? Don't mess with Lt. Col. Ahmed.

Lt. Col. Ahmed al Fahal was, nominally, the commander of the Riot Dispersal Unit (RDU). However, the RDU, despite its title, did everything *but* disperse riots. It was feared and respected both as the most effective anti–al Qaeda force in Iraq and as the unofficial muscle for the al Jibouri tribe of al Alam. Regardless of his official title, Lt. Col. Ahmed was easily the most powerful policeman in Salah ad Din province. The province's importance, in turn, made him the most powerful policeman in Sunni Arab Iraq.

One source of that power was Lt. Col. Ahmed Subhi al Fahal al Jibouri's closeness to coalition forces. He was the "go-to guy" for information or assistance. His RDU frequently participated in the most complex of military operations, including helicopter-borne air assaults, alongside coalition forces. His forces provided most of the obligatory Iraqi police escorts for each force that had had responsibility for Tikrit since the beginning of the war, including Task Force Steel and Task Force Patriot. This position as most-favored Iraqi force was important to Brig. Gen. (ret.) Abdullah Hussein al Jebarra al Jibouri and the al Alam al Jibouri tribe, as it allowed them to keep track of the movements of the US force commander and strategically position contractors along his route to solicit CERP projects.

The RDU's status as most-favored security force had, on at least one occasion, saved Lt. Col. Ahmed's job. It is unclear whether the source was Maj. Gen. Hamed, the provincial director of police, or the de-Ba'athification bureaucracy in Baghdad, but Lt. Col. Ahmed received a notice that he was being fired for his Ba'ath Party activities under the old regime. Because of the closeness of his relationship with Lt. Col. Ahmed, Steel 6, Lt. Col. Glenn Waters personally traveled all the way to the Ministry of the Interior in Baghdad to get the order rescinded.

It was obvious this evening at the Tikrit JCC that Lt. Col. Ahmed al Fahal's reach also extended upward into the Bronco Brigade. Lt. Col. Ahmed al Fahal arrived late, but as soon as he entered the room, his relative importance in the police hierarchy was obvious. He apologized for his lateness by patronizingly slapping S.Lt. Col. Khalil on the back and claiming he'd had to stop to rescue two of ERU 3's *shurta* from "terrorists." S.Lt. Col. Khalil remained submissively silent at the insult. A space was hurriedly cleared for Lt. Col. Ahmed at the head of the table, next to Col. Piatt. After the meal, as the gathering retired to the gaudy gold and yellow parlor furniture at the back of the conference room for *chai* (small glasses of heavily sweetened, hot tea), Lt. Col. Ahmed Subhi al Fahal al Jibouri sat hip to hip with Col. Piatt on a small love seat with one of his massive arms draped firmly over the American officer. The giant, grinning Arab clutched the pale, thin, obviously uncomfortable American like a brutish inmate tightly holding his new cell mate.

One last hurdle remained before Task Force Patriot could bid farewell to Task Force Steel and take over its area of operations: the TOP ceremony. Lt. Col. Waters insisted that the ceremony take place on COB Speicher and that Iraqis be invited. By then, a great number of his staff officers, including his S3, had departed. The Task Force Patriot staff objected to the plan on the grounds that it would be very difficult to get the nearly one hundred invited Iraqis through the gate of the base. Waters rebutted that it would be "good training" in the circuitous gate procedures at COB Speicher.

The ceremony was conducted in the gravel between the tactical operations center (TOC) and a conference room building in what was now Task Force Patriot's LSA on COB Speicher. Many of the most notable

The battalion commanders stand in the transfer of partnership ceremony in October 2009. From left to right in the foreground: Lt. Col. Glenn Waters (Steel 6), S. Lt. Col. Khalil (ERU 3 commander), Lt. Col. Ahmed al Fahal (RDU Commander), and Lt. Col. Bubba Cain (Patriot 6).

Iraqis in Salah ad Din, including provincial council member Brig. Gen. (ret.) Abdullah Hussein al Jebarra al Jibouri, Mayor Wai'el of Tikrit qa'da, and dozens of police and army leaders, were in attendance. Lt. Col. Ahmed Subhi al Fahal al Jibouri was one of two police commanders on the stage (the other was ERU 3 commander S.Lt. Col. Khalil). A platoon of Lt. Col. Ahmed's RDU, wearing black uniforms, black plate carriers (minimal-coverage body armor), black helmets, black stocking masks, and black sunglasses, stood in formation next to an American platoon. At the head of the platoon stood a *shurta* bearing a gaudy Iraqi flag ringed with gold thread tassels and mounted on a golden curtain rod.

During his speech, Steel 6 repeatedly broke down as he described his relationship with Lt. Col. Ahmed and the RDU. When Lt. Col. Ahmed gave his speech, he did so in passable English. The ceremony had the feel of a street festival, with Iraqis wandering on and around the stage throughout the event.

Following the TOP ceremony, before the stage even cleared, more RDU *shurta* appeared with bags full of gifts that they began distributing to all of the Task Force Steel staff officers and commanders. With that obligation completed, Lt. Col. Ahmed began working the crowd of new Task Force Patriot leaders.

It was not long before he had identified Lt. Chad Hunara, our acting S9 (civil affairs officer, coordinator of all CERP projects), and Cpt. Joe Breedlove, our Alpha Battery commander, who would have responsibility for Tikrit qa'da. With a broad smile, in his churlish English, Lt. Col. Ahmed indicated contractor Mithaq al Fahal at his side and said, "You will give him projects."

Cpt. Breedlove started to describe the CERP bidding process and the battalion's priorities for projects.

Lt. Col. Ahmed interrupted him, slightly less friendly and slightly more demanding, and said, "You *will* give him projects."

The reception, with food, cake, and sodas, in the battalion conference room adjacent to the stage, was an even more chaotic event than the ceremony. Iraqis piled into and poured out of the room, jockeying for position next to an American. Every passing US soldier was accosted by *shurta* for a 1st Infantry Division patch (the fabled "Big Red One") to replace the 25th Infantry Division patches that they were rapidly discarding from their patch-laden uniforms.

When the crowd finally departed and was ushered by bus back to the gate of COB Speicher, we surveyed the damage. The conference room was destroyed, with overturned cake plates and soda cans lying everywhere in the room. All of the food had been devoured. Someone had entered Lt. Col. Bubba Cain's office adjacent to the conference room and stolen his gloves and sunglasses. It was hard to decide whether the room looked like it had been the victim of a suicide vest or a plague of locusts.

• 2 •

Corporal Carrasco

$\mathcal{A}$lmost as soon as we took the reins of the fight, they were snatched from us by events beyond our control. At noon on 8 October 2009, acting on a list of "Ba'ath terrorists" provided by the Shi'a-led government in Baghdad, two emergency response battalions (ERBs), ERB 1 and 2 from Baghdad, partnered with US Special Forces, descended on the Khadasia neighborhood of Tikrit. They grabbed five Iraqis (as it later turned out, not the five they were looking for) right outside the Khadasia mosque (on the same steps where Lt. Col. Glenn Waters had been shot in the buttock a few months before). No one in the provincial government, not even Maj. Gen. Hamed, the provincial director of police (PDOP), was notified in advance. The commander of ERB 4, partnered with the US Special Forces operational detachment alpha (ODA) in Tikrit, wasn't notified until the raid was in progress.

The ERBs were gone as quickly as they had arrived, and Task Force Patriot (2nd Battalion, 32nd Field Artillery) was left to face the wrath of the Iraqi leadership in Tikrit. That afternoon, our key police commanders, including Lt. Col. Ahmed al Fahal of the Riot Dispersal Unit (RDU) and S.Lt. Col. Khalil of Emergency Response Unit 3 (ERU 3, not to be confused with the national police ERB), as well as the ERU 1 and 2 commanders, also based in Tikrit, came to Contingency Operating Base (COB) Speicher to meet with Lt. Col. Bubba Cain in the Task Force Patriot conference room. Lt. Col. Ahmed, as the most powerful of the four commanders, spoke for the group. He summed up their sentiments when he warned that he would "butcher" the Baghdad police if they set foot in Salah ad Din again.

Col. Hank Arnold, the Dragon Brigade commander, had Lt. Col. Bubba Cain represent him at a separate meeting the same evening with Maj. Gen. Hamed, the provincial director of police, and Sheikh Yahya, imam of the Saddam Mosque in Tikrit. That meeting didn't go much better.

No sooner had this row subsided than fresh ERB raids threatened the stability of the province. ERB 4 from Tikrit conducted a raid in Bayji to capture a woman named Hiba, the daughter of the infamous "Chemical Ali" (Ali Hassan al Majid of the albu Nasiri tribe, who got his nickname for using chemical weapons against Kurds in the 1980s). Bayji was about twenty kilometers north of Tikrit and just outside our area of operations (AO), in the AO of Task Force Rangers (2nd Battalion, 16th Infantry). The raid successfully captured a woman named Hiba, just not the right Hiba. The fact that they also captured her father should have been a clue that they had the wrong woman.

Once more, the province exploded. Rumors swirled of demonstrations to be launched in Bayji, and the PDOP threatened to launch an assault on the ERB 4 compound in Tikrit to recover the woman, until she was returned, along with her father, by helicopter from Baghdad. They were turned over to the PDOP and provincial political leaders, who escorted them back to Bayji.

The very next day, we got a list from Baghdad of personalities to be nabbed in a sweep of Tikrit for "Ba'athist terrorists," which confirmed our worst fears: the Shi'a-led government was trying to exploit the knowledge gap created by the transfer of partnership from the Bronco Brigade to the Dragon Brigade. The list contained twenty-six names, including some of the most prominent al Jibouris in the province, like Jassem Hussein al Jebarra al Jibouri (the head of the Salah ad Din office of the National Security Agency and Abdullah Jebarra's brother) and Lt. Col. Ahmed Subhi al Fahal al Jibouri (the RDU commander). The list also contained other Tikrit notables, like Mullah Jummah, the Khadasia Imam who had been present when Lt. Col. Glenn Waters, commander of Task Force Steel (3rd Battalion, 7th Field Artillery), was shot in the buttock, and Col. Iyad, the commander of the Tikrit joint coordination center (JCC).

US forces immediately concluded that this latest proposed operation was a ploy to weaken Sunni Arab Iraq ahead of the impending national elections. US pressure succeeded in getting the operation delayed twenty-four hours. The operation was delayed an additional twenty-four hours because the ERB in Mosul in the Ninewa province to the north (the unit selected to execute the raids) was having difficulty getting warrants. After a few more days, the operation was expanded, but the ambition of the list was reduced. The list was increased to thirty-four names in Tikrit and al Alam, but the only prominent figure remaining on the list was Lt. Col. Ahmed al Fahal. ERB 5 from Mosul would be joined by ERB 1A from Baghdad, and both would be supervised by Maj. Gen. Noman, commander of all the ERBs in Iraq.

US forces refused to provide any support except unmanned aerial vehicles (UAVs) for surveillance. They would not even allow the operation to be launched from COB Speicher, nor allow the prisoners to be evacuated through COB Speicher. The Iraqis briefly planned to launch the raid from Forward Operating Base (FOB) Dagger, the headquarters of the 4th Iraqi Army Division just north of Owja, before finally scrubbing the mission. While the mission was never revived, it did raise concerns that the Task Force Patriot staff had perhaps missed a huge problem: the uncertain future of Sunni reconciliation in Salah ad Din.

As if to underscore these concerns, we began to receive lists from the Ministry of the Interior (MoI), lists of police to be fired for former Ba'ath ties. The list of police in Salah ad Din alone numbered over 200. Many of them were either not in our AO or not of any significance, but others were. For instance, Col. Iyad, the director of the Tikrit JCC, was on a list and was eventually fired. Maj. Gen. Hamed, the PDOP, appeared on one list before he received word that he would be retained at least until after the national elections. Lists came and went. Some police lost their jobs; others did not.

This uncertainty was aggravated by the fact that nearly a third of the police in Salah ad Din did not have "orders" indicating that they were officially members of the MoI. Instead, they were "contract *shurta* [policemen]," with the authority to enforce the law but no benefits. If they were killed in the line of duty, the families of these contract *shurta* would get nothing.

In the end, a freeze was imposed on the firings until after the national elections, but not before many senior *shurta*, including Col. Iyad, had lost their jobs.

In the midst of these threats from Baghdad, another incident also shook our certainty that we had identified the most important problem in our area. On the evening of 13 October 2009, we detected what we believed to be an improvised explosive device (IED) along Highway 1 (the main artery through northern Iraq that US forces called Main Supply Route, MSR, Tampa) immediately south of the entrance to Owja and about ten kilometers south of Tikrit. We moved aerial surveillance to the location and spotted two men, triggermen for the IED, waiting in the tall grass on the outskirts southwest of Owja. The immediate concern was to prevent American or Iraqi forces from being attacked, so we contacted the nightly route clearance patrol from the Trailblazers (an engineer company) and had them quietly cordon the site. The Dragon Brigade tactical operations center (TOC) also sent an OH-58D attack helicopter scout weapons team (SWT) to the area and gave us tactical control of the aircraft.

With the immediate danger averted, we were faced with a decision. The simple solution would have been to kill the two men. Under the rules of engagement (ROE), we had every right to do so; they were engaged in a hostile act, waiting to attack Americans. A single burst of .50 caliber fire from the OH-58Ds would have ended their insurgent careers. But our charter in this new phase of the Iraq war was to advise and assist Iraqi security forces, to work "by, with, and through" the Iraqi police and army to provide security. The right course, we decided, was to contact the Owja police, and their chief, Lt. Col. Jamal, to make the arrest.

After the TOC made the call, we waited for nearly forty-five minutes, nervously watching the two triggermen from our full-motion video feed, hoping they would not flee before the police could arrive. We debated options, becoming convinced the Owja police weren't coming. We decided to call the real power in Owja, Sheikh Neda Mahmud Neda albu Nasiri, the caretaker sheikh of the town, to enlist his help. He was still on the phone, assuring us the police were on their way when we saw the unmistakable figure of a *shurta* approaching the two men in the night. His kneepads, worn by most *shurta* in Iraq, were clearly recognizable, even in the shadowy infrared feed we were watching. We were all smiling, expecting him to stop at any moment, draw his weapon, and apprehend the assailants.

Instead, the man ran right up to the two. They stood as he approached. We could clearly see the *shurta* point up in the air, right at us, watching from our video feed. The three men then broke into a run.

One ran toward the IED; the other two ran toward Owja. We received the radio report from the Trailblazers on Highway 1 that they had heard and seen an explosion, the man detonating the evidence. Then, through our video feed, we saw the third man run to join the other two in their flight. One of the Owja *shurta* had warned the insurgents they were being watched and was helping them escape.

From our vantage point high above, we continued to follow the men through the streets of Owja as they moved from house to house trying to find a spot to hide from our aircraft. Meanwhile, we debated what to do next. Finally, we brought Lt. Col. Bubba Cain's interpreter, Spc. Ortega, to the Task Force Patriot TOC and had him call Lt. Col. Ahmed al Fahal. Ahmed immediately dispatched the RDU to Owja.

Ortega was not the interpreter's real name. He was an 09L, pronounced "oh-nine-lima," an Iraqi-born US soldier-interpreter. He was a Shi'a, and his family still lived in Baghdad. For both of these reasons, he used an assumed name while operating in Sunni-dominated Salah ad Din province. Ortega was a talented interpreter. He could perfectly reflect the battalion commander's tone in a discussion and answer an Iraqi's questions, clarifying meanings, without constantly going back to the commander for clarification. He was also an excellent soldier. He was mature beyond his years, physically fit, and calm under pressure. On this night, with the TOC bustling with activity and a half dozen people all shouting directions at once, his poise was indispensible.

While we waited for the RDU to arrive, lest we believe that the *shurta* aiding the insurgents was just a bad apple, the three men stopped at the Owja police headquarters and were joined by a fourth man. The four men then traveled on foot to the home of Sheikh Neda Mahmud Neda albu Nasiri, caretaker sheikh of Owja. While it was impossible to be sure who they met, four men were sitting on plastic chairs in front of the *diwan* when the four fugitives arrived. They spent about ten minutes talking before the four fugitives walked calmly and confidently to another home, sat down, and began drinking *chai* (hot, sweet tea).

A few minutes later, eight trucks from the RDU arrived outside the home, guided onto the target by Spc. Ortega. The chase was on. Over the next three hours, the men ran like mad through streets, fields, and homes, trying to evade both the RDU and the ever-present eye hovering above them. The chase finally came to an end in the early morning of 14 October, when the men were cornered in a large house on the northern outskirts of town. One man was apprehended outside the compound, hiding under a blanket in the bushes. Another was caught hiding on the ground floor. The other two men had fled to the roof. One was captured immediately. The other had hidden inside a water tank. He sprang out, fleeing, when a *shurta* threw a concussion grenade into the tank.

The euphoria had barely worn off the next morning when reality began to set in. One of the suspects apprehended was a *shurta* lieutenant from the Owja police. The incident had been an embarrassment to the Owja police and Sheikh Neda to be sure. Moreover, both Sheikh Neda and Lt. Col. Ahmed al Fahal had told us on separate occasions that Neda was set to become the new executive officer (XO) for the RDU, so this embarrassment reflected on Lt. Col. Ahmed as well.

We asked Lt. Col. Ahmed to bring an investigative judge to watch the video from the evening, proof positive that the men had been involved in the crime. However, Lt. Col. Ahmed arrived the next day at COB Speicher alone. When he watched the video, he was visibly uncomfortable, especially when the suspects reached Sheikh Neda's house. He first claimed that the people outside of Neda's *diwan* (a sort of combination meeting hall, living room, and dining room) were women. Then Ahmed stepped out to "take a phone call" and did not return until after the video was complete. A few days later, we tried again but only got the RDU commander, S.Lt. Col. Khalil of ERU 3, and an "investigator" from the Salah ad Din branch of the National Iraqi Intelligence Agency. In the end, only one of the men was charged, after he supposedly confessed to full and sole culpability in the crime. The other three suspects, including the *shurta* lieutenant, were released.

It was clear that, at least in Owja, there was police collusion with insurgents. Lt. Col. Ahmed and the other Iraqi police who saw the video could clearly see this and, even if they were not complicit, did not try to stop it. If, as we suspected, these insurgents were affiliated with the Sunni separatist Jaysh Rijal al Tariqa al Naqshabandiyah (JRTN, literally "Army of the Men of the Order of Naqshabandi"), this suggested Sunni separatist sympathies within the Salah ad Din police. Combined with provocations from Baghdad, we began to suspect we might be seeing signs of a serious threat to Sunni reconciliation.

In late 2006, in the darkest days of the war in Iraq, the al Sawah ("the Awakening" movement) began in al Anbar province to challenge the power of al Qaeda in Iraq. When the movement came to Salah ad Din province in 2007, it was very much a matter of life and death. Many Sons of Iraq were killed, including the first leader of the Salah ad Din al Sawah council, Brig. Gen. (ret.) Abdullah Hussein al Jebarra al Jibouri's nephew, Sheikh Muawiya Naji al Jebarra al Jibouri. By late 2009, however, the Sons of Iraq program had become big business. There were over 1,500 Sons of Iraq in AO Proud Americans alone. Each was paid around $150 per month, but a percentage of the pay at each level went back up to the next higher level, through a kind of underground kickback system, to the senior al Sawah sheikhs in the province.

Since the beginning of 2009, when the government of Iraq reluctantly took over the Sons of Iraq program, pay had been an issue. They missed several months of payment. When they did pay, the pay invariably came late. By June 2009, the Ministry of Defense and the Iraqi Army had taken over the program, but without the funds from the Iraqi government, it did little to solve the problem. Some Sons of Iraq walked off of their checkpoints and quit, which was no doubt the government's objective in being consistently late in paying salaries (according to the program, when one of the Sons of Iraq quit, he could not return and could not be replaced). But the vast majority remained on the job. After all, the work was easy now that security had improved, and with unemployment rampant in Iraq, a job with late pay was better than no job at all.

But the program was coming to an end. On 21 October 2009, all of the sheikhs of the al Sawah council were called to a meeting at the Salah ad Din provincial council building. At the meeting were Maj. Gen. Salah, the commander of the 4th Iraqi Army Division, and Col. Hank Arnold, the commander of the Dragon Brigade. With them was a representative from the Ministry of Defense. His message was simple. The Sons of Iraq program would end on 1 January 2010. He promised that 20 percent would be hired into the Iraqi security forces and the remainder would get jobs in the Ministry of the Interior (the government agency responsible for the Iraqi police). However, he was short on specifics as to how this transition would occur.

Despite these troubling distractions, Task Force Patriot worked hard to try to confirm its original hypothesis about AO Proud Americans, that a tribal feud between the al Jibouris and al Duris was the source of ad Dawr's disenfranchisement. To solve this perceived problem, we had to both confirm that there was a feud and identify the highest sheikhs of each tribe. Lt. Col. Bubba Cain worked to find answers to both questions from within the al Alam al Jibouri camp.

His first stop was Mithaq al Fahal al Jibouri, a wealthy al Jibouri contractor. Mithaq enjoyed favored status with his cousin, RDU commander Lt. Col. Ahmed al Fahal. For a cut, Mithaq enjoyed rights of first refusal on all contracts that passed within Lt. Col. Ahmed's orbit. Mithaq couldn't illuminate our questions about the relationship between the al Jibouri and al Duri tribes, but we were treated to a tour of a girls' school in al Alam that Mithaq wanted to renovate and six Commander's Emergency Response Program (CERP) project packets, ready to submit for approval.

Lt. Col. Bubba Cain next met with Brig. Gen. (ret.) Abdullah Hussein al Jebarra al Jibouri, the powerful provincial council member for al Alam. The meeting did little to further Task Force Patriot's objective of identifying or healing a tribal rift (though Lt. Col. Cain did leave with the name of the chief sheikh of the al Alam al Jibouri, Sheikh Khemis Naji al Jibouri). However, it did illuminate some of the dynamics within the al Alam al Jibouri tribe.

Lt. Col. Ahmed Subhi al Fahal al Jibouri and his RDU may have been the muscle for the al Alam al Jibouris, making him Brig. Gen. (ret.) Abdullah Hussein al Jebarra al Jibouri's political ally, but this did not mean the two were friends. Lt. Col. Ahmed clearly did not recognize the authority of Brig. Gen. (ret.) Abdullah Jebarra, frequently making side deals or engaging in his own, countervailing political activities. In fact, one of the first things Lt. Col. Ahmed told Lt. Col. Bubba Cain after they met was that he was going to run for a seat in the Council of Representatives in the next national elections.

On 20 October 2009, Lt. Col. Cain went to see Brig. Gen. (ret.) Abdullah Jebarra at the provincial joint coordination center (PJCC) adjacent to FOB Danger in east Tikrit. FOB Danger had once been the northern palace for Saddam Hussein when he visited his home province. The compound featured a huge man-made lake, a luxurious midriver island in the Tigris, and a massive palace complex that sat atop high cliffs overlooking both al Alam across the river and, downstream, Saddam's home village of Owja. The front of the compound was dominated by the massive "Horse Gate," an ornately decorated stone gate directly west of the palace along the east side of Business 1, the branch of Highway 1 that went through the middle of Tikrit.

Immediately following the coalition invasion of Iraq, FOB Danger was established as a forward base from which coalition forces could maintain security in the rough-and-tumble city of Tikrit. They erected massive "T-wall" barriers (the omnipresent four-meter-high concrete walls with broad bases that could be interlocked to create long walls of any shape or length) that extended north and south from the Horse Gate and curved east to the edge of the cliff overlooking the Tigris. The wall was periodically interrupted by ten-meter-high concrete towers from which guards could watch over the angry city outside.

In late 2005, this compound was turned over to the Iraqi police and became the headquarters for Iraqi justice in Salah ad Din province. It housed the headquarters of ERU 1 and 3, the High Crimes Division (where terrorism suspects were housed until trial), the Salah ad Din office of the Iraqi National Security Agency, and the Salah ad Din courthouse. FOB Danger was also home to all of the province's judges and the Salah ad Din Iraqi High Elections Commission (IHEC) office. The governor's residence on FOB Danger's high bluffs sat above the palatial island compound in the Tigris River below, home to the RDU.

Immediately adjacent to FOB Danger, with a small connecting walkway, was the Salah ad Din PJCC. This small, squat structure, manned by two dozen Dragon Brigade soldiers and a handful of Iraqi *shurta*, housed an operation center that, theoretically, kept the Dragon Brigade connected to the PDOP and all of the qa'da (district) police districts across Salah ad Din. In practice, the PJCC was more of a permanent conference center for meetings between US forces and various political, military, police, and business leaders.

At his meeting at the PJCC with Brig. Gen. (ret.) Abdullah Jebarra, Lt. Col. Cain mentioned Lt. Col. Ahmed's political ambitions. Brig. Gen. (ret.) Abdullah sneered, obviously irritated by the suggestion that Lt. Col. Ahmed al Fahal might enter the political arena. "Lt. Col. Ahmed is from the old Iraq," Abdullah explained. "His methods were effective three years ago, but they have no place in the new Iraq."

Almost as if he had heard the reproach, Lt. Col. Ahmed arrived and began visibly vying for Patriot 6's attention. Tension gradually rose between the two until Lt. Col. Cain finally got up and left to defuse the situation. The two men depended on one another, Brig. Gen. (ret.) Abdullah for protection and Lt. Col. Ahmed for position, but it was clear the men didn't like one another.

Cpt. Scott Steele, our Bravo Battery commander, with responsibility for ad Dawr qa'da, had been busy trying to confirm or deny the existence of a feud from the al Duri perspective. He had already confirmed that, while ad Dawr did not have seats in the provincial council, there were meetings taking place between the ad Dawr qa'da council and the provincial council. In October alone, Sheikh Mahsood and his deputy chair, Sheikh Ali Nwaf Diab al Shimiri, had made multiple trips to Tikrit to meet with the council.

Lt. Col. Bubba Cain was impatient to get to the bottom of the relationship between the al Jibouris and the al Duris, so he decided to meet Sheikh Kaseeb al Duri, who we were told was the head sheikh of the al Duri tribe. Sheikh Kaseeb was also the elder brother of Sheikh Mahsood al Duri, chairman of the ad Dawr qa'da council.

Sheikh Kaseeb al Duri arrived at Patrol Base (PB) Woodcock in what appeared to be a 1970s-era Cadillac. He was visibly old, his *dishdasha* (robe) and *abaya* (cloak) unable to conceal his thin, frail frame. He walked slowly toward the wooden building that housed the PB Woodcock conference room, pausing at each step of the short stairs, gathering strength for the next step. Sheikh Mahsood walked a respectful distance behind him, watching but not helping as he made his way. As he sat down at the long conference room table, his gaunt features and thin white moustache seemed almost translucent in the fluorescent light.

The first half hour of the conversation was dominated by talk of the good old days, before the fall of Saddam. "Things were better then," Kaseeb repeatedly told us. "Everyone had a job."

Lt. Col. Cain tried to turn the conversation to matters of more immediate concern. Only a few days earlier, Task Force Patriot had taken its first enemy contact, an IED consisting of two mortar rounds and a bottle of gasoline (designed more to look fearsome on camera than to do real damage) on the ad Dawr–Tuz road (what US forces called Route Mango). But Sheikh Kaseeb quickly turned the conversation back into a lament of Saddam's passing. "Kids did not have to lay IEDs along the road for money in those days. The sheikhs had money and power and could control the tribe so they didn't get in trouble, commit crimes, and disrespect their elders."

Sheikh Mahsood sat silent, saying nothing. It was odd to see the head of the ad Dawr government in a subordinate role.

In late October 2009, Task Force Patriot finally met Sheikh Kaseeb al Duri. From left to right: Cpt. Scott Steele (Bravo Battery commander), Lt. Col. Bubba Cain (Task Force Patriot commander), Spc. Ortega (interpreter), Sheikh Kaseeb al Duri (al Mua'shit sheikh), and Shiekh Mahsood al Duri (ad Dawr qa'da council chairman).

Lt. Col. Bubba Cain grew impatient with the diatribe and was eager to get to the reason we had come. He wanted to know about the al Jibouris and whether the al Duris resented being shut out of the provincial council and provincial resources. Sheikh Kaseeb smiled, amused by the question. "Why should I be angry with them?" he asked. "They are in charge, and they are taking what is theirs to take. If we were in charge, we would be doing the same thing. It is the Iraqi way." Lt. Col. Cain pressed, but Sheikh Kaseeb insisted that there was no feud between the al Jibouris and the al Duris.

Lt. Col. Cain was thrown off script by the revelation and started talking instinctively about elections. He told Sheikh Kaseeb that the Iraqis should elect honest people that wouldn't steal from them. Sheikh Kaseeb laughed, saying, "You should run for president. If you put an Iraqi in charge, he will take care of his tribe."

As he continued, Sheikh Kaseeb revealed something very interesting. He said that he was the sheikh of a tribe of 5,000 people from Basra to Mosul. We had been led to believe he was the sheikh of the al Duri. There were at least 25,000 al Duris in the city of ad Dawr alone. If this wasn't the head sheikh of the al Duris, who was?

After our meeting with Sheikh Kaseeb, we stopped for dinner in al Alam, at the home of Sami, one of Lt. Col. Bubba Cain's local Iraqi interpreters. Watching the interpreter, the police, and the nahiya officials socializing with Task Force Patriot leaders at the dinner, it all started to come together. While we had been wrong about the feud between the al Jibouris and al Duris, we had completely underestimated the power of the tribes in Salah ad Din. Tribes were the organizing principle for everything that was happening in AO Proud Americans. Brig. Gen. (ret.) Abdullah Jebarra gave the al Alam al Jibouri tribe access to the halls of government and, perhaps with top al Alam al Jibouri sheikh Khemis (whom we had yet to meet), ran the tribe. Lt. Col. Ahmed al Fahal and his RDU provided both the muscle to protect the tribe and access to US forces to get CERP contracts. Contractors like Mithaq al Fahal and Mohammed Ibrahim al Jibouri brought money into the tribe through CERP contracts. And interpreters like Sami provided the tribe with intelligence on US forces activities and intentions. Each tribe was a massive, self-contained moneymaking and security-providing machine.

It must be the same for the al Duris, the Task Force Patriot staff decided when I returned with this new insight. Sheikh Mahsood provided access to the strings of government. The al Duri–dominated police force provided the tribe with security. Before that day, we had thought Sheikh Kaseeb ran the tribe. But we now understood that he was not the top sheikh of the al Duri. Who was? Additionally, there was very little CERP money flowing into ad Dawr. How was the al Duri tribe making its money?

It was clear that there was a serious flaw in the logic of Task Force Patriot's original campaign plan; there was no feud between the al Jibouris and the al Duris. Even if there were a political rift, we would not be able to solve it. The ad Dawr's qa'da council was already having meetings with the Salah ad Din provincial council, the end state we hoped we could achieve. It was time to start from scratch.

When the Task Force Patriot staff assembled, we began by discussing the new perspective we were developing on AO Proud Americans. It was then that our assistant S2 (intelligence officer), 1st Lt. Peter Song, brought new information. According to the analysis of Multi-National Corp-Iraq (MNC-I), Izzat Ibrahim al Duri, former vice president of Iraq, was the head sheikh of the al Duri tribe. Moreover, 1st Lt. Song also found an old patrol debrief written by Cpt. Scott Steele in which he mentioned that many al Duris disliked the city of Samarra and the al Samarra'i tribes rather than the al Jibouri tribe. The staff needed to know more, so I hopped on one of our provincial reconstruction team (PRT) escort missions to the Samarra JCC to meet its Iraqi police director, Lt. Col. Guyath Sami Shoki al Duri. (One of our responsibilities as "land-owner" of Tikrit qa'da was to escort PRT members wherever they wanted to go in Salah ad Din province; this almost always meant patrols to the provincial council building in Tikrit, but sometimes patrols as far away as Bayji or Samarra.)

Samarra, about thirty kilometers south of ad Dawr and also on the east side of the Tigris, was an ancient center of Tigris River valley trade. It had been the principal city of the region now known as Sunni Arab Iraq since the ninth century, when it became the capital of the Islamic world, the home of the Abbasid Caliph al Mu'tasim. The city also held one of the holiest sites in Shi'a Islam, the al Askari Mosque (also called the Golden Mosque), burial place of the tenth and eleventh Shi'a imams and site of the occultation (heavenly ascension) of the twelfth imam, the Mahdi, a kind of "messiah" in Shi'a theology.

In the years after Saddam Hussein took over Iraq, Samarra was intentionally marginalized in favor of Tikrit, the city, close to Saddam's home village of Owja, that Saddam Hussein intended to make the new principal city of Sunni Arab Iraq. A bypass was built on Highway 1 to allow travelers to bypass Samarra on their way south to Baghdad or north to Tikrit. The tribes of the Tikrit and Bayji qa'das were showered with riches, power, and opportunity at the expense of the al Samarra'i, the tribes of Samarra.

After the invasion of Iraq, Samarra, with a predominantly Sunni population, became a center of al Qaeda in Iraq's Sunni insurgency against US forces and the government of Iraq. Shar'ia (Islamic law) was imposed over the city. The anti-American Muslim Brotherhood offshoot, the Iraqi

Islamic Party (IIP), took over the politics of the city, possibly with the backing of the Jaysh al Islami fil Iraq (literally "Islamic Army of Iraq," IAI). The fervent Sunni political Salafism that overtook the city culminated in the 2006 bombing of the al Askari Mosque, which in turn set off the sectarian carnage that plunged Iraq into a civil war. After security in the city was restored by a US-led clear-and-hold operation during the surge, a Shi'a national police brigade from Baghdad occupied, and even in December 2009 still occupied, the city.

It was in the midst of this chaos that Mike Craft, satellite PRT, arrived in Samarra. Mike was a tall, elderly man. Bespectacled and bald, with a scholarly tone, he seemed more like a college professor than a diplomat or city planner. His efforts initially focused on rebuilding the infrastructure and economy of Samarra. Those efforts bore fruit; within two years, the city had restored its sizable electric grid (powered by its hydroelectric dam across the Tigris), the medicine bottle plant on the northwest of Samarra reopened, and shops sprang up in the old city around the al Askari Mosque to cater to Shi'a pilgrims. But then Craft decided to delve into provincial politics. In 2008, he helped the IIP organize and campaign. That effort also, unfortunately, bore fruit. The massive 400,000-strong population of Samarra—roughly as big as that of Tikrit (200,000) and Bayji (200,000) combined—mobilized with the help of the PRT, created a tectonic shift of political power that reversed Salah ad Din's thirty years of Tikriti rule. Mutashar Hussein al Aliwi, sheikh of the al Aliwi tribe and leader of the Salah ad Din IIP, was appointed governor of Salah ad Din province by the new Samarra majority in the provincial council.

Lt. Col. Guyath Sami Shoki al Duri, Samarra JCC director, provided us with more background on ad Dawr. The city of ad Dawr was dominated by the al Duri tribe. In fact, the tribal name "al Duri" did not indicate a bona fide tribe (i.e., a lineage tracing its roots back to the Nejd and Hejaz, the ancestral homeland of the Arabs on the southwest Arabian Peninsula). Rather, the name al Duri simply indicates a tribe from ad Dawr. Within the al Duri tribe were five subtribes. Chief among them were the albu Jummah, Lt. Col. Guyath's tribe, and the al Mua'shit. The albu Jummah dominated ad Dawr and the al Duri tribe until late 2006, when the bombing of the old ad Dawr JCC violently tipped the balance of power in ad Dawr in favor of Sheikh Mahsood Shahab Ahmed and the al Mua'shit. Sheikh Mahsood was the brother of Sheikh Kaseeb Shahab

Ahmed, senior sheikh of the al Mua'shit. Both were nephews of Izzat Ibrahim al Duri through Izzat's sister.

Izzat Ibrahim al Duri was ad Dawr's favorite son. Gaunt and pale, but with bright red hair and a wide, matching moustache, he stood out from his fellow al Duris. Izzat Ibrahim al Duri first met Saddam Hussein in the early days of the Iraqi Ba'ath Party and, like Saddam, was one of the plotters in the coup that brought the Ba'ath Party to power in 1968. In 1979, Izzat al Duri became Saddam Hussein's vice president. Later, Izzat's daughter married Saddam's son, Uday.

As a result of his close ties to Saddam, Izzat rose to the role of titular head sheikh of the al Duri tribe, and ad Dawr prospered. The town began to grow from a sleepy village into a cosmopolitan vacation home for the rich and powerful of the Iraqi Ba'ath Party—senior ministry officials and generals of the Iraqi army—many of them al Duris. Izzat al Duri also solved one of ad Dawr's enduring issues.

Since the formation of Salah ad Din province, ad Dawr had fallen inside the Samarra qa'da. This meant that all money and resources for the city had to flow through the Samarra qa'da council before it could reach ad Dawr. Tiny ad Dawr was dwarfed by the huge population and prosperous industry of ancient Samarra and, as a result, was neglected by its larger, more powerful neighbor. This all changed when Izzat Ibrahim al Duri rose to power. One of his first acts was to use his influence to form a new ad Dawr qa'da that could directly engage the provincial government for resources.

The Task Force Patriot staff now believed that Izzat Ibrahim al Duri was the elusive sheikh of the al Duri tribe that we had been seeking, which of course would make a *sulh*, a tribal reconciliation, impossible (and, as we had already found, unnecessary). This answered the question of who ran the al Duri tribe, but it still left the question of how the tribe made its money. We theorized that JRTN, the insurgent group that was perpetrating attacks across our area, was in fact a big moneymaking scheme for the al Duris. This explained why the Task Force Patriot patrol had been attacked with an IED built for dramatic effect rather than to damage our vehicles or injure our soldiers. They were putting the video on the Internet (through media cells like the one in Mujamma that had just been captured by ERB 4) to solicit donations from across Iraq and the broader Arab world. If we were right, JRTN was the economic engine of the city of ad Dawr and the al Duri tribe.

Armed with this new information, what, then, should we be doing in AO Proud Americans? What was the most important problem we needed to solve? It was Cpt. Dan Peck who provided an answer. Cpt. Peck was our fires and effects coordinator (FECC); his job was to manage the weekly process by which we assigned missions to our subordinate companies and batteries and decided where we would send the battalion commander to influence our area or gather information. He was tall and thin, smart, and physically fit. Despite his relatively short time in the Army, he was already a master of counterinsurgency from his time in Afghanistan as a company fire support officer (FSO) with the 82nd Airborne Division. Cpt. Peck suggested that we should focus on the other big problem that had been looming since our arrival in Salah ad Din province. "We have to keep Baghdad from monkey-stomping the province after we leave."

Cpt. Peck was right. As we mined back through the engagement notes from all of the commanders who had been traveling AO Proud Americans for the past month, the universal theme among Iraqis was fear of Baghdad. It drove security leaders to hoard supplies and ammunition; when we first arrived, the 4th Iraqi Army Division executed a live fire, for which the Bronco Brigade provided tens of thousands of rounds of ammunition and hundreds of gallons of fuel, yet when the actual live fire was executed, it was done on foot with only 5,000 rounds fired. This fear almost certainly also drove them to tolerate JRTN insurgents, like the four men caught in Owja; these would be the foot soldiers for the war to come after we left, if we did nothing to alleviate the fear of Baghdad.

If this was the problem, how would we solve it? To answer this question, we asked ourselves another. Baghdad didn't go to Irbil or Sulimaniya, in Iraqi Kurdistan, and try to catch political opponents. Why not? First, of course, the Iraqi Kurds had their own formidable security force, the Peshmerga. But they also had a strong political bloc, the Democratic Patriotic Alliance of Kurdistan (an alliance of all of the Kurdish parties in Iraq), that worked against the larger Shi'a and Sunni factions to protect Kurdish interests in the Council of Representatives. Finally, it was the most economically viable region of Iraq; in addition to the oil fields the Kurds controlled in and around Kirkuk, Iraqi Kurdistan was also the fastest-growing economic zone in Iraq, with industry and tourism growing at an exponential rate. All of these reasons—security, political, and economic—prevented Baghdad from using excessive means to enforce its will in Iraqi Kurdistan.

As the unit responsible for the capital of Salah ad Din province, the economic, intellectual, and cultural center of Sunni Arab Iraq, Task Force Patriot was in a unique position to affect this problem. In the security realm, we would redouble our efforts to build capability in the Iraqi security forces by concentrating on the lagging police battalions, like ERUs 1 and 2, to bring them up to the capabilities of ERU 3 and the RDU. Politically, we could encourage the key Sunni Arab tribes, all with representation in Tikrit qa'da, to form a political bloc to run a unified list of candidates in the upcoming national elections. And, finally, we would find economic opportunities that we could further with CERP projects or through political influence in order to create new economic engines in Salah ad Din that could augment the Bayji Oil Refinery. This last effort would have the added benefit of finding employment for the soon-to-be-unemployed Sons of Iraq and, possibly, creating economic opportunities for the al Duris that would obviate their need for JRTN.

The idea was to create disincentives for Baghdad to, as Cpt. Dan Peck had put it, "monkey-stomp" Salah ad Din. We were trying to create an obstacle too high for Baghdad to overcome. To communicate this idea, we created a PowerPoint slide showing a tall, three-legged table—the legs labeled with "Security," "Political," and "Economic." On top of the table was a fishbowl containing a goldfish. On the floor, at the base of the table, sat a black cat. While the slide occasionally inspired satires (one version of the slide mocked Lt. Col. Bubba Cain's love of Alabama football by labeling the goldfish "national championship" and the cat "University of Alabama," complete with a little capital *A* on the cat's chest), it was an elegant way to convey this new intent.

On 23 and 24 October, a pair of confusing events took place in Tikrit that undercut the confidence the staff had just built. On the night of 23 October, we received a report from the Tikrit JCC that they had heard a loud explosion only blocks away from their location. Only minutes later, they called back, saying that the Tikrit police who shared the JCC with them were saying it was another magnetic IED. Since we had taken over AO Proud Americans, there had been several magnetic IEDs found on the private cars of Tikrit police officers. Most were discovered before they exploded, but a few did detonate. None had yet caused casualties. We believed these to be JRTN intimidation attacks to intimidate overeager police.

An hour later, however, the full chilling report came in. When the police arrived at the site of the explosion, a nondescript home in the northwest of Tikrit, they found a garage devastated by a prematurely detonated car bomb. The renter of the home had fled, but his wife and children remained at the location and identified him as a bomb maker from Mosul and a wanted member of al Qaeda in Iraq. This had been the first car bomb detonation in Tikrit qa'da since 2008.

We had barely processed this information when, the next afternoon, Tikrit suffered an even more dramatic attack. At about 3 p.m. on 24 October 2009, a man in a winter coat approached the entrance of the National Unity Collective Party headquarters. He was about to turn and enter the gate when a security guard, leaving his shift and walking toward his car, turned and called after him. The man turned, met the guard's eyes, and then detonated a suicide vest he was wearing under his coat. The wave of concussive force and ball bearings obliterated the suicide bomber and killed three men, including the security guard. Two more men who had been painting the outside wall of the party headquarters were severely wounded.

The Tikrit police and Iraqi police explosive ordnance disposal team (IPEOD) were first on the scene. The Task Force Patriot TOC sent out the quick reaction force (QRF) and the US explosive ordnance disposal team (EOD), both stationed on a rotating basis at the Tikrit JCC. Their mission was to collect any evidence they could gather. They took a lot of pictures, as well as tissue samples from the attacker, but otherwise they were not able to gain any intelligence from the site; it had already been picked clean by IPEOD. The QRF platoon leader did note that a *shurta* had taken the head of the suicide bomber and mounted it on a stake in front of the party headquarters.

We learned a week later that Lt. Col. Ahmed al Fahal, presumably pursuing his political ambitions, had left the site of the suicide bombing—the party headquarters—only a few hours before. While there was no evidence that the attack was meant for him, it seemed Lt. Col. Ahmed had made the connection; two days later, while Lt. Col. Bubba Cain was meeting with Sheikh Hassan albu Nasiri and his nephew, Sheikh Neda, in Owja, Lt. Col. Ahmed stopped by to tell Cain he was leaving for Jordan, supposedly to seek female companionship. The meeting might have gone unnoticed except that, when he returned, he began to appear everywhere in civilian clothes. His political ambitions had kicked into high gear.

To successfully build a unified Salah ad Din political bloc, we would have to sell the idea to Brig. Gen. (ret.) Abdullah Hussein al Jebarra al Jibouri, the most powerful political leader in Salah ad Din province. We still were not sure who held the power within the al Alam al Jibouri tribe, Brig. Gen. (ret.) Abdullah or his nephew, Sheikh Khemis Naji al Jebarra al Jibouri, purportedly the senior sheikh of the al Alam al Jibouris. The only way to be sure would be to see them together, at the same place, so we called Brig. Gen. (ret) Abdullah to set up a meeting. We accepted his invitation to go with him to meet Sheikh Khemis at the sheikh's farm. Abdullah suggested we meet him in al Alam and then follow him to the farm.

Joining us on the trip was Michael Boyle, our new "satellite PRT" (the provincial reconstruction team, PRT, the representative assigned responsibility for Tikrit and ad Dawr qa'da). Michael Boyle was a tall but unassuming man whose manner and appearance reminded one of Christopher Reeves playing Clark Kent. Before joining the PRT as a contract hire, he was a business information technology specialist in the state of Washington. He first came to Iraq to serve in the Sharqat qa'da in the extreme north of Salah ad Din province. He was wounded in an IED explosion that cost him his right arm below the elbow. After a half year of convalescence, he was back in Iraq, serving as our satellite PRT.

Lt. Col. Bubba Cain was immediately skeptical, saying, "No right arm? That's going to go over well with the Arabs." (In a country without toilet paper, being touched with the left hand was taboo.)

But the Iraqis seemed to accept Michael Boyle and were genuinely fascinated first by the mechanics of his cable-operated prosthetic arm and then by his determination to return to Iraq after such a grievous wound. Boyle integrated well with the unit, as well. While, nominally, he had veto power over the CERP process, he did not wield it. He diligently accompanied us on those patrols where he was wanted, bowed out where he was not, and had the good sense to know the difference. Boyle also integrated well into the Task Force Patriot staff by identifying and concentrating on those points where the PRT shared our objectives, rather than pushing into areas where our interests diverged.

When our patrol arrived in al Alam, we took off our heavy body armor and helmets (the town was the only place in AO Proud Americans safe enough to do so in the open, outside of a closed compound) and greeted Brig. Gen. (ret.) Abdullah al Jebarra. He had had us meet him at the site of the al Jebarra family *diwan* (a combination meeting hall, family room, and dining room). The al Jebarra family, we had already learned from our discussions with the sheikhs of other tribes, was one of the most prestigious families in the al Jibouri tribal confederation. The family had historically been at the center of the leader caste of the tribe. Such was certainly the case among the al Alam al Jibouris; both Brig. Gen. (ret.) Abdullah and Sheikh Khemis were of this family. But, seeing the al Jebarra neighborhood and *diwan* gave one no hint of their stature. The homes and buildings were no more ostentatious than others in al Alam. In fact, they were a bit more modest.

Brig. Gen. (ret.) Abdullah had shed his normal business suit for a *dishdasha* and a thick, brown, insulated vest that seemed too thick for the warm day. The *diwan* was a simple gathering hall with a grass courtyard, browned and dormant for want of water. We sat outside the *diwan*, on a stone porch, in the inevitable white plastic chairs, sipping *chai* (very sweet, hot tea served in small, ornate tea glasses) and listening as the family's elders shared the trivial comings and goings of their neighborhood.

As the gathering broke and we prepared to walk out of the family compound, I stole the chance to peek inside the *diwan*. On the wall near the door, opposite where the guests of honor would sit—the wall normally reserved for portraits of the honored dead of the family or tribe—were three pictures. The first two I recognized to be Sheikh Naji Hussein al Jebarra al Jibouri and his first son (Sheikh Khemis' older brother) Sheikh Muawiya Naji al Jebarra al Jibouri, both slain by al Qaeda in Iraq. The third was an al Jibouri general I did not recognize. As I followed the back wall to the center, to the place of honor where the portrait of the highest living member of the family or tribe would normally hang, there was a picture of Brig. Gen. (ret.) Abdullah al Jebarra.

Next, we took a short walk through the al Jebarra neighborhood of al Alam (which was unsettling without body armor, despite the minimal risk) to Abdullah's youngest son's school. While in good repair and freshly painted, Abdullah insisted it required a CERP project for renovation. Then we were off to Sheikh Khemis' farm, a long, bumpy ride over rutted dirt roads (which Abdullah also insisted required a CERP project to repair). We were soon at the extreme eastern edge of the arable land in Tikrit qa'da, at the verge of the al Jalaam al Tikrit (literally "the desert east of Tikrit"), at Sheikh Khemis' farm.

It was difficult to judge the amount of land that belonged to the farm, but by Salah ad Din standards, it seemed exceptionally large and well

Brig. Gen. (ret.) Abdullah Hussein al Jebarra al Jibouri (provincial council member) and, to his right, Lt. Col. Bubba Cain (Task Force Patriot commander) walk through the al Jebarra neighborhood of al Alam in mid-November 2009.

irrigated. The al Alam al Jibouri *diwan* and home were not particularly large or ornate, just small, squat, concrete buildings. The only particularly luxurious feature of the home was a square of lush green grass, perhaps thirty meters on a side, ringed by pink-flowered bushes and bifurcated by a small irrigation ditch.

It was here that we sat with Sheikh Khemis and the perhaps thirty al Jibouris present and ate in the traditional Sunni Arab Iraqi style, with our hands from huge, communal plates of goat on mountains of amber rice with almonds and sweet golden raisins. The goat was prepared in the traditional Iraqi style, complete with the liver and entrails. As a sign of respect, one of the elder men who shared a plate with Lt. Col. Bubba Cain and me grabbed a fistful of meat, fat, and entrails and placed it in front of me.

No matter how many meals one shares with Arabs, it is hard for Westerners to get used to having meat, let alone goat intestines, handed to them with a bare hand. Still, I concealed my discomfort and rendered a polite "shukran jazeeran" (thank you very much).

As soon as the man turned away, I gingerly scooted the entrails over, in front of Lt. Col. Cain. He, in turn, rendered a "shukran habibi" (thank you, dear friend).

Throughout the meal, Brig. Gen. (ret.) Abdullah walked among the diners, moving food closer to the guests and distributing fresh bottles of water, the role of the senior host at a traditional Arab meal. After dinner, as everyone washed their hands, mingled, and smoked, the dinner guests thanked Abdullah, rather than Sheikh Khemis, for the generous meal. It was clear throughout the afternoon that Brig. Gen. (ret.) Abdullah was the senior member of the al Alam al Jibouri tribe.

As I made my thanks, Brig. Gen. (ret.) Abdullah produced his nephew (and Sheikh Khemis Naji al Jebarra al Jibouri's younger brother) Sheikh Wanus. Wanus was a young, tall, thin man, perhaps nineteen or twenty years old, with a thin, barely detectable moustache. He wore a modern-looking, black leather jacket over his *dishdasha* and had his *shem-agh* and *agal* tightly gathered up on top of his head in a way that made it look more like a turban.

Cpt. Hicks, commander of the Tikrit ODA, had told me in a sepa-rate discussion that Sheikh Wanus Naji al Jebarra al Jibouri, in addition to being the al Alam Sons of Iraq chief, was also heavily engaged in the elicit arms trade in the area. The report was dissonant with the Task Force Patriot staff's understanding of the al Alam al Jibouris, so, having no other foundation for suspecting Wanus, I dismissed the statement as background noise. Now, meeting Sheikh Wanus, I found the report even less credible. Wanus was still nearly a boy.

A few weeks later, Task Force Patriot would receive another bit of information that seemed dissonant with everything we understood about AO Proud Americans. According to the report, passed by an informant to US forces inside the Salah ad Din PJCC, Sheikh Khemis Naji al Jebarra al Jibouri, the nominal head of the al Alam al Jibouris, had, with his brother Riyad, purchased $250,000 worth of weapons on behalf of an organiza-tion the informant called the "New Iraqi Resistance." Having no other evidence to implicate Sheikh Khemis as an insurgent, we dismissed the report as someone trying to create suspicion about the al Alam al Jibouris among US forces. There was certainly no evidence of insurgent ties here, this late afternoon, at his farm.

After dinner, a long-barrel shotgun appeared, and the guests took turns shooting bright orange clay pigeons. Abdullah and Cain were both lethal shots. Having only fired a shotgun a handful of times in my life, I embarrassed myself badly.

As the crowds broke into smaller conversations, Brig. Gen. (ret.) Abdullah Hussein al Jebarra al Jibouri, Michael Boyle (our new satellite PRT), and I retired to the *diwan*. Once we sat down, Brig. Gen. (ret.) Abdullah shared another vision of his, an airport for Salah ad Din. His dream was to take an old, abandoned airstrip, bordered on the west by the village of abu Ajil, on the north by the Tikrit–Kirkuk road (what US forces called Alternate Supply Route, ASR, Clemson), and on the east by Highway 2. The project would be exorbitantly expensive, and before I could balk he told me he understood it was beyond the capability of CERP to finance.

Abdullah explained, "I have tried to get the government in Baghdad to fund the project. An airport could bring Shi'a pilgrims safely from Baghdad to the al Askari Mosque [the famed "Golden Mosque" in Samarra]. They won't give us the money."

I saw the opportunity to press the battalion's new objective, using the national elections to build a strong proreconciliationist Sunni Arab bloc. I told him, "Salah ad Din and Sunni Arab Iraq need a strong political bloc in the Council of Representatives to press this airport project." I then explained what we proposed, and the other sheikhs to whom we had talked.

He seemed unmoved, giving a halfhearted "enshallah" (literally "if Allah wills it," a catchall phrase that, in this context, dismissed the idea as far-fetched).

I must have appeared despondent, because Brig. Gen. (ret.) Abdullah volunteered, "Perhaps Sheikh Khemis can make this an element of his campaign. He is running for the Council of Representatives."

On the morning of 4 November 2009, Cpt. Scott Steele departed with his 1st Platoon, Bravo Battery, from PB Woodcock to ad Dawr. He had a full day of scheduled meetings that day, aimed at identifying economic opportunities for the qa'da. As had been their tactic for patrols in the city since arriving in Iraq, they dismounted from their MRAPs at the edge of the city and walked the remaining few hundred meters into town. They were accompanied by a force that Americans called ADSWAT (pronounced "add-swot," ad Dawr special weapons and tactics team), a component of the ad Dawr police that was stationed inside PB Woodcock and seemed more willing than the city police to work with US forces.

Cpt. Steele, Bulldog 6, began the day by meeting with the ad Dawr qa'da service manager for agriculture to discuss points where CERP could reinvigorate agriculture in the qa'da. The meeting was unproductive, so he continued on to his next meeting.

When 1st Platoon arrived at their next stop, the service manager for education, the platoon quickly secured the location, posting soldiers outside the compound at the corners, more soldiers in the courtyard, and soldiers and ADSWAT on the roof. Cpt. Steele went inside and spent about thirty minutes discussing educational opportunities that could train the city's "concerned local citizens" (ad Dawr residents use this term, rather than "Sons of Iraq," to refer to the unofficial security forces operating in their town). He was just packing up to leave when he heard a shot outside. The shot was followed by a hail of gunfire, mostly from the ADSWAT on the roof, firing in all directions in response to the enemy fire.

Cpl. Tony Carrasco Jr., a twenty-five-year-old with a new, pregnant wife waiting for him in Texas, had been shot in the forehead just above the left eye. The bullet was traveling so fast that it penetrated the back of his helmet and went out the other side. The platoon called forward its vehicles and requested an immediate medical evacuation (MEDIVAC) helicopter, but Carrasco was already dead.

· 3 ·

Lt. Col. Ahmed al Fahal

*P*atriot 6, Lt. Col. Bubba Cain, had already been scheduled to go to ad Dawr to discuss the formation of a unity slate of candidates with Sheikh Kaseeb al Duri. The Task Force Patriot (2nd Battalion, 32nd Field Artillery) staff was now sure he was not the top al Duri sheikh but still believed he was the senior sheikh currently living in ad Dawr. Sheikh Ali Nwaf Diab al Shimiri, whom we believed to be the most influential sheikh of the al Shimiri tribe, the second-largest tribe in ad Dawr qa'da (district), would also be present.

The death of Cpl. Tony Carrasco changed the agenda. Lt. Col. Cain was joined by Col. Hank Arnold, commander of the Dragon Brigade (4th Brigade, 1st Infantry Division, Task Force Patriot's higher headquarters). They were also joined by Lt. Col. Ahmed Subhi al Fahal al Jibouri, commander of the Riot Dispersal Unit (RDU) and the most powerful *shurta* (policeman) in the province.

As they departed, I reminded Patriot 6 that Sheikh Ali was only the deputy chairman of the qa'da council and none of his tribe lived in the city; I was concerned that we might unintentionally alienate a potential ally. Lt. Col. Cain reluctantly agreed, but it was clear he was going to ad Dawr to lay blame for Carrasco's death.

When they arrived at Patrol Base (PB) Woodcock, they found the sheikhs joined by Mayor Uthman al Duri and Lt. Col. Khatan Mawlud Tawfiq Kudir al Duri, the deputy chief of police for the ad Dawr police district (and recent releasee from the US detention facility at Camp

Bucca). Lt. Col. Bubba Cain barely spoke, deferring to his commander. Col. Arnold's message was simple: "The violence ends now, or the CERP [Commander's Emergency Response Program] money ends and combat operations begin in ad Dawr."

This was not the first time these men had heard this message. In fact, everywhere Lt. Col. Cain had gone since we arrived in Salah ad Din province, his first message had always been that CERP projects were tied to security. No security, no projects. In fact, earlier that day, the Task Force Patriot staff had pulled from consideration all of the proposed projects for ad Dawr and had begun the process of canceling the one ongoing project, the construction of the ad Dawr joint coordination center (JCC) next to Sheikh Mahsood's office.

From PB Woodcock, the patrol traveled to ad Dawr. They were "rolling heavy," with two platoons of mine-resistant armored personnel carriers (MRAPs). They didn't bother with stopping on the edge of town and walking in; they rolled right to the scene of the previous day's attack and established a perimeter. Cpt. Scott Steele and 1st Lt. Javier Sanjuan, Cpl. Tony Carrasco's battery commander and platoon leader, respectively, had traveled to the site with the two senior commanders and recounted the attack. When they indicated the direction from which they believed the shot had come, Lt. Col. Ahmed al Fahal took two *shurta* and stormed the house, kicking in the door and ransacking the home. Ahmed emerged with an AK-47 assault rifle and a small bag of ammo (neither of which was illegal).

While the search was taking place, Lt. Col. Bubba Cain looked off to the northwest of the attack site, to a gas station just across the alley. Standing in the middle of the station was a thin, Arab man in khaki pants and a dirty button-down shirt. The man stared back at Patriot 6 with obvious contempt, but also a sort of smirk, a look of baleful satisfaction. Lt. Col. Cain turned to gather a few soldiers to investigate, but when he turned back, the man was gone.

With everything gleaned from the site that could be, Lt. Col. Cain and the Proud Americans loaded their MRAPs and headed back to PB Woodcock. Col. Hank Arnold and his personal security detachment, PSD, turned north and headed back through Tikrit to Contingency Operating Base (COB) Speicher. On the way back, just after the Tikrit bridge, two young men emerged from behind two parked cars and threw two RKG-3s (hand-thrown antiarmor grenades) at his convoy. It was the weapon of choice of Jaysh Rijal al Tariqa al Naqshabandiyah (JRTN, literally "Army of the Men of the Order of Naqshabandi"). Both grenades missed, and the two insurgents escaped, but the Dragon Brigade had gotten its answer to Col. Arnold's ultimatum to ad Dawr.

Over the next week, Task Force Patriot cast a broad net across every source at our disposal, including the US Special Forces operational detachment alpha (ODA) living and working in Tikrit, looking for information on the shooting of Cpl. Tony Carrasco. We received word that three men working at the gas station right across the street from where Carrasco was shot—one of which looked just like the man who had stared down Lt. Col. Bubba Cain the day after the attack—were part of a JRTN cell operating in ad Dawr. The three men, three of the eight sons of a man named Jadir al Duri, had all worked as bodyguards for former Iraqi vice president Izzat Ibrahim al Duri, the current head of JRTN. Since the war began, the three had been implicated in numerous attacks against US forces.

The man who shot Carrasco had been in the open, one hundred meters away from two US platoons, and we had let him go.

There was absolutely no response from the Iraqi police in Salah ad Din to the increase in violence against US forces. When Lt. Col. Bubba Cain went to meet with the provincial director of police (PDOP), Maj. Gen. Hamed, he was infuriatingly noncommittal and apologetic for the ad Dawr police. Cain abruptly ended the meeting, telling the PDOP that the al Duris were stuck in the past and he wanted the PDOP to remove the district chief of police for ad Dawr, Col. Sayeed al Duri, who had been unreachable since the incident.

Even the response of Lt. Col. Ahmed al Fahal, the real top *shurta* in Salah ad Din and a stalwart partner of US forces since the beginning of the war, was suspect. He was purportedly "cracking down" on JRTN in ad Dawr after the death of Cpl. Carrasco, but we had no way to independently verify that he was conducting operations or even had forces in the town. He wasn't inviting us to join him in these operations, which was suspicious in and of itself. Nearly every time he saw Lt. Col. Bubba Cain, he invited him to join in some raid or cache hunt. But he wasn't inviting us to join his purported operations in ad Dawr.

It was clear to us that we had misread ad Dawr and the al Duris' motivation for supporting JRTN. In the days leading up to Cpl. Carrasco's memorial ceremony at PB Woodcock, the Task Force Patriot staff began to reexamine everything, from the engagement notes for all of the discussions that all of the battalion's leaders had had since we arrived in Iraq to the secret and unclassified sources that we had passed over in our first two iterations of planning. We were, simply put, reevaluating the fundamental assumptions on which our entire approach in the Tikrit and ad Dawr qa'das was based.

In the process of this reexamination, a much different picture of ad Dawr began to emerge. When the Iraqi army dissolved before the advance of coalition forces during the initial invasion of Iraq and the Ba'ath regime fell, those senior government leaders who were not important enough to make the Americans' "deck of cards" (its fifty-two most-wanted Iraqi leaders) retired to their vacation homes in ad Dawr with their millions of Iraqi dinars plundered from Iraqi treasuries. After all, many of them were al Duris; next to Saddam Hussein's albu Nasiri tribe, the al Duris had more people in high-level Ba'ath Party jobs than any other tribe. When Coalition Provisional Authority (CPA) administrator Paul Bremer officially dismissed the Iraqi army, these disgruntled government leaders were joined by disgruntled Iraqi generals, many also al Duris and also armed with piles of Iraqi dinars. Thus, it is not surprising that ad Dawr quickly emerged as the epicenter of the Ba'athist insurgency in Sunni Arab Iraq.

It was also not surprising that former President Saddam Hussein chose ad Dawr as his hiding place in 2003. Ad Dawr had a high concentration of former Ba'ath government and military leaders and the plunder from Iraq's coffers. It was also just a short row across the Tigris from ad Dawr to Saddam's home village of Owja, giving him easy access to the remnants of his tribe and his family still living in the village. Saddam Hussein was found in a spider hole beside a small farmhouse only a few hundred meters northwest of the Khadasia neighborhood of ad Dawr, on the banks of the Tigris River, within sight of Owja.

In late September, during our relief in place of Task Force Steel (3rd Battalion, 7th Field Artillery), Lt. Col. Ahmed al Fahal had told us, "AQI [al Qaeda in Iraq] or JRTN, they are the same people with a new banner." At the time, we had dismissed the comment as his typical bravado, but now we began to see the statement in an entirely new light.

By 2008, years of US-sponsored messaging against al Qaeda in Iraq, generated by UK public relations contractor Bell Pottinger, had hammered away at the violence perpetrated by al Qaeda in Iraq against Iraqi civilians. The campaign had taken a toll. The Iraqi populace, even the Sunni Arab Iraqi populace, had turned against al Qaeda in Iraq. The Sunni al Sawah ("the Awakening" movement) and the Sons of Iraq phenomenon it spawned were a rejection of the methods (if not necessarily the ideology) of al Qaeda in Iraq.

For the power brokers of ad Dawr, the al Duri former Ba'ath officials and generals, and their patron, former vice president Izzat Ibrahim al Duri, this presented a crisis of branding. For five years, al Qaeda in Iraq had been the nom de guerre through which the New Ba'ath Party had attacked coalition forces and furthered its goal of a separate Sunni Arab Iraq, independent of the rule of the Shi'a-dominated government in Baghdad. There was a real al Qaeda in Iraq, which operated quite independently from the New Ba'ath Party and ad Dawr. But its fragmented, nonhierarchical nature allowed the ad Dawr power elite to co-opt the brand name, at least in Salah ad Din and Kirkuk. It had provided the New Ba'ath Party with a "front" organization for those Sunni Arabs who supported separatism but resented the excesses of the former Ba'ath regime. It had also provided a convenient standard to draw those who opposed the occupying infidels on religious grounds and wished to fight in the defensive jihad to expel them from Muslim lands. Now, with the al Qaeda in Iraq brand name plummeting in value, this front organization was unable to draw young men to fight and die for the New Ba'ath Party.

The al Duris needed a new banner to unify the secular and religious wings of Sunni separatism in opposition to the Americans and the Shi'a government of Iraq. It found that organization to the southeast, in the province of Diyala. JRTN was a tiny insurgent group organized around the Sufi mystical order of Naqshabandi, a branch of Sufi Islam that taught its adherents to draw themselves closer to Allah by chanting or silently contemplating his ninety-nine names.

The brand name was perfect. Its association with a Sufi cult would make it impervious to co-option or confusion with al Qaeda in Iraq; Salafist jihadist al Qaeda considered all forms of Islam except Sunnism (including both Sufism and Shi'ism) to be heretical. JRTN also originated among the Sunni Arabs of Diyala in opposition to Shi'a rule of the province; it could serve as a banner to unify Sunni Arab separatists.

Finally, and perhaps most importantly, in addition to being the former vice president of Iraq—making him head of the New Ba'ath Party—and head sheikh of the al Duri tribe, Izzat Ibrahim al Duri was also a sheikh of the Naqshabandi order. In the 1990s, as Islamism began its dramatic rise throughout the Arab world, culminating in the attacks of 11 September 2001, the secular Arab regimes searched for ways to inoculate themselves against political Salafist dissidence. Eventually, President Saddam Hussein decided to establish the Saddam Fedayeen and rebrand himself as an Islamic leader. But, before he settled on this solution, the Ba'athist elites first tried a series of other strategies to deal with the problem. One solution that attracted many, including Vice President Izzat Ibrahim al Duri, was to sponsor the rise of Sufi cults and brotherhoods. It was during this period that the vice president had himself ordained a sheikh of the Naqshabandi order.

In the process of being ordained, Izzat Ibrahim al Duri no doubt developed contacts with many of the same people who were behind JRTN in Diyala in 2008, including its elusive founder who went by the nom de guerre Sheikh Naqshabandi. This was no doubt his avenue for co-opting the organization and making it his own. And herein lay the most important element of the New Ba'ath Party's move from al Qaeda in Iraq to JRTN. The Ba'athists were never really part of al Qaeda in Iraq. Their operatives were simply pretending to be from the organization in order to attract young men. With JRTN, they *were* the organization. They did not have to pretend to be something they were not or hide from some real organization seeking to eliminate poseurs.

After they co-opted and dramatically expanded JRTN, the New Ba'ath Party moneymen in ad Dawr sought to correct another problem they had had when they fought under the guise of al Qaeda in Iraq; that organization had fallen from the graces of Sunni Arabs because its attacks killed more Iraqis than US troops. Thus, as soon as the Ba'athists assumed control of JRTN, they began to emphasize as part of their new trademark that they only attacked coalition forces, not Iraqis. This proved the decisive point in the rebranding of the Sunni Arab insurgency. Young men from across Sunni Arab Iraq, disenchanted with al Qaeda in Iraq and the remnants of the dozens of other splintered Sunni insurgent groups, but still hungry to attack the occupiers, flocked to the JRTN standard.

In practice, of course, any insurgency that wishes to survive must occasionally wield violence against the population in which it exists. Some people will be motivated to support an insurgency out of sympathy, but others only respond to fear. Even those who sympathized with JRTN, if sufficiently pressured by US forces, might give up the insurgents. JRTN had to walk a thin line, wielding enough violence to intimidate the population into silence and Iraqi police into inaction without wielding so much force that they drew the same ire that had eventually undone al Qaeda in Iraq. In practice, this violence took the form of magnetic improvised explosive devices (IEDs) affixed to the automobiles of overeager *shurta*. Some went off with the Iraqi inside, but most exploded at night, in front of the offending officer's home. Either way, the message was clear: turn a blind eye and keep your mouth shut or this will happen to you.

The New Ba'ath Party, thinking beyond the occupation, was also fighting a halfhearted insurgency against the coalition. After all, al Qaeda in Iraq didn't just disappear because of bad press. The relentless pressure of the US military, including both the security operations of conventional forces and the targeted raids of special operations forces, had bled al Qaeda in Iraq white. Yet the New Ba'ath Party had to keep JRTN growing and alive for the next war, after the departure of US forces, with the Shi'a government of Iraq. The Ba'athists had to walk a fine line here as well. They had to conduct attacks against the coalition in order to keep young men enlisted in their movement. In order to edge out competitors, they also had to conduct attacks to bolster their credibility as the only legitimate Sunni Arab resistance to the occupiers. But, perhaps most importantly, they had to conduct attacks in order to keep the cash flowing. At its heart, JRTN was a moneymaking scheme. By filming attacks and posting them on the Internet, JRTN could draw money from devoted Muslims from across the Arab world. (It is a commandment of the Qu'ran that each Muslim give *zakat*, alms, a percentage of which must go to jihad.) But their attacks could not be *too* effective, lest they draw the concerted attention of the entire US military and suffer the same fate as al Qaeda in Iraq.

The Task Force Patriot staff slowly came to the realization that the fatal assumptions on which we had based our approach to ad Dawr were the fundamental assumptions of our new Army dogma, counterinsurgency. We arrived in ad Dawr, saw a disenfranchised population and insurgents, and assumed that we needed to prosecute a counterinsurgency. But the situation in ad Dawr defied counterinsurgency as a solution because it violated the assumptions on which counterinsurgency doctrine was based. We were supposed to be separating the populace from the insurgents, but the populace of the city of ad Dawr *were* the insurgents. We were supposed to be addressing the grievances of the population, but the only way to address their grievances would be to put Saddam Hussein back in charge of Iraq. We were in uncharted territory. We were going to have to start from scratch and build a completely novel approach without counterinsurgency doctrine as a crutch.

JRTN was a mortal threat to Sunni reconciliation, the "goldfish" we were trying to protect by building the security, political, and economic strength of Salah ad Din. The presence of JRTN, the armed wing of the New Ba'ath Party, in Salah ad Din provided justification for Shi'a fears of a Ba'athist resurgence and encouraged Baghdad to take excessive measures with the province. If Task Force Patriot did nothing, then after the departure of US forces, the Shi'a-dominated government would feel compelled to be heavy-handed. This could reignite sectarian conflict and potentially lead to civil war.

Our new theory was that the political disenfranchisement of ad Dawr we had observed even before we arrived in Iraq was real and intentional. The other tribes in the area had decided to join the political process and participate in the future of Iraq, and as a result they had turned their backs on the al Duris and the city of ad Dawr, the spiritual center of JRTN, which chose to remain in the past. Rather than hinder that isolation, we decided, we should be hastening it.

The Task Force Patriot staff came to a sudden and startling realization. The Proud Americans battalion had Tikrit, the capital of Salah ad Din province, the intellectual, cultural, and economic center of Sunni Arab Iraq, in its AO. The battalion also had ad Dawr, the center of the JRTN Sunni separatist insurgency, in its AO. If we could beat JRTN and the New Ba'ath Party at its source, we could end the single greatest threat to Sunni reconciliation and end the threat of a future sectarian civil war in Iraq.

With this new realization, the staff developed the following problem statement:

> The ad Dawr district government is dominated by al Duris, which causes the whole qa'da to be ostracized by the province, blocks rural access to provincial resources, creates a JRTN safe haven in the city, and feeds government of Iraq charges of Salah ad Din's Ba'ath ties. Left unchecked, al Duri/JRTN domination of ad Dawr could drive the Shi'a-dominated government of Iraq to respond militarily, potentially reigniting sectarian warfare.

To stop this from happening, we had to defeat JRTN.

We knew we were not going to defeat JRTN by taking a heavy-handed, purely military approach to the problem. That hadn't worked in the year since JRTN arrived in Salah ad Din. We certainly weren't going to get a different result with our tiny, 450-man task force. We needed a different approach.

Iraq had never had nationwide qa'da elections. While some US forces had held elections in their areas to select qa'da councils, most of the qa'da councils in Iraq were either appointed by US forces or selected by the most powerful factions in each qa'da. This was a source of continuing friction in many provinces of Iraq. Provincial leaders in our area and in the Council of Representatives had already signaled that there would be qa'da elections in late 2010, after the national elections. We could leverage these elections to change the balance of power in ad Dawr qa'da, robbing the al Duris of legitimate power and access to government funds to fuel their JRTN insurgency. With no government money, no CERP funds, and no economy, the al Duri's JRTN insurgency would fade away for lack of resources.

The Task Force Patriot staff arrived at a three-pronged approach:

1. Use Iraqi security force partnership to stay abreast of the security situation and disrupt JRTN across AO Proud Americans.
2. Use key leader engagements combined with CERP projects as leverage to unite the rural leaders in the ad Dawr qa'da in preparation for qa'da elections that we thought might take place in late 2010.
3. Use CERP projects and provincial reconstruction team (PRT) expertise to help rural ad Dawr build sustainable industries that create jobs—especially for former Sons of Iraq and other would-be JRTN members—and have the realistic potential to become vital to the broader Iraqi economy after the departure of US forces.

We would use force to keep the pressure on JRTN, but the most important component of our approach would be to unify the sheikhs of rural ad Dawr marginalized by the al Duri-dominated qa'da government. To empower these sheikhs, we would focus on building industries—primarily agriculture—in rural ad Dawr and employing Sons of Iraq and other potential JRTN recruits. We were going to co-opt the al Duris and JRTN politically and economically and move both the political and economic center of power out of the city of ad Dawr and into the rural areas of the qa'da.

The only problem was we didn't really know who the most powerful rural ad Dawr sheikhs were. In fact, the only sheikh from a tribe outside of the city of ad Dawr in the qa'da that we knew well was Sheikh Ali Nwaf Diab al Shimiri. Sheikh Ali was the deputy chairman of the ad Dawr qa'da council (a largely irrelevant role as the council never met and the qa'da was run autocratically by Sheikh Mahsood al Duri). Ali was also a Sons of Iraq chief for the stretch of Highway 2 (what US forces called Alternate Supply Route, ASR, Dover) from ad Dawr to Mujamma (literally "the factory," a housing complex immediately south of PB Woodcock). As a successful CERP contractor, he was also a fixture at PB Woodcock.

Sheikh Ali had a home in al Nammah, along the ad Dawr–Tuz road (what US forces called Route Mango), about halfway between ad Dawr and the Hamerine Mountains. However, he spent most of his time at his home in Mujamma. It was never clear whether he preferred this location because it kept him close to his job (his Sons of Iraq along Highway 2 near Mujamma), close to his paycheck (the Americans at PB Woodcock), close to his patron (Sheikh Mahsood al Duri in ad Dawr), or away from his rival (Sheikh Sabah al Shimiri in al Hamerine).

Sheikh Ali was not the real sheikh of the al Shimiri. However, his cousin, Sheikh Sabah Muntasir Diab al Shimiri, who was the real sheikh, was disliked by everyone we asked, including Brig. Gen. (ret.) Abdullah Hussein al Jebarra al Jibouri and Sheikh Hassan albu Nasiri. In fact, as an alternative to Sheikh Sabah, Sheikh Ali was preferred by all of the other leaders with which we engaged in Salah ad Din province. At a meeting on 28 September, Sheikh Hassan, the senior sheikh of Saddam Hussein's albu Nasiri tribe still living in Salah ad Din (most of his relatives were hiding in Syria), told me that his sister was married to Sheikh Ali. On a separate occasion Sheikh Ali showed up at an al Alam qa'da council meeting attended by Cpt. Joe Breedlove (our Alpha Battery commander with responsibility for al Alam) and was greeted as a friend of the al Jibouris. While Ali didn't supplant Sheikh Sabah as sheikh of the al Shimiri, he had certainly forged closer ties with the other tribes of AO Proud Americans.

By 10 November 2009, the day of Cpl. Tony Carrasco's memorial at PB Woodcock, the battalion had charted a new course. After the ceremony, after all of the well-wishers from the Dragon Brigade,

10 November 2009, the memorial for Cpl. Tony Carrasco, killed in ad Dawr six days earlier.

Multi-National Division–North (MND-North), and Multi-National Corps–Iraq (MNC-I) had departed by MRAP and helicopter, Task Force Patriot got to business. Cpt. Scott Steele, Bravo Battery commander, with responsibility for ad Dawr qa'da, went with Lt. Col. Ahmed al Fahal to ad Dawr to meet with Mayor Uthman al Duri (Col. Sayeed al Duri, the police chief, predictably missed the meeting). Their message was simple. "Cooperation with the ad Dawr police is over," Steele told Uthman. "The RDU now runs ad Dawr."

The meeting was intended as much to corner Lt. Col. Ahmed Subhi al Fahal, the RDU commander, into backing up a threat as it was to communicate the threat to the mayor.

But the most important meeting that day was with Sheikh Ali Nwaf Diab al Shimiri. When Sheikh Ali arrived at PB Woodcock, he was visibly nervous. Only days before, he had been present when the Dragon Brigade commander, with Task Force Patriot's commander at his side, leveled a flurry of threats at Mayor Uthman al Duri, Sheikh Kaseeb al

Duri, and the deputy police chief, Lt. Col. Khatan al Duri. He almost certainly feared he was about to be pressured or, worse, arrested.

It took a while to get past his initial nervousness. The task of putting him at ease was made all the more challenging by the mood of the day. Lt. Col. Bubba Cain had, only hours before, rendered a final salute before the picture, boots, rifle, and helmet of one of his soldiers, a moment that had drained him of his signature wit and Alabama charm. But Lt. Col. Cain rose to the occasion.

"We are done with the al Duris," Cain began, matter-of-factly. "We are ready to take all of the money we were going to spend on them and spend it on you. Where do you want it?"

Sheikh Ali was stunned. After a few moments, he began to list a few farmers he thought should get microgrants. These were small, $5,000 awards, intended to assist small businesses to expand or hire more people.

I interrupted. "You need to think bigger, Sheikh Ali. We were going to spend two million dollars on ad Dawr." I watched as the number was translated to him and his cheeks flushed in realization. "We want to restart all of the farms in al Nammah. Do you need irrigation? Tell us what you need."

Sheikh Ali began to talk about an old irrigation canal, stretching northeast from the banks of the Tigris, north of Samarra, around Mujamma and out into the desert east of the city of ad Dawr into al Nammah. It needed to be cleared of debris, and its water-pumping stations needed to be repaired. "Just don't let Tikrit get involved," Sheikh Ali said. "They will take all of the money and we won't get anything."

"I also have fifty names in my car for farmers who need microgrants," he added.

The meeting concluded with commitments for further meetings and enthusiastic handshakes and embraces. His enthusiasm was so infectious that, for a moment, we forgot the sad event that had brought us to PB Woodcock that day.

Provincial council chairman Ahmed Abdullah abd Khalaf al Jibouri, commonly known as abu Mazen, hailed from the town of al Hijai, south of Bayji. There were rumors, often spread by abu Mazen himself, that he was the CIA spy identified in a *Time* magazine article in October 2003 as working with the Americans to gather intelligence on the eve of the Iraq war. According to the news story by Timothy J. Burger and Michael

Ware, which may or may not have been about abu Mazen, the spy had been a dissident Iraqi in exile in Jordan before being recruited, sent to America for training, and then returned to Iraq to spy on the regime. He was captured and beaten and tortured for weeks before the Americans reached abu Ghraib prison during the invasion and his captors fled. After his liberation, he was paid $75,000 and returned to his home near Bayji.

Abu Mazen certainly did not look the part of a debonair, international superspy. He was a short, stocky man, with a closely cropped haircut that accentuated the roundness of his face. His used-car-salesman smile was crowned with a full but pale, graying moustache. His eyes always seemed half closed, as if he were trying to discern something not easily understood. But his shifty appearance was significantly muted by the fine, slightly shiny suits he wore and the smoothness of his speech.

Whether or not this story of international intrigue was true, by 2008, he had parlayed his wealth, family ties inside the Bayji Oil Refinery, and closeness to the Americans into a burgeoning enterprise in fuel trucking, smuggling, and black market sales. He had parlayed that economic power, in turn, into a close alliance with the powerful al Alam al Jibouris.

While the al Alam al Jibouris had, by being the first to work with the Americans, cornered the market on CERP projects and secured many of the most important political and security positions in Salah ad Din, their success did not necessarily transfer across the al Jibouri tribe in other areas. For instance, in Bayji, the al Jibouri tribe had traditionally been under the thumb of the more powerful al Qaysi tribe. To counterbalance the might of the al Qaysi economic-political-military juggernaut, the Bayji al Jibouris made an alliance with the al Alam al Jibouris. In repayment for what was almost certainly a huge cut of their fuel trucking and illicit oil profits, the Bayji al Jibouris received several key postings in the al Alam al Jibouri regime. Sheikh Hamid Ibrahim Salim al Jibouri was made the chairman of the al Sawah council, from which he could control (and skim) payments to the Sons of Iraq. Brig. Gen. Eisa al Jibouri was given command of the provincial joint coordination center (PJCC), from which he could bully and fleece the Americans for CERP and work contracts for his cronies. The biggest prize went to abu Mazen, who was made provincial council chairman.

In his heart, abu Mazen was a scoundrel. In addition to his smuggling and black market fuel business, abu Mazen also had a lucrative trade in political favors. He used his position to fire the director general (DG) of health for Salah ad Din province and replace him with the chairman's cousin, a fellow Bayji al Jibouri (the latter hoped to parlay the position into a bid for the Council of Representatives in the upcoming national elections). But perhaps his most ambitious scheme of all was his plan to depose Governor Mutashar Hussein al Aliwi and become the provincial governor. Abu Mazen had been the visible leader of the movement that ended in the provincial council's vote to depose the provincial governor. And, as the power struggle continued and the governor refused to step down, it was abu Mazen who appeared on Salah ad Din Television each night, pressing the case for him to leave.

While it was impossible to prove, there were also accusations that Lt. Col. Ahmed was involved in a scheme with abu Mazen to extort money from wealthy families in Tikrit and Bayji qa'da. According to a report we received through the Iraqi Advisor Task Force (IQATF, a group of Iraqi contractors that work on American bases but maintain contact with people in cities across Iraq and provide "man-on-the-street" perspectives on perceptions in each town), Lt. Col. Ahmed al Fahal arrested the sons of wealthy patsies selected by abu Mazen. Abu Mazen then approached the mark, offering to intervene to get the son out of jail for $65,000. Abu Mazen and Lt. Col. Ahmed then allegedly split the proceeds.

Lt. Col. Ahmed Subhi al Fahal was also causing us concern for other reasons. In multiple reports we received through the IQATF, locals accused Lt. Col. Ahmed and his RDU of conducting unjustified "raids" simply to rob owners of their money and valuables. There were also accusations of RDU *shurta* beating, intimidating, and extorting protection money from locals. Of course, because the locals feared Lt. Col. Ahmed and knew he was close to the Americans, none of these reports ever reached us directly. And, because his force was so effective and always available when needed, it was easy for us to dismiss these negative reports as lies from political opponents.

While these reports deeply concerned the Task Force Patriot staff, Lt. Col. Bubba Cain dismissed them out of hand. Lt. Col. Ahmed al Fahal was the most powerful *shurta* in Salah ad Din province, which, by virtue of the province's prominence, made him the most important *shurta* in Sunni Arab Iraq. Partnership with Lt. Col. Ahmed also provided us with access to the al Alam al Jibouris, the power brokers of Salah ad Din province. Additionally Ahmed's RDU provided Task Force Patriot with an entire battalion for everything from the obligatory, security-agreement-mandated US-Iraqi police escort when leaving COB Speicher to highly capable quick reaction forces for operations like the one in Owja.

But, beyond all of that, Lt. Col. Ahmed al Fahal was Lt. Col. Cain's friend. They traveled virtually everywhere on the battlefield together. Cain had been to Ahmed's home and dined with his family on multiple occasions. "He may be a criminal," Cain would frequently say, "but he's our criminal."

Finally, however, even Cain began to become suspicious. Lt. Col. Ahmed al Fahal appeared uninvited during a visit to PB Woodcock by Brig. Gen. Patrick Donahue II, the deputy commanding general for maneuver of MND-North (which had just been assumed by the 3rd Infantry Division). Lt. Col. Ahmed was wearing civilian clothes, in full campaign mode. He first praised Lt. Col. Bubba Cain and Task Force Patriot. Cain responded by handing him a dollar bill, joking that it was prearranged "payment" for the service of "talking him up" to his boss.

After this levity, Lt. Col. Ahmed began to brag about his participation in the operation in Owja the previous month to catch men who had laid an IED on Highway 1 (what US forces called Main Supply Route, MSR, Tampa), which had netted four detainees (which the battalion had begun to refer to as the "Owja Four"). Not surprisingly, he failed to mention that one of the detainees was a *shurta* or that the men had met with his new executive officer (XO), Sheikh Neda albu Nasiri, only minutes before they were captured.

Ahmed continued, "All four terrorists have been sentenced to death."

He also claimed he had just rounded up three members of JRTN in ad Dawr who had been involved in Cpl. Carrasco's shooting.

Brig. Gen. Donahue was visibly pleased and asked us to provide him with more information on both claims. The only problem was, when we investigated later, neither claim turned out to be true. In fact, all but one of the Owja Four had already been released.

Even Lt. Col. Bubba Cain's strong attachment to Lt. Col. Ahmed al Fahal was shaken by the lies Lt. Col. Ahmed told at PB Woodcock during the meeting with Brig. Gen. Donahue. "If he would lie about this," Cain asked me a few days later, "what else is he lying about?" We began to suspect that it may have been no accident that Lt. Col. Ahmed al Fahal had remained on Baghdad's anti-Ba'athist hit list well after all of the other powerful al Jibouris were removed.

On Thursday, the last day of the Iraqi workweek, Lt. Col. Bubba Cain went to RDU Island, on Forward Operating Base (FOB) Danger, to meet with Lt. Col. Ahmed al Fahal, commander of the RDU, and S.Lt. Col. Khalil, commander of Emergency Response Unit (ERU) 3. They first discussed a joint operation that the two Iraqi commanders had conceived to interdict IED materials that they said were being ferried across the river from ad Dawr into Owja. The two police battalions wanted to execute the hammer-and-anvil operation to catch JRTN in the act but needed US helicopters to move them rapidly to ad Dawr's side of the river. Otherwise, the network of al Duri "concerned local citizens" (CLCs) and *shurta* in checkpoints around the city would provide advance warning of their approach and allow the insurgents to escape. Lt. Col. Cain was sold on the operation and promised to get them the needed resources.

Talk then turned to the stalemate between the governor and the provincial council. Only days before, abu Mazen al Jibouri, the provincial council chairman, had told Barbara Yoder, governance lead for the Salah ad Din PRT, that if the governor didn't step down, he was going to use every means at his disposal, including the media, the Iraqi police, and US forces, to force him out of office.

Now Lt. Col. Ahmed Subhi al Fahal al Jibouri told Cain he expected to get an order at any moment to arrest the governor. "When I do," Ahmed asked, "will US forces help?"

Patriot 6 demurred, unwilling to commit to such a highly politically charged operation without the express permission of Col. Hank Arnold, the Dragon Brigade commander. Lt. Col. Ahmed al Fahal didn't press. He seemed confident he had the capability to accomplish the task on his own, despite Governor Mutashar al Aliwi's rumored one-hundred-man PSD.

As the meeting concluded, Lt. Col. Ahmed invited Lt. Col. Cain to accompany him to the amusement park, a small, ramshackle collection of game booths and little rides that ran every Thursday night, occupying a city block in the middle of Tikrit just south of the Saddam Mosque. Ahmed was going to hand out toys to kids, he told Cain. Cain politely refused, making up the excuse that he had a meeting with Col. Arnold, and left.

After Lt. Col. Bubba Cain left RDU Island, Lt. Col. Ahmed left as well. He traveled out of the massive "Horse Gate" of FOB Danger and a few blocks south, toward the amusement park. He had to get out of his vehicle and walk once he reached the amusement park street, as the road was closed at Business 1 (the offshoot of Highway 1 that went through the middle of Tikrit and in front of FOB Danger). As he walked west toward the amusement park, he stopped at a jewelry store and spoke briefly to the store owner.

While they were speaking, a young, male, mentally handicapped teen that Lt. Col. Ahmed al Fahal may have known ran toward him. Lt. Col. Ahmed's PSD *shurta*, instantly alert and suspicious, raised their weapons. However, as the boy approached, he called out a word that in Iraqi culture compels one to provide protection or sanctuary. Accepting the request, Lt. Col. Ahmed al Fahal motioned for the boy to approach.

The boy stepped forward, hugged Ahmed, and detonated his suicide vest. At least seven people were wounded. The jewelry store owner, RDU Sgt. Maj. Jassem, two members of the RDU commander's PSD, and Lt. Col. Ahmed Subhi al Fahal al Jibouri were ripped apart by the explosion.

· 4 ·

The Jadir Brothers

$\mathcal{L}$t. Col. Cain's impulse upon hearing the news of Lt. Col. Ahmed al Fahal's death was to take his personal security detachment (PSD) and go to the scene of the attack. Only a concerted effort by Maj. Tim Blackwell, the battalion executive officer (XO), and me dissuaded him from leaving. We convinced him that, in the chaotic first few hours after the attack, the focus had to be on helping the living. Many of the wounded *shurta* (police) were arriving at the front gate of Contingency Operating Base (COB) Speicher within the first half hour. The COB Speicher "garrison" headquarters was directing the Nigerian guards to refuse them entry. The combat surgical hospital (CSH, pronounced "cash") was threatening to refuse them treatment based on medical rules of engagement (ROE) that were intended to develop Iraqi medical capability by forcing Iraqis to use Iraqi medicine. Lt. Col. Cain, incensed, loaded up the PSD and went to the gate to escort the wounded onto COB Speicher and the CSH. Cpt. Dan Peck, our fires and effects coordinator, followed and led a second wave of wounded to the CSH. Fed up with the circumvention of their procedures, a CSH doctor went to the front gate of COB Speicher and turned away six more wounded Iraqis. The patients that did make it to the CSH were eventually evacuated by helicopter to Joint Base Balad (JBB) where they could receive more intensive medical treatment.

At the end of the evening, we called Brig. Gen. (ret.) Abdullah Hussein al Jebarra al Jibouri, provincial council member for al Alam and de facto head of the al Alam al Jibouri tribe. He was crying inconsolably, despondent and incoherent. We also received a call from the United States, from Lt. Col. Glenn Waters, commander of Task Force Steel (3rd Battalion, 7th Field Artillery) that we had replaced in Salah ad Din province only months ago. When we confirmed that the news was true, that Lt. Col. Ahmed al Fahal was dead, he began crying as well.

A night's sleep did not improve Lt. Col. Bubba Cain's mood. The Dragon Brigade (4th Brigade, 1st Infantry Division) commander, Col. Hank Arnold, insisted on going with Lt. Col. Cain to Lt. Col. Ahmed's funeral. Cain resented his presence and disapproved of his manner at the event. Cain returned from the funeral with S.Lt. Col. Khalil, the 3rd Emergency Response Unit (ERU) commander.

If Lt. Col. Ahmed al Fahal had been the most powerful *shurta* in Salah ad Din, S.Lt. Col. Khalil al Dulaymi was perhaps the most capable. He was tall and not excessively overweight (practically slim for a middle-aged Iraqi). He shaved his head, which made his bushy dark eyebrows and moustache seem more prominent. He was soft-spoken, lacking Lt. Col. Ahmed's bravado; instead, he seemed to exude a kind of quiet, confident professionalism. He held the title of "staff" lieutenant colonel because he had attended Iraq's prestigious military staff college. He was also studying nights at Tikrit University to earn his juris doctorate and become a judge. Khalil was a pious Muslim. He didn't drink, and, unlike most every other Iraqi in Salah ad Din, he didn't smoke either.

After the Riot Dispersal Unit (RDU), his ERU 3 was the most capable police battalion in Salah ad Din. It was frequently tapped by US special operations forces to provide security or assist in their targeted raids across the province. ERU 3 also did a great number of unilateral operations, with no US assistance at all.

Lt. Col. Cain had returned expecting a medical update on the wounded Iraqis at JBB from our medical officer, Cpt. Gabriel Gandia, and an intelligence update from our S2, our intelligence officer, 1st Lt. Josh Jeffress. Cpt. Gandia angered the commander with news that Mahmood, the most critically wounded of Ahmed's PSD, was being sent by US forces back to Tikrit teaching hospital to complete his recovery. Jeffress' update failed to satisfy him either; we had few leads. We believed the suicide bomber had been recruited by an organization called the Birds of Paradise, an offshoot of al Qaeda in Iraq that used disadvantaged or mentally handicapped children to execute suicide attacks. Beyond that, there was no information at all.

That night, US special operations forces conducted an operation in Mukashifa, a rough town immediately northwest of Samarra, a stronghold of Jaysh al Islami fil Iraq ("Islamic Army of Iraq," IAI). The operation netted their target plus three brothers, all part of an IAI or al Qaeda in Iraq improvised explosive device (IED) cell. On the target's cellular phone was a text message, sent only moments after the attack on Lt. Col. Ahmed, indicating that an operation had been successful. The message was sent to a number of suspected insurgents, including an insurgent who had, in the past, sent messages to our friend Sheikh Neda albu Nasiri, the caretaker sheikh in Owja.

The Task Force Patriot (2nd Battalion, 32nd Field Artillery) staff believed that the car bomb in northwest Tikrit and the suicide vest attack on the National Unity Collective Party headquarters that had occurred in the weeks leading up to Ahmed's death had been failed prior attempts by the same perpetrators who finally killed Ahmed. Beyond that, the staff had two working theories. The first was that al Qaeda in Iraq alone had selected Lt. Col. Ahmed al Fahal as their target. Ahmed had certainly drawn the anger of al Qaeda in Iraq; he had put many of them in jail and many more in the grave. Only a few months before we arrived in Iraq, Ahmed was featured in a news story on Salah ad Din Television claiming he had killed over 200 al Qaeda terrorists. He was a lucrative target.

The second, more dangerous possibility was that Governor Mutashar Hussein al Aliwi; the Iraqi Islamic Party (IIP); and possibly the IAI, al Qaeda in Iraq, or both had killed Lt. Col. Ahmed. The governor certainly had the motive; killing Ahmed would both weaken the al Alam and Bayji al Jibouris and cripple the security force most likely to prosecute an operation to remove the governor from office. Additionally, the text message evidence, linking the attack to Mukashifa, strengthened the case for IAI involvement. The timing of the attack, just as the al Jibouris were preparing to arrest the governor, was too convenient to ignore.

A few days after the funeral, Patriot 6, Lt. Col. Cain, learned another detail that strengthened the case for IIP collusion in the attack. One of the RDU PSD *shurta* told Lt. Col. Cain that Lt. Col. Ahmed had been having an affair with the sister of Deputy Governor Ahmed abd al Jabar Ali Kareem albu Issa (a close ally of Governor Mutashar from Mukashifa). She called him only minutes before the attack, asking where he was. She had also called Ahmed only a few hours before the suicide vest attack on the National Unity Collective Party headquarters a few weeks earlier.

Whoever the perpetrators, if the attack had been intended to weaken the RDU, it had certainly succeeded. Lt. Col. Ahmed had been the glue that held the RDU together. Without him, the battalion plunged into recrimination and suspicion. The al Jibouris wanted one of two candidates, either Ahmed's uncle from Baghdad, Col. Aswad al Fahal, or his brother from Kirkuk, Col. Salah al Fahal, to take over the RDU. But the provincial director of police (PDOP) was not eager to have his authority supplanted by yet another "top cop" in Tikrit qa'da (district). He was satisfied to see the RDU go leaderless.

Without a leader, the RDU clung to Lt. Col. Bubba Cain. Competing bands of *shurta* frequently cornered Cain alone to accuse others in the police battalion of complicity in the attack on Lt. Col. Ahmed. In an effort to hold the battalion together, Lt. Col. Cain gathered them all in a formation at RDU Island and gave them a pep talk. They responded by declaring in unison that he was now their commander. When the PDOP refused to give them fuel or resources, the RDU pressured Lt. Col. Cain to intervene on their behalf; without leverage, his demands simply weakened his standing with the police leader. Mahmood, the RDU PSD *shurta* most severely wounded in the attack on Lt. Col. Ahmed, became another pressure point the RDU used against the commander. Mahmood's wife and family and the rest of the RDU PSD pressured Lt. Col. Cain to fly them to Balad to see him, and then pressured Cain to fly him back from Balad when he had recovered enough to go home to convalesce. Task Force Patriot's PSD ended up mounting a patrol to bring him back to his home from COB Speicher. Both Mahmood and Lt. Col. Cain were welcomed as returning heroes at his home when he arrived.

The al Fahal family exerted tremendous pressure on the Task Force Patriot commander as well. A few days after Ahmed's funeral, Lt. Col. Cain went to visit Lt. Col. Ahmed's mother, a large, weathered, old woman that Lt. Col. Ahmed had jokingly called "the tank"—perpetually dressed in flowing black from head to toe with only her tattooed face exposed. While Lt. Col. Cain sat in her *diwan*, she dismissed all of the other men from the room and brought in Lt. Col. Ahmed's two young wives. "You are my son, now," she told Cain through his female interpreter, Simone. These gestures had a powerful impact on Lt. Col. Cain, a passionate man who valued family, interpersonal relationships, and loyalty above all else.

As a new "son," the al Fahal family put demands on Lt. Col. Cain as well. He was expected to support a number of Commander's Emergency

Response Program (CERP) projects proposed by Mithaq al Fahal, the proceeds of which would purportedly help the widows of Lt. Col. Ahmed. He was also expected to press the case for either Col. Aswad al Fahal (Ahmed's uncle) or Col. Salah al Fahal (Ahmed's brother) to succeed Lt. Col. Ahmed as RDU commander. Finally, he was also constantly hounded for updates on the investigation, forcing him to repeatedly travel to Forward Operating Base (FOB) Danger to see High Crimes officials and judges and pressure them for information and progress in the investigation.

The RDU and the al Fahal family had their hooks in Cain, and they never let go.

As the turmoil surrounding Ahmed's death receded, Task Force Patriot tried to get back on track with its most important operation, changing the balance of power in ad Dawr qa'da. Lt. Col. Bubba Cain took a patrol to Patrol Base (PB) Woodcock to meet with two sheikhs we believed could help, Sheikh Sabah Muntasir Diab al Shimiri and Sheikh Shakur Mubarrak Muhammad albu Issa. The patrol took the military bypass around ad Dawr. The trip seemed to go without incident, but when we stopped inside PB Woodcock, the crew in the trail vehicle, which included our S7 (information operations officer), 2nd Lt. Caleb Riggs, piled out of their vehicle saying they had heard a large "thud" as they passed the southeast corner of ad Dawr, where the houses were only a few dozen meters from the road. By the time I reached their vehicle, they had identified a prominent, bullet-shaped dent on the rear passenger-side corner of their up-armored high-mobility multiwheeled vehicle (HMMWV, pronounced "hum-vee"), where a large-caliber round had made a glancing blow on the truck.

The excitement passed as soon as Sheikh Sabah and Sheikh Shakur arrived. Much of PB Woodcock had already been packed up, anticipating our turnover of the base to the Iraqi army, so we were forced to sit on wooden benches around a smaller table at the foot of the large conference table in the conference room.

Sheikh Sabah Muntasir Diab al Shimiri was overweight, but not excessively so. His facial hair was cropped into a neat goatee that accentuated the fullness of his face. He wore a simple *dishdasha* (traditional Arab robe) and *shemagh* and *agal* (traditional Arab headdress). In the photos I had seen before meeting him, his dark eyebrows had a sinister tilt, but in person, he was gracious, welcoming, and engaging. While his voice was much smoother, his manner of speaking reminded one of the movie *Lawrence of Arabia* and Anthony Quinn's Sheikh Auda abu Tayi telling Peter O'Toole's Lt. Col. T. E. Lawrence, "I am a river to my people."

Sabah spoke with an aristocratic tone. When asked what we could do for him and his people, he spoke of his tribe like children. "They are simple farmers," he explained. "All they know is that they put seed in the ground and it grows into grain. They feed and water their animals and they grow healthy and strong. Their needs are simple." He said more than once, "I am happy to talk to educated officers." He had the tone of a man who had been lost in the wilderness with primitives for a long time, finally returning to civilization.

Sheikh Shakur albu Issa shared none of Sheikh Sabah's confidence or refinement. He was quiet, clearly the subordinate at the table. But there was more. He seemed to be in beyond his depth. Even when directly engaged in conversation, he instinctively looked to Sheikh Sabah Muntasir Diab al Shimiri before answering. When he did answer, his answers were simple and ineloquent but quiet and respectful.

Sheikh Shakur, unlike Sheikh Sabah, was not a sheikh. In fact, he was not even the head of his subtribe or family. That honor belonged to his brother, Sheikh Faner Mubarrak Muhammad albu Issa. Sheikh Faner had served as part of the ad Dawr qa'da council under the more inclusive albu Jummah regime. When the al Mua'shit made their grab for power, Sheikh Faner was accused of being a member of al Qaeda in Iraq, arrested, and sent to the coalition detention facility at Camp Bucca. Now, with Sheikh Faner albu Issa in prison, Sheikh Shakur was in charge of the area. He knew he was not up to the task, so he clung closely to Sheikh Sabah, sheltered under his wing. The two were seldom separated.

Both sheikhs agreed that the stranglehold of the al Duris over the ad Dawr qa'da must be broken. The meeting closed with us agreeing to visit Sheikh Sabah at his home soon.

The closure of PB Woodcock, the first major operation in the Dragon Brigade's "responsible drawdown of forces," was turning out to be a huge, complicated operation. First, the base contained dozens of connexes (shipping containers) full of unaccounted-for material—some junk, some important communications and force protection equipment—stockpiled at the base since the beginning of the war. After briefly trying to inventory and properly account for the thousands of items at PB Woodcock, Bravo Battery, with the help of Golf Company (Task Force Patriot's logistical support company), finally just moved the connexes to COB Speicher so their contents could be turned over to an "excess yard" in a more deliberate fashion.

The next question was to whom Task Force Patriot should transfer the base. Before the war, the site had been the home of the Salah ad Din Company, a state-owned enterprise that built electric towers. Engineer Dhaif al Duri, the current director of the factory and a member of Sheikh Mahsood's ad Dawr qa'da council, had campaigned hard for the base to be turned over to him. While Cpt. Scott Steele, the Bravo Battery commander, was sympathetic, the Task Force Patriot staff had no intentions of turning over a lucrative source of government income to the al Duris. Besides, the battalion still needed the facility for the national elections as a base of operations from which to stage combat platoons to respond to emergencies in ad Dawr qa'da. Additionally, we feared Engineer Dhaif would demand that we remove the hundreds of T-wall barriers (four-meter-high concrete wall sections) and watchtowers—he just happened to have the cranes that could do the job, for a fee. The Iraqi army would let us keep the barriers and towers in place. The best solution was to turn the base over to them.

That, however, turned out to be another complicated ordeal. The senior leaders of Iraq's new army had been the junior leaders of Saddam's old army. One of the first rules of survival in that army had been to avoid direct credit, responsibility, or culpability whenever possible. Failing to do so could mean death if your name was attached to the wrong activity. We needed someone from the 14th Iraqi Army Brigade to sign for the base, but it was incredibly difficult to get a senior Iraqi commander to accept responsibility for anything, let alone a multimillion-dollar installation.

Maj. Brian Bettis was a military police officer who was added to the Dragon Brigade just before our deployment as part of a twenty-four-man stability training team (STT) package—a novel development that was being implemented Army-wide for brigades deploying to Iraq in the new "advise-and-assist" role that would become the norm as combat operations ended in August 2010. Bettis was actually a promotable captain (a captain who had been selected by the Army for promotion but had not yet reached his promotion date) who had been frocked (officially allowed by the Army to wear his new rank early) to facilitate his responsibilities as a liaison in the very rank-conscious Iraqi police and army culture. He was attached to Task Force Patriot to act as our liaison to the 14th Iraqi Army Brigade after we arrived in Tikrit.

Bettis still had the aggressiveness of a seasoned captain. When combined with his personable nature and his practical approach to problems, this made him incredibly effective in dealing with the nuances of life at the provincial joint coordination center (PJCC). He was constantly on the move, getting resources for his Iraqi brigade. In fact, he was able to build an entire firing range in the 14th Iraqi Army Brigade's compound at FOB Scimitar, directly adjacent to the PJCC compound, simply by scrounging from adjacent units and getting supplies "under the radar." While his inexperience and unorthodox methods drove Maj. Tim Blackwell mad, I generally appreciated Maj. Bettis' efforts, even if they did occasionally cause headaches. His infectious energy, wit, and enthusiasm made it easy to forget his faults as a new major.

While Maj. Bettis assured us that S.Brig. Gen. Abdullah, the 14th Iraqi Army Brigade commander, would be happy to sign for the base, pinning him down to do so turned out to be an adventure. In the end, his XO signed on his behalf. We prayed no one would notice before the base was turned over.

The next hurdle was a huge cache of bombs, explosives, and other captured IED-making materials, stockpiled since the beginning of the war, that Bravo Battery found at the edge of the base only days before the handover. We feared that if the base were turned over with these items present, they might end up back on the battlefield as IEDs. When the US Navy explosive ordnance disposal (EOD) team arrived at PB Woodcock, they found everything from artillery rounds to a huge naval mine. Rather than move the ancient explosives, they chose to blow up the ordnance in place. The resulting explosion shook windows in Tikrit and Samarra, each thirty kilometers away.

On 9 December, only two weeks before the base was supposed to close, the 14th Iraqi Army Brigade, based in Tikrit with forces from Tikrit to Samarra, was ordered to switch places with the 48th Iraqi Army Brigade, with forces from Bayji qa'da north to Sharqat. Apparently, the 48th Iraqi Army Brigade, especially its commander, S.Brig. Gen. Majid al Qaysi, had become so embroiled in his tribe's exploitation of the transport of fuel out of the Bayji Oil Refinery and the security of the oil pipeline transporting oil into the refinery that the brigade was being moved in favor of a less corrupt force. Task Force Patriot certainly was not getting the better end of that deal. The only bright spot in the 48th Iraqi Army Brigade was the 2nd Battalion, commanded by S.Lt. Col. Uday al Jibouri (an al Alam resident), who was very capable, with an equally capable battalion.

Maj. Bettis assured the Task Force Patriot staff that S.Brig. Gen. Majid would be at PB Woodcock on 18 December for the mandatory joint inventory of the base, in which the Iraqi army was supposed to acknowledge all of the US property we would be transferring. However, on the day of the event, only a lieutenant from the 4th Iraqi Army Division's G4 (logistics) staff arrived. Again, we let him sign for the hundreds of thousands, if not millions, of dollars worth of property and hoped no one would notice before the transfer was complete.

The morning of the closure, 20 December, was equally chaotic. That morning, one of the platoons leaving the base, 3rd Platoon, Bravo Battery, took a southern route out of PB Woodcock toward Samarra. An extra route-clearance patrol, scheduled by the Task Force Patriot staff, had ensured that both the northern and southern routes out of PB Woodcock were clear of IEDs the night before the closure ceremony. Yet, the next morning, only a few kilometers outside the base, 3rd Platoon was attacked by an IED. At first it appeared that there had been no damage or injuries. However, as they approached COB Speicher on Highway 1 (the main artery through northern Iraq that US forces called Main Supply Route, MSR, Tampa) at the bypass around Samarra, one of the gunners, who had dropped down into his hatch during the attack and hit his head, first vomited and then lost consciousness. The patrol had departed without proper communications with the Task Force Patriot tactical operations center (TOC) at COB Speicher, so they were not able to call for help or medical evacuation (MEDIVAC) until they were so close to COB Speicher that it made more sense to just continue on to the CSH. The soldier survived the injury, but only after weeks of treatment at Joint Base Balad, in the extreme south of Salah ad Din province.

The closure ceremony itself went only slightly better. The Task Force Patriot commander arrived at PB Woodcock at 10 a.m. and was soon joined by S.Lt. Col. Uday, the 2nd Battalion, 48th Iraqi Army Brigade, commander, and S.Brig. Gen. Majid, the 48th Iraqi Army Brigade commander. S.Brig. Gen. Majid was in rare form. He wouldn't sign for the base, he insisted, unless the 4th Iraqi Army Division G4 was also present. The whole transfer seemed on the brink of collapse until one of the general's PSD *jundi* (soldiers) stole Lt. Col. Bubba Cain's helmet. The incident so severely threatened S.Brig. Gen. Majid's reputation that he relented to signing for the base in order to cover the embarrassment.

Mr. Samir al Haddad, the receivership secretary from Baghdad, arrived at 4:15 p.m. (thirty minutes late) and immediately began playing for the Salah ad Din Television cameras, closely inspecting every room of the facility and raising objections that caused Iraqis and Americans to scramble to address his concerns. Then Engineer Dhaif al Duri, the Salah ad Din Company director, showed up to protest the transfer of the facility to the Iraqi army rather than to him. The transfer again seemed on the brink of collapse. However, Mr. Samir al-Haddad, tired of the event, told Dhaif to make his protests to the courts and finally signed the documents to relieve Task Force Patriot of responsibility for the base.

Engineer Dhaif did appeal to the courts and eventually did get the facility back by allowing a company of infantry from 2nd Battalion, 48th Iraqi Army Brigade, to occupy the compound across Highway 2 (what US forces called Alternate Supply Route, ASR, Dover) from PB Woodcock. As soon as he got control of the compound, Dhaif blocked off the remaining entrances with T-walls to prevent US forces from entering with their mine-resistant armored personnel vehicles (MRAPs). Bravo Battery soldiers had to stake out the factory compound one morning and corner Dhaif as he entered the compound to get him to at least open access so the battery could reach the acting ad Dawr joint coordination center (JCC), inside the former PB Woodcock.

As we discussed the confrontation later, I told Cpt. Scott Steele, the Bravo Battery commander, "In the end, we gave JRTN a walled fortress." (JRTN was Jaysh Rijal al Tariqa al Naqshabandiyah, literally "Army of the Men of the Order of Naqshabandi," the armed wing of the New Ba'ath Party).

With the elections approaching, the political battle between Samarra and Tikrit was heating up. In a meeting with Dr. Hatem, the director of the Salah ad Din office of the Iraqi High Elections Commission (IHEC) and a Samarra native, he volunteered that he would soon bring suit on behalf of IHEC against Brig. Gen. (ret.) Abdullah Jebarra. He said that the papers the former deputy governor had obtained to clear him in the de-Ba'athification hearings in Baghdad before running for the provincial council were forged.

A few days later, the other shoe dropped. Brig. Gen. (ret.) Abdullah was still joking on the floor of the provincial council chambers about the suit brought against him when the provincial council chairman, Ahmed Abdullah abd Khalaf al Jibouri (commonly known as abu Mazen) was sued as well. According to the suit, his high school diploma was forged. If true, he did not meet the minimum requirements to be in the provincial council, let alone be its chairman. Within twenty-four hours, both men were on Salah ad Din Television nearly nonstop, accusing the governor and IHEC of collusion. Two weeks later, yet another salvo was launched at the al Jibouris; the IHEC director in Baghdad "disqualified" abu Mazen from the provincial council based on an old conviction for car theft, for which he was supposedly sentenced to fifteen years. Apparently, for reasons we did not completely understand, Prime Minister Maliki in Baghdad had aligned himself with Governor Mutashar Hussein al Aliwi and against the al Alam and Bayji al Jibouris.

Neither Lt. Col. Bubba Cain nor the Task Force Patriot staff was terribly concerned about the conflict between the governor and provincial council per se. The staff was, however, concerned about the potential for violence on election day as a result of the conflict. Lt. Col. Cain was also concerned about reports he had received from the RDU that the governor's PSD had been firing at them on RDU Island from the governor's compound on the east edge of FOB Danger on the high bluffs overlooking the island.

When the governor asked to meet with Patriot 6, he was eager to oblige in order to raise the issue. The Task Force Patriot staff was still trying to piece together the governor's potential role in the death of Lt. Col. Ahmed al Fahal. The staff had devised a test: if the governor was *not* an ally of Deputy Governor Ahmed (whose sister was supposedly sleeping with Lt. Col. Ahmed and had allegedly tipped off his attackers as to his whereabouts), then it was unlikely that Mutashar was involved in the attack. Therefore, the staff, too, was eager for the meeting with the governor to take place in order to gather information on these relationships.

In the end, neither Patriot 6 nor the staff got what they wanted. Governor Mutashar arrived for the meeting at the Tikrit JCC with a squad of television reporters in tow and played for the cameras with US forces as the backdrop. He was trying to create the perception that the Americans still supported him; Task Force Patriot had been duped. We were luckily able to get the story killed. Salah ad Din Television got a huge amount of revenue from US forces; the vast majority of its commercials were progovernment or anti–al Qaeda public service announcements, shown on airtime purchased by the United States of America. Disaster was narrowly averted.

Task Force Patriot remained adamant that no good could come from US involvement in the dispute between the governor and the provincial council; whichever side lost the battle would accuse the United States of neoimperialism. American interference could create a backlash that would undermine all of the United States' efforts in Salah ad Din. Besides, Task Force Patriot calculated, Governor Mutashar was running for the Council of Representatives. If he won, he would leave. Engineer Khalid (the provincial council's pick to be the new governor, a provincial council member from Samarra who was, for reasons that were not readily clear, less objectionable than Governor Mutashar) would take office, and the dispute would resolve itself.

Apparently the State Department did not agree. Once the High Court in Baghdad finally endorsed the provincial council's decision to impeach the governor, a senior representative from the US embassy in Iraq went to the Iraqi Presidential Council and convinced them to do the same, in writing. A few days later, at the insistence of the Salah ad Din PRT, Dragon Brigade commander Col. Hank Arnold accompanied Barbara Yoder, the governance lead for the PRT, to notify Governor Mutashar that they no longer recognized him as governor. This was followed by a PRT dinner at Deputy Governor Amin's home, to, in essence, coronate him as the interim governor of Salah ad Din. A few days later, the PRT doubled down on the United States' commitment to the ouster of Governor Mutashar; Barbara Yoder appeared on Salah ad Din Television alongside a stoic Col. Arnold to announce that America no longer recognized the former governor.

In the end, the maneuvering settled nothing. Governor Mutashar remained in the governor's residence on FOB Danger and continued to act as the governor, appearing frequently at public gatherings and on Salah ad Din Television in that role. Abu Mazen, in a meeting with Lt. Col. Bubba Cain, remained belligerent. He frequently traveled with the provincial council to Baghdad to ask the Iraqi prime minister for an arrest warrant. Col. Salah Subhi al Fahal al Jibouri, Lt. Col. Ahmed al Fahal's brother and the acting commander of the RDU (still without orders from the PDOP), went to the MoI in Baghdad, presumably for the same reason. Brig. Gen. (ret.)

Abdullah continued to insist that the prime minister wanted to keep the IIP in charge of Salah ad Din to allow Dr. Hatem to steal the election and neutralize al Iraqiya support in the province. The battle raged on.

In 2004 and 2005, at the same time the US Army was relearning the lessons of counterinsurgency, a colloquialism came into broad usage to describe the natural inclinations of a conventional army faced with an insurgency: when you are a hammer, everything looks like a nail. The US Army was built to carry out violence, a tendency that is frequently at odds with the demands of counterinsurgency. Overcoming this tendency required vigilant, disciplined restraint. Never was that discipline more surely tested than when a unit was blooded, losing one of its own. Lt. Col. Bubba Cain had lost two of his own: his soldier, Cpl. Tony Carrasco, and his friend, Lt. Col. Ahmed Subhi al Fahal al Jibouri. Despite the fact that the latter attack was almost certainly perpetrated by al Qaeda in Iraq, Samarra, or both, momentum steadily grew inside Task Force Patriot for a "kinetic" response (i.e., the use of force) in ad Dawr.

This is not to say that everyone was in favor of a heavy-handed military operation in the city. On the evening of 23 December, I convened an "ad Dawr focus group" to discuss our options in ad Dawr. I invited Cpt. Skip Turner, our Headquarters and Headquarters Battery (HHB) commander, and Cpt. Simon Welte, my assistant S3 and soon-to-be Bravo Battery commander. Both had been in battalions responsible for ad Dawr in past tours in Iraq. They related a picture of ad Dawr that was eerily familiar. During each of their tours, ad Dawr had been an insurgent city. Each of their units had begun their tour trying to use a standard counterinsurgency approach, strengthening local police and providing projects to the local government to separate the populace from the insurgency. When this approach failed, each battalion tried to clear and hold the city, just as many in Task Force Patriot now wanted to do. After a few months of hard fighting, the insurgency would subside. But as soon as each force turned the city back over to the local police, the city again reverted to insurgent control. The big money in ad Dawr, the Ba'athist former officials and generals, provided insurgent leadership in the town with a steady flow of money to replenish their ranks and arm themselves for new attacks.

It had become clear that Lt. Col. Cain would insist on some force in ad Dawr, so before I took the staff's recommendation to him, we also discussed a plan for Iraqi security forces to occupy the city. S.Lt. Col. Uday al Jibouri, the commander of the 2nd Battalion, 48th Iraqi Army Brigade, had responsibility for this area and had two companies already stationed in ad Dawr qa'da, one across the street from the former PB Woodcock, the other several kilometers east of abu Dalef on the ad Dawr–Tuz road (which US forces called Route Mango). I recommended to Patriot 6 that, rather than a large operation including multiple police battalions, we help the Iraqi army occupy the city.

Lt. Col. Cain listened patiently to my recommendation and then told me we were doing the bigger, kinetic operation anyway. He added, "*Then the Iraqi army can occupy the city.*"

A week later, Bravo Battery took fire while boarding their MRAPs after a dismounted patrol in ad Dawr. The MRAPs were parked in the cemetery (the same place where I had dismounted on my patrol a few months earlier). As the doors were opening to accept the patrol, a gunman fired about forty rounds from an AK-47 at the platoon. Luckily, no one was injured, but the insurgent got away. After the attack, the last resistance inside Task Force Patriot to a kinetic operation in ad Dawr faded away.

The operation the staff developed was called Operation Patriot Raptor. Half of Bravo Battery, in conjunction with S.Lt. Col. Khalil's ERU 3, would encircle the city from the north, out of the Tikrit JCC. The other half of Bravo Battery, traveling with Col. Salah's RDU, would depart from the Samarra JCC and encircle the city from the south. OH-58D Kiowa attack helicopters, operating in scout weapon teams (SWTs), and a platoon from Alpha Battery on the west bank of the Tigris, south of Owja, would watch the river to stop stragglers from fleeing the city to the west. Once the town was surrounded, the ERU and RDU would then enter the town and capture their targets. Surveillance aircraft would provide full-motion video from overhead throughout the operation. The battalion commander's PSD would act as the TAC (a mobile tactical operations center) for the operation.

As it turned out, this small operation was the biggest kinetic operation that had been planned anywhere in Iraq for months, and, as word of it got out, it began to grow exponentially. Task Force Black Lions (1st Battalion, 28th Infantry) to our south, in Samarra and Balad qa'da, wanted to participate. We asked them to establish a screen line south of the city, behind our encirclement, to stop stragglers from escaping. (On the night of the operation, they actually staged almost every combat platoon in their battalion, "just in case" their assistance was needed during the operation.) The combat observation and lasing team (COLT) platoon, attached to Alpha Battery as another maneuver platoon, wanted to participate in the operation as observers, so they were integrated into the plan to watch approaches to the city for people trying to enter or leave during the operation. The brigade public affairs officer (PAO) asked us to take the division's combat camera team (COMCAM) to record the event. When Patriot 6 briefed the PDOP on the plan, he insisted that we also include ERU 1 and ERU 2 in the operation. We had to partition the city into quadrants to keep them from running into each other, or worse, shooting at each other.

The first joint planning session with the Iraqi Army was a free-for-all. The commanders of the RDU and ERU 1, 2, and 3 were all present. We presented them with maps showing the location of targeted individuals we had identified in the town. They had been asked to come with targets of their own, but no one had brought any. To save face, they all began talking about their individual organizations and how they were better suited to this US target or that. Then Lt. Col. Khalil started talking about other targets that he had east of the city, in the al Jalaam ad Dawr (literally "the desert east of ad Dawr"), that he could prosecute instead. This enraged Col. Monsour, the commander of ERU 1, who wanted to know why ERU 3 should be allowed to prosecute its own targets, outside of the city. "Are his *shurta* braver than mine? No!"

The meeting and the operation were both in danger of collapse. Lt. Col. Bubba Cain, the master improviser, salvaged the meeting at the last moment. He dramatically stood up and then waited stoically until the room fell silent, everyone listening for him to speak. "I lost a soldier in ad Dawr," he finally said. "We are doing our first operation there. After that operation is over, we will do the operations you want to do."

The room fell silent for another moment. Then Lt. Col. Khalid, the grandfatherly, doddering commander of ERU 2 said, "We should do this operation in ad Dawr!"

"Thank you, Khalid," Patriot 6 said. The meeting concluded with all of the commanders promising to return a few days later with targets.

They did bring more targets, and the remaining disputes between the commanders were resolved. The next week was a flurry of meetings, rehearsals, and refinements to the plan. Platoon leaders from Task Force Black Lions, the company commander in command of the SWTs, and

On 7 January 2010 at the Tikrit JCC, the police battalion commanders fight over targets in Operation Patriot Raptor. From left to right: Col. Salah al Fahal (RDU commander, partially obscured), Cpt. Fayez (RDU intelligence officer), Lt. Col. Monsour (ERU 1 commander), Muzahim (RDU intelligence operative), Spc. Ortega (interpreter, looking up), Lt. Col. Khalil (ERU 3 commander), Lt. Col. Khalid (ERU 2 commander), and Maj. Kareem (RDU operations officer).

all the other last-minute additions to the operation passed through the battalion area for the briefings and meetings as the plan coalesced into discernable form.

While we were preparing for our first kinetic operation, Emergency Response Battalion (ERB) 4 and the Tikrit US Special Forces operational detachment alpha (ODA) had apparently been planning an operation of their own. The mission was based on a warrant generated in Baghdad, so the Iraqi commander over all of the ERBs, Brig. Gen. Noman, accompanied the operation as well. The target was the al Othaim area, on the north bank of the Othaim River, in the furthest southeastern extent of our area of operations, at the edge of the al Jalaam as Samarra (literally "desert east of Samarra"). In the "bad old days" of 2006, the area had been a hotbed of al Qaeda in Iraq activity, but it had been years since there had been any attacks there. The persistent Iraqi suspicion about the area was a symptom of the very human need to believe that people who would commit terrorism against innocent civilians must be "others" from far away in the eastern desert rather than friends and neighbors.

Task Force Patriot was notified of the raid early in the evening before it was executed, but in the swarm of activity surrounding Operation Patriot Raptor, the staff failed to notice that one of the targets was the younger brother of Sheikh Shakur albu Issa. (Shakur was Sheikh Sabah al Shimiri's vassal and a key member of our proposed rural ad Dawr coalition.)

As the ERB/ODA patrol approached al Othaim, Sheikh Shakur was at a checkpoint on Shara al Mel'ha (literally "Salt Road," a reference to the fact that the road passes through the southern tip of the Salt Flats on its way from Samarra to al Othaim). He was, after all, also an al Sawah ("Awakening" movement) leader and had a large contingent of Sons of Iraq in his charge. When he saw the large convoy, suspecting they might be after his brother, a former insurgent now living quietly in Sheikh Shakur's home, Shakur pulled out his phone to call his brother. The ODA, spotting an Arab male making a phone call, stopped him and checked his phone. When they discovered he was calling one of their targets, they detained him as well.

The Task Force Patriot staff did not discover that Sheikh Shakur had been detained until the next day, when 1st Lt. Jay Urban, the platoon leader for 2nd Platoon, Bravo Battery, brought the news. It then took several more hours to piece together how he had been detained and by whom. With this established, it took several more hours to determine that he was being held by the Salah ad Din branch of High Crimes (a sort of combination prison and courthouse inside FOB Danger designed specifically to prosecute terrorism cases) and to begin petitioning for his release. Maj. Dave Collins, the chief of operations (CHOPS) for the Dragon Brigade, helped by asking Multi-National Division–North (MND-North) to intervene on our behalf; because of the frequent targeting of reconciled former Sunni insurgents in the al Sawah program, the detention of an al Sawah sheikh was reportable to the Multi-National Corps–Iraq (MNC-I) commander.

The ODA understood our concern and was sympathetic, but with the prisoner in Iraqi hands, they had little leverage to assist us. We wanted to do a formal prisoner release; Sheikh Shakur could be transferred to the Tikrit JCC and met by US forces and Shakur's family to ensure maximum dignity was afforded and his innocence in the eyes of Iraqi justice was acknowledge publicly. It would be damage control to protect our objectives in rural ad Dawr. However, before we could secure his release, Sheikh Shakur was transferred to the ad Dawr police district headquarters.

We were now concerned for his safety. He was a non–al Duri in an al Duri jail. He was also a key player in our strategy to take political and economic power away from the al Duris and give it to the rural tribes. If they realized this, they might pressure him to oppose us, or worse. We needed to make sure they knew that *we* knew he was in their custody. We also wanted to make sure Sheikh Shakur albu Issa knew we were concerned for his safety and were trying hard to secure his release. To achieve both ends, Cpt. Scott Steele, the Bravo Battery commander, and 1st Lt. Jay Urban went to the ad Dawr police district headquarters and demanded to see Shakur. They were initially rebuffed, but when Cpt. Steele made it clear he was not leaving until he saw Sheikh Shakur, the al Duri police relented. The Americans were relieved to find the sheikh rattled but otherwise unharmed. He told Cpt. Steele that he was being held on an old warrant related to a feud between his tribe and a tribe on the other side of the Hamerine Mountains, in Tuz qa'da—a matter that had been cleared up years before.

As 2nd Platoon's patrol was leaving the district headquarters, the people of ad Dawr registered their dissatisfaction with Cpt. Steele's conduct with twenty rounds of AK-47 fire from the same troublesome southeast corner of ad Dawr, closest to the military bypass, that had been the site of so many other attacks. The ad Dawr police at the checkpoint only one hundred meters away did nothing, but the Americans had been ready for trouble. Two MRAPs tore off through the break between the two buildings where the fire had come from, blocking off two of the three exits to the alley complex. The rest of the platoon, still on the road, watched the remaining exit with their M240B machine guns mounted on top of their MRAPs. Unfortunately, the insurgent escaped by ducking into a building and exiting through the other side.

The Dragon Brigade staff continued to apply pressure as well. The brigade judge advocate (BJA, the brigade's legal counsel), Maj. Wade Faulkner, was pressing the province's head judge, Judge Faisal. Faisal was able to establish that ad Dawr's ultraconservative Judge Fadal would be handling the case. We had heard deeply disturbing (and, admittedly, possibly apocryphal) stories about the judge, like the story that he had acquitted a *shurta* for shooting two teenage boys because they were playing pool in a pool hall, which the judge believed was against Shar'ia (Islamic law). Normally, Judge Fadal's involvement in a case would be a cause for alarm, but Sheikh Shakur was a deeply pious man who neither drank nor smoked and prayed five times a day. In short, he was Judge Fadal's kind of guy.

In the end, Sheikh Shakur albu Issa was released, none the worse for wear. His family arrived at the ad Dawr police district headquarters to find Bravo Battery soldiers present to officiate the release. In a strange way, Sheikh Shakur seemed happy that the whole thing had happened; the fuss US forces had made over him improved his stature with the al Duris and with his own tribe. This made it that much easier for us to build a coalition of rural sheikhs. Oddly enough, this US force screwup had ended up moving the ball forward in our effort to undermine the legitimate power base of JRTN.

By the evening of 13 January, we had run through Operation Patriot Raptor so many times that it seemed as if the battle had already taken place and the actual execution would only be a formality.

It was a formality that almost didn't happen. That evening, a huge sandstorm blew through, and visibility dropped to nearly nothing. Without visibility, air MEDIVAC would be unable to fly should a soldier or *shurta* be injured, an abort criterion for the mission.

The operation was saved by a bit of last-minute deal making between Lt. Col. Bubba Cain and Lt. Col. Rich Menhart, the commander of the 701st Brigade Support Battalion. Menhart offered up his surgeon, Maj. Raja Kolli, and a vehicle full of medics as a mobile surgical team. I was reluctant to add yet another variable to the operation, but, as the weather refused to abate, I had little choice. I was reminded of that old military axiom that all battles occur at night, in the rain, at the junction of four map sheets (a corollary to the much older observation from the venerable Prussian general and military theorist Carl von Clausewitz that, "In war, everything is simple, but even the simple things are difficult"). After some difficulty getting Maj. Kolli linked up with his escort, we were finally assembled and ready to roll to the Tikrit JCC.

The next crisis was fuel: not that there was not enough, but that the police wanted more. One of the big reasons Iraqi police were so eager to do operations with US forces was that they got all kinds of extras, like extra ammunition and free fuel, infrared chem-lights and flashlights, and a number of other goodies. (The police resold the vast majority of these items either to other police or on the open market as an additional source of revenue for their units and, of course, their commanders.) On this evening, Maj. Kareem, the RDU S3 (operations officer) was upset that there was not more fuel to go around. He was threatening not to participate if more fuel was not brought in.

When I arrived at the Tikrit JCC, I pulled him aside and called his bluff. "No more fuel is coming," I told him. "Go ahead and leave." He skulked away and the RDU was on the road to their appointed staging area at the Samarra JCC without further incident.

As the time to launch the attack approached, what we were about to do finally started to feel real. We were going to surround the spiritual home of JRTN in the middle of the night and flood it with Iraqi police. We were going to round up some of the heaviest hitters in the city, including Brig. Gen. Nuamah Khalil Kareem, a high-level Ba'athist general in the former regime, and Dr. Omar, purportedly Izzat Ibrahim al Duri's dentist and contact inside ad Dawr. We also intended to round up a number of cell leaders the police battalion commanders said were living in the town. We were obviously interested in grabbing the three Jadir brothers, the gas station employees we believed had perpetrated the attack that killed Cpl. Carrasco. But, for the Proud Americans, our number-one target was Mohammed Khalaf Rashid al Duri, who our sources said was the leader of the JRTN in ad Dawr.

As everyone did final precombat checks—verifying that their radios, digital devices, weapons, and ammunition were all in order—and the realization of what we were about to do settled in, the adrenaline finally began to pump. Soldiers became stony faced, sharing cigarettes or jokes followed by nervous laughter. Even that chatter fell silent as we loaded the vehicles.

The actual encirclement of ad Dawr nearly didn't happen either. ERU 2 arrived at Tikrit JCC late for its trip with the RDU to the Samarra JCC and arrived there just in time to continue moving to ad Dawr. When we departed for ad Dawr, we were held up at the Tikrit bridge by the route clearance patrol we had coordinated to clear our path of IEDs. Once they were out of the way, we had to pick up the pace to keep our time line and hit the city at the same time as the RDU. As it turned out, the RDU was late, too. They had been held up at a checkpoint in Samarra, manned by local police who believed the Tikrit police were preparing to conduct some kind of operation inside their city. It took half an hour to clear up the dispute. The delay ended up being fortuitous, allowing the northern force time to catch up. The cordon of the city was established. Each police or concerned local citizen (CLC) checkpoint around the city was occupied by an MRAP using its phone-jamming capability to prevent the al Duris on the checkpoints from warning the town.

While the SWTs were unable to fly due to weather, our surveillance aircraft was up, giving us an unobstructed view as the police battalions poured into the city. We followed an insurgent fleeing ERU 3 and watched him enter a house. We wanted to pass the location to S.Lt. Col. Khalil, but our police liaison in the TAC vehicle (an MRAP we had specially configured with maps, digital devices, and radios to make it a command and control vehicle) was fast asleep. Two of Lt. Col. Bubba Cain's interpreters, Spc. Ortega and Simone, pulled out their cell phones and began to coordinate the police battalions. We watched as the ERU 3 trucks passed by the house three times, unable to spot the location. In frustration, I sent 1st Lt. Jay Urban with his local quick reaction force (QRF) platoon to link up with S.Lt. Col. Khalil and use his global positioning system (GPS) and map to point out the location to the ERU 3 commander. We watched from full-motion video as the ERU 3, finally fixed on the correct house, swarmed over it like locusts, emerging five minutes later with the dazed insurgent.

We were less fortunate with another insurgent we spotted fleeing the police. We followed the man for over an hour via full-motion video from high overhead. He passed through the areas of three of the four police battalions in the town that night, often within a few meters of *shurta* or police trucks. I shouted directions and distances, landmarks and road intersections, which Simone and Spc. Ortega tried to pass to the police. But the man was just too wily. At one point he lay motionless in the middle of Highway 2 (which ran right through the middle of town), while confused police platoons passed by him on either side of the road. We finally thought we had him cornered in a house in the Khadasia neighborhood on the northwest corner of ad Dawr. ERU 1 surrounded the house and stormed it with concussion grenades but emerged without the suspect.

Amazingly, hardly a shot was fired that night. There was certainly some fire from the police, mostly warning shots. Concussion grenades sounded like 2,000-pound bombs in the still desert night in the narrow streets of ad Dawr. But the insurgents did not shoot back. They ran like hell to evade capture, but they knew the situation—they were surrounded by four police battalions and half of a US Army battalion—and knew our rules of engagement (ROE): we couldn't shoot them unless they shot back or in some other way showed the intent to harm someone.

By 4:30 a.m., the police had expended their target lists and their patience and were ready to go home. Each battalion dropped its prisoners at High Crimes for processing and went home. The Task Force Patriot PSD arrived at High Crimes and began processing the prisoners, running their biometric data to see if it matched any outstanding warrants, photographing and questioning the prisoners. Mr. Frazee, our law enforcement professional (LEP, a civilian contractor who worked with the battalion), came to FOB Danger to help. He was an old New York cop who had turned in his police uniform and revolver for an army combat uniform and an M-16 assault rifle. He seemed back in his element, running prints, taking pictures.

We had netted thirteen prisoners that evening. The Jadir brothers were not among our detainees. They remained at large. The detainees we did have all looked cold, tired, and miserable, blindfolded and bound, sitting on the cold tile floor in the early morning chill. One of the detainees was so cold that his hands wouldn't register on the fingerprint scanner until we warmed them up.

It was easy to tell the prisoners who had been detained before. They "knew the drill," opening their eyes for the iris scan without being asked, placing their fingers on the print scanner in the correct order without being told. They were also brazen; one of the men, a particularly tough-looking character in a long black coat, when asked his profession, answered matter-of-factly, "sniper."

The RDU *shurta* still present at High Crimes immediately added that he was the sniper that shot Carrasco, making me suspicious. It was just a bit too neat. The RDU claimed that another of the detainees was Mohammed Khalaf Rashid al Duri, though he did not match the picture we had for the JRTN cell leader. Moreover, the man admitted that he and his brother, Jassem, were JRTN "financiers," but he claimed that his name was Mohammed Abdullah Halul al Duri. We were able to verify that the man he said was his brother was in fact Jassem Abdullah Halul al Duri. I began to suspect that the RDU was trying to feed us an open-and-shut case.

Things got even more suspicious. The next day we found out that the Salah ad Din director general (DG) of health had called the PDOP, insisting that Dr. Omar be released. We were incensed; Dr. Omar had outstanding warrants from both Tikrit and Baghdad. We called the PDOP to let him know we had heard the rumor that he was being pressured. The PDOP told us not to worry. "If I tell them not to release him, a million dinars won't get him out of jail."

We had reached a crossroads in our quest to build a rural ad Dawr coalition and build the economy of the al Jalaam ad Dawr. On the one hand, we had Sheikh Ali Nwaf Diab al Shimiri. He had been our first contact in the al Shimiri tribe and seemed very pro-Western. We were already doing contracts with him and had offered him the opportunity to do many more. But, as we got to know him, we were becoming concerned that he was too close to the al Duris, in particular ad Dawr qa'da council chairman Sheikh Mahsood al Duri.

A few weeks before Operation Patriot Raptor, we had accepted an invitation from Ali to come to his home in al Nammah and meet his subtribe sheikhs and family heads. The attendees were all eager to discuss their needs and the challenges they faced on their farms. But when talk turned to Sheikh Mahsood and the excesses of the ad Dawr qa'da council, the men became restive, visibly uncomfortable criticizing Mahsood in front of Sheikh Ali.

On the other hand, we had Sheikh Sabah Muntasir Diab al Shimiri. We already knew that he was the real sheikh of the al Shimiri, and he definitely had the support of at least Sheikh Shakur albu Issa. The Bravo Battery leadership, 1st Lt. Jay Urban and Cpt. Simon Welte (who had just replaced Cpt. Scott Steele as the Bravo Battery commander), believed we should be supporting Sheikh Sabah rather than Ali. However, he was not supported by many of our other key leaders in Salah ad Din province. Sheikh Hassan albu Nasiri and Brig. Gen. (ret.) Abdullah Jebarra both recommended that we deal with Sheikh Ali instead.

We decided the best way to settle the argument was to put them both in a room with the subtribe sheikhs and family elders of the al Shimiri, pitch our idea to both of them, and see how each reacted. We arrived at the Tikrit JCC just as the sheikhs and the family heads were taking seats in the lounge *diwan* area, behind the conference table in the long conference room. Sheikh Ali took the seat closest to Patriot 6. To his left was Cpt. Welte. To Cpt. Welte's left was Sheikh Sabah al Shimiri. I sat closest to Patriot 6, opposite Ali. The subtribe sheikhs and family heads sat along the wall to my right in the massive, gaudy gold chairs and sofas of the Tikrit JCC. I immediately noticed that none of the men were the family heads we had seen at Sheik Ali's home.

Lt. Col. Cain began his pitch, which he had honed to something of a stump speech. He began with the story of his first meeting with Sheikh Mahsood at his qa'da office. Mahsood, when prompted for how we could help ad Dawr qa'da, asked for a new office building with new furniture. Patriot 6 then described the trouble we had had with JRTN in the city of ad Dawr and the intransigence of the police in addressing the problem. Then he made the pitch. "We are done with the al Duris. They are standing in the way of your qa'da." Both men had heard it before, but not in front of their family heads and subtribe chiefs. The room fell silent. We watched for any hint of their reaction.

Sheikh Sabah said nothing. He sat motionless, almost stoic. He watched Sheikh Ali as a lion watches its prey. Sheikh Ali stunned us with his response. He praised Sheikh Mahsood. He began to talk about all of the good Mahsood had done for the qa'da and how he had brought $4 million in aid from the provincial government. He agreed that the district police chief, Col. Sayeed al Duri, had to go, but insisted we could not blame Mahsood for the faults of the police. The soliloquy went on for nearly fifteen minutes. As he finally wound down, Lt. Col. Cain tried to solicit a response from Sheikh Sabah. "What do you think, Sheikh Sabah?"

Sheikh Ali shifted uncomfortably in his chair.

"Sheikh Mahsood is a dog," Sheikh Sabah said calmly, quietly. "And the al Duris are the scum of the earth. Everything you have said, Lieutenant Colonel Cain, is absolutely true. We are with you, whatever you want to do."

With that Sheikh Ali al Shimiri leaned over to Spc. Ortega, Lt. Col. Bubba Cain's interpreter, and whispered something. Spc. Ortega announced, much louder than Sheikh Ali would have liked him to, "Sheikh Ali is sorry but he has to leave. Sir," he said to Lt. Col. Cain, "he wants to talk to you alone before he leaves."

With that, we stood up, and the formal portion of the meeting was over.

As Lt. Col. Bubba Cain departed, Sheikh Sabah excused himself to the restroom, and the family heads and subtribe sheikhs descended upon me. "Sheikh Sabah forgives your ignorance, but you have insulted him by making him sit in the same room with Ali," one of them said, noticeably omitting the title of sheikh. "Ali is Mahsood's errand boy," another one said. "Why are you even talking to Ali?" another asked. "He has no authority in our tribe." The barrage continued for five minutes before I was finally released.

A few minutes later, Sheikh Sabah returned, sat down, and lit a cigarette. I overheard him talking to Cpt. Welte and 1st Lt. Urban. He was telling them he had attended another meeting in at FOB Dagger, the 4th Iraqi Army Division headquarters south of Tikrit. "The Sons of Iraq program will continue until after the elections," he told them. "After that the province will take over paying al Sawah."

While he shared light banter with the two Bravo Battery officers, I stole a moment with Proty. The category 2 (secret clearance) interpreter, who went by "abu Ibrahim" among other Iraqis, had been a Shi'a gas station attendant in Baghdad when the war began. He used the interpreter visa program to travel to the United States and get his citizenship, but now the prematurely elderly man was back, working with US forces. He had been at PB Woodcock for years, working with all of the personalities in the qa'da. He knew all of the stories from ad Dawr. He began to tell me the story of the feud between Sheikh Ali and Sheikh Sabah.

A few years earlier, Sheikh Sabah was briefly thrown in jail over charges related to his leadership in the Sons of Iraq program. While he was in jail, Sheikh Ali Nwaf Diab al Shimiri had tried to usurp him by holding an election among all of the subtribe sheikhs in which he was elected the new sheikh of the al Shimiri. This was an unforgivable affront as it struck at Sheikh Sabah al Shimiri's very identity and prospects for survival. Taking away his role as sheikh of the al Shimiri was very literally taking away everything he had.

The threat to his legitimacy was short-lived; Sheikh Sabah managed to get out of jail and get the charges cleared, but he never forgave Sheikh Ali.

Task Force Patriot was running out of time and needed to make a choice. That choice was clear. Sheikh Ali had cast his lot with Sheikh Mahsood and would not help us. Sheikh Sabah would carry the battalion forward toward a rural ad Dawr coalition.

When the meeting reconvened, only Sheikh Sabah Muntasir Diab al Shimiri remained, having driven his cousin Sheikh Ali from the field.

Lt. Col. Bubba Cain resumed, "What can we do to help the people in your area?" It was a question layered with meaning. The cautionary tale of Sheikh Mahsood that had begun the meeting almost certainly weighed on Sheikh Sabah; if his answer was self-serving, he would permanently damage his standing with Patriot 6. The question was also an acknowledgement that he had won, that he was our choice for the future of the al Shimiris. Finally, the question was a necessary one. After all, Task Force Patriot's strategy was not just about electing a new qa'da council. It was also about making rural ad Dawr economically stronger than the city.

Sheikh Sabah's answer would set us on a path that would consume hundreds of man-hours and countless patrols over the remainder of our time in Iraq. "Electricity! Al Hamerine, al Nammah, al Othaim, we all need electricity to water our crops. Without electricity our farms will never grow and our people will continue to starve and live like insects."

We had found the "Afghan road" Col. Hank Arnold had charged us to find four months earlier at the Counterinsurgency–Stability Operations Course (COIN-SOC) in Taji.

At the end of January, a decision was finally made on how the Dragon Brigade would "thin the lines" and execute a phased withdrawal. Because Task Force Patriot was the battalion with responsibility for the provincial capital and because Patriot 6 already had relationships with all of the key political and police leaders in the province, the Dragon Brigade commander, with the approval of the MND-North commander, made the decision that Task Force Patriot would remain in Salah ad Din until August. Task Force Rangers (2nd Battalion, 16th Infantry) would redeploy in May, and the Proud Americans would assume responsibility for Bayji and Sharqat qa'da. Task Force Wolverine (4-1 Brigade Special Troops Battalion) would leave in June, and Task Force Patriot would assume responsibility for Tuz qa'da as well. Task Force Black Lions would remain in Samarra and Balad until August, though around half of their battalion would leave early.

Of course, the Proud Americans soldiers and families were disappointed that they would not be going home early, but the extension of our time line did mean that everyone would be taking rest and relaxation (R&R) leave. Across both Iraq and Afghanistan, there was a strictly enforced policy that any soldier on the ground for twelve months would receive two weeks of R&R leave, generally back home in the United States.

Now that we were staying for twelve months, everyone had to go. Lt. Col. Bubba Cain asked me to go in February, so that I would be back for the national elections and he could return home in May to attend his son's high school graduation. I was, of course, thrilled to be going home to see my family, but as I got on the plane to depart COB Speicher, I could not help feeling that I was abandoning another family in Iraq.

Just as this change in our time line was taking place, the time was also arriving for our second and final "base closure," the transfer of the Tikrit JCC at Mahmoon Palace in northwest Tikrit. The base was much smaller, with a much smaller US contingent than PB Woodcock (only a dozen permanent residents, mostly TOC personnel). The main challenge with the handover of the JCC, much like PB Woodcock, was figuring out who would assume responsibility for the palace. We originally hoped that ERU 2, which had its headquarters across the street, would assume responsibility for the base, but Lt. Col. Khalid refused; he was already getting a new headquarters built for his battalion and didn't want to jeopardize that appropriation by taking over this large compound. In the end, the PDOP decided that Internal Affairs, which already had offices in the compound, would assume control.

The actual base closure went much better the second time; we had learned the lessons of the previous closure: chief among them, don't invite the media. Without cameras to play to, the receivership secretary, Mr. Samir al Haddad, had little patience for prolonging the process. He landed in an American helicopter, signed the papers in the JCC conference room, and was back in the air within fifteen minutes.

The PDOP had told us he wouldn't let Dr. Omar out of jail for a million dinars. Apparently someone had come up with 13 million dinars, because within a week all thirteen prisoners were out of jail and back on the street. Yet this did little to dampen the momentum of kinetic operations. Operation Patriot Raptor had been the highlight of the Dragon Brigade's brief to the division, the highlight of MND-North's brief to MNC-I. Everyone seemed to be pressing for more operations. The PDOP told Lt. Col. Bubba Cain he wanted us to do operations with the police battalions in the mythical den of al Qaeda iniquity, al Othaim, in the far southeast extreme of our area of operations (AO). He also wanted us to do an operation in Tuz, which wasn't even in our AO.

Lt. Col. Bubba Cain was eager to do both missions but decided to begin with al Othaim. He wanted to hand more of the planning responsibilities over to the Iraqis to improve their competence but soon found this easier said than done. The targets the police commanders identified in the area fell inside three villages. The only problem was that these villages didn't appear on any of our maps, and neither the targets nor the villages were mentioned in any of our intelligence reports. When we asked the Iraqis to point out the locations on a map, all four commanders identified different locations for the three villages, two of them pointing to spots outside of Salah ad Din. This would not be a problem for an independent Iraqi police operation; they almost certainly already had informants who could drive them directly to the spot on the ground. But the Iraqi police wanted the US to provide aircraft and aerial surveillance, which needed exact locations to operate.

In the end, after three weeks of coordination meetings, rehearsals, and negotiations—as well as a risky ground recon in which Lt. Col. Monsour, the ERU 1 commander, physically accompanied an informant to the three locations with a GPS—the locations were finally determined and Operation Bright Eagle was ready to launch. On 24 February, helicopters launched from the staging area at FOB Danger full of *shurta* from all four battalions—ERU 1, 2, and 3 and the RDU. I returned to the TOC from R&R leave at 4 a.m. on 25 February to find Bravo Battery spread out across al Othaim, cordoning the area. However, all of the police converged on the one village with the most certain and lucrative targets. The ground convoy that was supposed to extract the Iraqis, consisting of both Iraqi trucks and the battalion commander's PSD platoon, stopped at the first, most appealing objective as well. To rapidly shift to support the impromptu change by the Iraqis, the most distant US soldiers had to commandeer a "bongo" truck (the Americans' nickname for the ubiquitous Japanese minitrucks with snub-nosed cabs), piling into both the front and the back to reach a new mutually supporting position to protect the police and isolate the objective. The situation became so fluid that, at one point, Lt. Col. Bubba Cain's PSD inadvertently left him alone, in his vehicle, in an open field, before being recalled by a two-minute, expletive-laden radio diatribe to retrieve him.

The operation was otherwise unremarkable. The mission netted twenty-four detainees, mostly poor farmers from these remote desert villages. Yet the mission again received huge play across the brigade and

MND-North. Pictures of Iraqis pouring out of twin-propellered CH-47 Chinook helicopters in the dark of night graced "storyboards" (one-PowerPoint-slide summaries used to highlight significant events, good or bad, that occur in an AO) all the way up to MNC-I.

Unfortunately, the effort expended on Operation Bright Eagle stole precious weeks from our most important operation, the economic and political empowerment of rural ad Dawr. While I was gone, Cpt. Simon Welte recalled many of the approval packets for microgrants to help farmers buy new livestock in the al Jalaam ad Dawr. Many of the missions I had helped plan for Patriot 6 before I left—a meeting between Lt. Col. Bubba Cain and all of the sheikhs of the al Jalaam ad Dawr and al Jalaam as Samarra and a meeting between Sheikh Sabah Muntasir Diab al Shimiri, Brig. Gen. (ret.) Abdullah Hussein al Jebarra al Jibouri, and the provincial DG of electricity Sabhan—were canceled. It was probably unfair of me; there were almost certainly good reasons that these engagements did not occur. But I could not help but feel that the battalion had drifted back to its comfort zone—kinetic operations—without me there to keep it on course. I felt terribly guilty for having left, even though I had had no choice but to do so.

I was determined to get us back on course to the final defeat of JRTN. By the afternoon, I had convinced the battalion commander to meet all of the proposed sheikhs of our rural ad Dawr coalition, a motley crew cobbled together by Cpt. Simon Welte and his platoon leaders from across rural ad Dawr. By the evening, I had also convinced him to chair a meeting between Sheikh Sabah al Shimiri and Brig. Gen. (ret.) Abdullah Jebarra and DG Sabhan. I had to concede ground as well; both meetings would occur in one day.

The meeting on electricity for the desert happened first. We met Brig. Gen. (ret.) Abdullah and DG Sabhan at an American-built building beside the PJCC. The CERP project for the building had originally been sold to the Americans as a building for the Iraqi High Elections Commission (IHEC). In fact, it was sold to the Americans twice; the Iraqis exploited a gap in the handover of the project from the Bronco Brigade (3rd Brigade, 25th Infantry Division) to the Dragon Brigade to get the project paid for twice. The final project, a small, one-story building of less than 3,000 square feet, cost the American taxpayer nearly half a million dollars. After the building was complete, it ended up being, not an election headquarters, but a suite of new offices and conference rooms for the provincial council to meet with Americans at the PJCC. To make the bait and switch more palatable, Brig. Gen. (ret.) Abdullah Jebarra named the hall the Lt. Col. Ahmed al Fahal Memorial Conference Center and invited Lt. Col. Bubba Cain to the grand opening.

We brought large maps of ad Dawr to the meeting, maps showing the trace of power lines into and through ad Dawr qa'da. When we arrived, Abdullah and Sabhan began poring over them. They explained that there were two lines that entered the qa'da. The first trailed south from Tikrit, around the east side of the city of ad Dawr, and then south along Highway 2 toward Mujamma village (the housing complex to the south of the former PB Woodcock). This power line, DG Sabhan explained, was moving electricity at an acceptable level. The second power line stretched along the al Alam–Tuz road (what US forces called Route Pepper) west from Tuz toward ad Dawr. Immediately after it crossed the Hamerine Mountains and entered the qa'da, it turned south, along the Sheikh Mohammed Road (what US forces called Route Grape) through Sheikh Sabah's area of al Hamerine and Sheikh Shakur's area of al Othaim. At the al Othaim River, it turned southwest and stretched toward Samarra along the Shara al Mel'ha, stopping perhaps twenty kilometers northeast of the city. This power line, DG Sabhan explained, had been cut by "terrorists" in 2004, repaired in 2005, and cut again in 2006. It carried no power beyond FOB Bernstein, the joint American-Iraqi army base just west of the city of Tuz.

At this point, Sheikh Sabah Muntasir Diab al Shimiri arrived. I immediately noticed three things. First, Sheikh Sabah was well dressed, having added a red-and-white-striped suit coat over his *dishdasha* in lieu of an *abaya* (cloak). Second, Brig. Gen. (ret.) Abdullah Hussein al Jebarra al Jibouri greeted the sheikh with more outward respect than I had ever seen him show any Iraqi, shaking hands very formally and deliberately kissing him first on one cheek, then the other, and then the other. Finally, while the greeting was respectful, there was a coldness to it, as if two adversaries were meeting before a duel.

Sheikh Sabah took a seat, smoking, aloof, hardly paying attention as conversation resumed over the map. Brig. Gen. (ret.) Abdullah traced out a trail from the east edge of ad Dawr, along the al Alam–Tuz road, toward the corner, at which the Tuz–al Hamerine power line turned sharply south into al Hamerine. "There are control stations at each of these corners," he

In early 2010, we met with Director General (DG) of Electricity Sabhan (left) and Brig. Gen. (ret.) Abdullah Jebarra (middle) about electricity for al Hamerine and al Othaim, in ad Dawr qa'da (district). They pour over a map of the qa'da, discussing power lines.

indicated the northeast corner of ad Dawr and the northwest corner of the Tuz power line. "We can build a line that connects them along this road."

"We can't, General Abdullah," Sabhan interrupted. "This control station in ad Dawr is faulty." He indicated the corner closest to ad Dawr. "We must begin from the end of the ad Dawr line, here." He indicated a point near Mujamma. "Then we can build a line that stretches across the desert toward the al Hamerine control station." He traced an impossibly long line that stretched through dozens of kilometers of open desert across the Salt Flats, a huge, ancient, dry lake bed that separated the al Hamerine and al Othaim regions from the city of ad Dawr and the Tigris River valley.

"But there is no control station at the end of this line," Brig. Gen. (ret.) Abdullah began. By now it was obvious that this whole conversation had been prepared in advance and was taking place for our benefit.

"I understand that Samarra is building a new control station. When it is complete, we can take their old, mobile control station and place it here." He indicated the end of the ad Dawr line. Now they were getting to the point. Brig. Gen. (ret.) Abdullah was constructing a pretext to take something from Samarra.

"But can we build a line that goes all the way across the desert?" Brig. Gen. (ret.) Abdullah asked. "Perhaps Lt. Col. Bubba Cain can take us in a helicopter to survey the path for the line." That must have been the other thing they were after, a helicopter ride.

Lt. Col. Cain, cornered and looking to move the theater along, offered to try to get them an aircraft.

Brig. Gen. (ret.) Abdullah continued, "Such a line would be terribly expensive. Perhaps twenty million dollars." Cpt. Simon Welte started to protest that it was too much for CERP to fund by about forty times, but Brig. Gen. (ret.) Abdullah Jebarra was not done reciting his prepared line.

"Perhaps if the US forces could put up some small amount, perhaps $500,000, the government in Baghdad would give us the rest."

I had had my fill of the two actors. I sat down next to Sheikh Sabah. He motioned for Cpt. Welte's interpreter, Proty, to join us. "That electric line," he said through Proty, "it goes right past DG Sabhan's house in abu Dalef as Samarra [a small village northeast of Samarra and on the southwest corner of the Salt Flats]. He has been trying to get the Americans to build it for his village for years."

I started to ask him what course he would suggest, but he raised a single finger to stop me and then motioned toward the two Iraqis still speaking to Lt. Col. Cain and Cpt. Welte over the map. I understood his meaning—not in front of Brig. Gen. (ret.) Abdullah.

After the meeting broke up, it was on to the Tikrit JCC to meet with the sheikhs of the fledgling rural ad Dawr coalition. Three days before, when I had been trying to convince the battalion commander to do the engagement, Cpt. Welte had told me that the sheikhs of abu Dalef as Samarra and Sheikh Mohammed Village, southeast of the Salt Flats, had been very upset that the battalion commander had stood them up two weeks earlier. Apparently they were more upset than he thought, because when we arrived, they were not at the Tikrit JCC.

The only sheikhs who showed up were the subtribe sheikhs and family heads of the al Shimiris (excluding Sheikh Ali) and Sheikh Shakur albu Issa. Sheikh Sabah made an attempt to gather the al Jalaam as Samarra sheikhs to the meeting, but they said they had misunderstood the day of the meeting and were unavoidably detained in Samarra.

As was generally the case when a meeting took place with Iraqis without an agenda, the meeting rapidly descended into a litany of complaints. Projects took too long to get approved, which in Iraqi eyes was equivalent to making promises one couldn't keep. Not all of the projects were going to them, which in Iraqi eyes was equivalent to favoring other tribes more than them. Sheikh Sabah sat silent, allowing his subordinates to vent their anger. Sheikh Shakur, mimicking his patron, said little. Lt. Col. Bubba Cain soon became exasperated and excused himself for an extended break from which he never returned.

I felt his frustration and disappointment, in fact, more than he did. I was beginning to realize that, while he logically understood that building the rural ad Dawr coalition and making it economically strong made sense, he did not share my passion for the idea.

I hoped to salvage something of the day, so, before we departed, I stole another aside with Sheikh Sabah. I wanted to know the suggestion he was unwilling to share in front of Brig. Gen. (ret.) Abdullah Jebarra. He became animated, as if he had been waiting for me to ask. As Cpt. Welte drew closer, newly interested in the conversation, Sabah produced a single sheet of paper with numbers and tables in Arabic. "This is the solution to our electric problem. We need to repair the Tuz–al Hamerine electric line. I have counted the poles and wire needed, and the cost is small, only $75,000."

"How will we protect the line from being destroyed," I asked.

Sabah seemed happy to hear the question. He knew the answer. "Ah ha! I have that problem under control. I have an agreement with Sheikh Sami al Bayati from Tuz qa'da. We will protect the line together. It will be our shared responsibility as sheikhs."

I gestured for the paper, and he gave it to me, satisfied.

The idea was a wonderful one, but there was a lot of work to be done. The piece of paper might as well have been written in crayon. Approval of a project required mountains of paperwork of which Sheikh Sabah al Shimiri was blissfully ignorant. Moreover, every piece of paper in a CERP packet came at a price from some Iraqi official who lorded over its stamping and approval. A $75,000 project could easily mushroom to $500,000 or more. What we needed was a wily contractor who knew the system and how to make it produce money. What we needed was an al Jibouri.

Despite the lackluster results of the first two kinetic operations, there was still an appetite within the battalion for more. Since the conclusion of Operation Patriot Raptor, Lt. Col. Bubba Cain had wanted to do simultaneous operations in Owja and Wynot (a small town about six kilometers south of Owja and across the river from ad Dawr). In many ways, Operation Bright Eagle had been a nod to the wishes of the Iraqi police in order to predispose them to participate in this mission with us.

Nor was the operation totally unjustified. Over the previous month there had been a marked increase in JRTN attacks against US forces in AO Proud Americans. On two separate occasions, Alpha Battery patrols were attacked by a sniper with some sort of armor-piercing projectile. One single-round attack nearly hit a soldier standing watch in a turret, instead striking the interior of the turret and spraying his body armor with hot metal. The other attack struck the driver's door of an MRAP, nearly penetrating the vehicle's armor. Bravo Battery had also been attacked by an RKG-3 (a hand-thrown antiarmor grenade) on the outskirts of ad Dawr. JRTN was getting bolder in its attacks.

I was not averse to doing another operation. It built confidence inside the Iraqi police battalions and built public confidence in the police as well. Hopefully, getting their insurgents out of jail was also costing JRTN money. I just didn't want to risk soldiers for no reason. I recommended to the battalion commander that we wait until right before the elections so that we could take insurgents off the street during the critical period of the elections. Patriot 6 agreed.

As was the case with Operation Patriot Raptor, once proposed, the mission took on a life of its own and started to grow exponentially. Within a week, the operation was expanded to also include abu Dawr and Tarabala (small towns another six kilometers south of Wynot) and abu Ajil (a small town immediately south of al Alam, on the east side of the Tigris River, south of the Tikrit–Kirkuk road, what US forces called ASR Clemson). This consumed all four police battalions—ERU 1, 2, and 3 and the RDU.

When Lt. Col. Uday, commander of the 2nd Battalion, 48th Iraqi Army Brigade, heard about the mission from Bravo Battery, with whom he had been closely partnered since the closure of PB Woodcock, he too insisted on participating. Thus, ad Dawr was also added to the operation, dubbed Operation Miami-Dade. Without really trying, the operation had mushroomed into the first battalion-sized kinetic operation in Iraq in nearly a year. To cover all of the Iraqi units in the operation, we even had to include as a maneuver force our attached military police (MP) company, 363rd MPs, which normally maintained partnership with the many local police chiefs throughout our AO.

The weeks leading up to Operation Miami-Dade were a flurry of activity. An operation of this scale required detailed planning, but that planning was constantly complicated by changes the Iraqis made each time they were brought together. The staging plan for forces changed from FOB Danger, to FOB Sa'ad (the long, narrow base of the 2nd Battalion, 48th Iraqi Army Brigade, that stretched from Tikrit to Owja along Highway 1), to, finally, both places. Of course we had to bring fuel, infrared chem-lights, and other goodies for the Iraqis, which now had to be split between two separate locations. The preparation also included possibly one of the most massive joint US-Iraqi rehearsals ever staged for a kinetic operation. Every commander or platoon leader in the battalion, including our MPs and other attachments, crammed in a room at the Lt. Col. Ahmed al Fahal Memorial Conference Center, with the Iraqi police or army commander with whom they would operate, to walk through the plan. Whereas in an American-only rehearsal, this might have been an orderly process, run by one central figure who choreographed the entire rehearsal, in this case it was thirty separate conversations, all taking place at once in a room full of smoke, chatter, and *chai*.

The operation itself began on the evening of 2 May 2010, only five days before the national elections. It was a masterpiece, the culmination of lessons learned from two previous operations of increasing complexity. The battalions all departed their staging areas roughly on time and, by being closely paired with American counterparts, arrived at their separate objectives rather than all converging on the most lucrative target.

Before 2nd Battalion, 48th Iraqi Army Brigade, even reached ad Dawr, they happened upon and stopped a suspicious vehicle trying to flee ad Dawr and bypass them. Inside they found four brothers, Jamal, Nemer, Ali, and Mohammed Jadir Ali al Duri, the ring of JRTN operatives we believed had shot Cpl. Carrasco. Bravo Battery soldiers at the scene positively identified one of the men as having been present on the street when Carrasco was shot and another as the man who had thrown an RKG-3 at them only weeks before. The immediate success exhilarated Iraqi and American alike and began a game of one-upmanship that made this the most lucrative raid of our time in Iraq.

Each US battery or company cordoned its area of operations while its police or army partner went from street to street, from target house to target house, rounding up its prey. From our TAC location, we watched on full-motion video and coordinated the movement and targeting of OH-58D Kiowa helicopter SWTs between the four large target areas. By daybreak the Iraqi police and army battalions had netted thirty-two prisoners.

Only the RDU (now led by a major handpicked by the PDOP and starved of both leadership and resources) came up empty, operating in Wynot, Tarabala, and abu Dawr. They had departed FOB Danger late because they were more interested in draining the last drops of free fuel at FOB Danger than participating in the operation.

On the night Lt. Col. Bubba Cain conceived of Operation Miami-Dade—the day the prisoners from Operation Patriot Raptor had been released—I told the battalion commander I wished we had used the OH-58D SWT to shoot those two insurgents in Owja all those months ago, while they lay in wait to attack one of our convoys. I wasn't joking. By now, only one of the "Owja four" captured on that night was still in jail, and he would probably be released as soon as we stopped asking about him.

Thirty-six hours after Operation Miami-Dade, Task Force Patriot drew the line on the revolving door of Iraqi "justice." When we called High Crimes to coordinate for permission to interrogate the four Jadir brothers, they told us the brothers had been released! A quick overflight of their home with reconnaissance aircraft confirmed that they were at home, literally celebrating with a welcome-home lawn party.

After a quick round of recriminations, delivered telephonically by Spc. Ortega on behalf of Patriot 6 to all of the prominent judges, the PDOP, and the RDU (who had allegedly effected their release), the battalion began crisis action planning for Operation Bright Hawk.

Bravo Battery would link up with a company of the 2nd Battalion, 48th Iraqi Army Brigade, at the Tikrit JCC, conduct a quick rehearsal, and then move to ad Dawr. Once in ad Dawr, an SWT and aerial recon would provide over-watch while Bravo Battery isolated the section of town where the Jadir brothers lived and 2nd Battalion, 48th Iraqi Army

Brigade, moved in and detained them. Lt. Col. Uday sounded genuinely enthusiastic to be going back to ad Dawr to reclaim the glory he had secured only two days before.

Word of Operation Bright Hawk spread quickly. As Bravo Battery moved toward the front gate of COB Speicher—only three hours after we had learned of the Jadir brothers' release—angry calls began to flood the Dragon Brigade headquarters. Col. Hank Arnold contacted Lt. Col. Bubba Cain and, concerned about the uproar, asked that we postpone the mission until we had warrants. We called the PDOP, who had told us weeks ago he had warrants for the four. He now denied ever having made such a claim. A quick call to Lt. Col. Uday confirmed that he could obtain a warrant through the 4th Iraqi Army Division from Baghdad within an hour, so, with the permission of the Dragon Brigade commander, Bravo Battery continued on to the Tikrit JCC to begin rehearsals while we waited for the promised warrants.

As soon as the first platoon left COB Speicher, the RDU called the Task Force Patriot TOC to assure us they had already recovered three of the Jadir brothers and had the fourth on the way. We had had to release our aerial recon so that it would be available during Operation Bright Hawk, so we could not verify that the recapture was taking place. Instead, we told Maj. Kareem, the RDU S3, that we were on our way to FOB Danger to verify that the Jadir brothers were back in custody. By the time Bravo Battery arrived in force at High Crimes, they found that all thirty-two of the Miami-Dade prisoners, as well as twenty-two of the twenty-four Operation Bright Eagle prisoners (two had been released with our knowledge, as they had been victims of mistaken identity), were back in custody.

• 5 •

Sheikh Sabah al Shimiri

$\mathcal{I}$n January 2005, Sunni Arab Iraqis largely boycotted the elections to elect a transitional national assembly. As a result, they had little voice in the writing of the Iraqi constitution. They did participate in the late 2005 referendum on the constitution but opposed it by 96.9 percent. They also came out in droves for the 2006 national elections, but the rules—set by the transitional authority that Sunni Arabs had refused to help select—were grossly disadvantageous to the Sunni minority. As a result, they were grossly underrepresented in the Council of Representatives. Only an eleventh-hour, backroom deal granted them enough seats to minimally represent their interests. Now, with elections slated for January 2010, Sunni Arab Iraqis were very motivated to vote and increase their voice in the Iraqi government.

By election day, 7 March 2010, a vast amount of effort, steadily, day by day, had been expended to help the Iraqis prepare for the national elections. The elections had initially been planned for January but, due to wrangling in the Council of Representatives over the allocation of seats, they were delayed until March. Would there be a census which might shift the balance of power in Kirkuk toward or away from Kurds? How many seats would be allocated for women? How many seats would be allocated for voters outside the country? There were dozens of other questions that had to be settled before an election law was passed and an election could be held.

While the election law remained in question, of course, Iraqi Ground Forces Command (IGFC, the high command of the Iraqi army) and the

Ministry of the Interior (MoI, the government agency in charge of all Iraqi police) refused to issue an order directing security for the elections. And commanders in Salah ad Din, conditioned by thirty years of the Saddam Hussein regime *not* to show initiative or outshine their peers, adamantly refused to plan or prepare for elections. Task Force Patriot (2nd Battalion, 32nd Field Artillery) did what it could; it surveyed predicted election sites itself and tried to anticipate the requirements for each. But without willing Iraqi participation in the survey, it was impossible to anticipate their every need.

Once the IGFC and MoI orders were published, only weeks before the election, the Iraqi security forces were finally willing to prepare for the elections and flooded us with demands. We had anticipated many of them, but many more we had not. Filling those requests was frustrated by the same byzantine rules that made it so difficult to get Commander's Emergency Response Program (CERP) money for schools, electric lines, or other projects. We couldn't purchase barrier materials for the Iraqis until they submitted a request to the Iraqi High Elections Commission (IHEC) and were refused help in writing. Once the materials were purchased and emplaced, there were more ridiculous rules to navigate. Even though the items had been purchased for the Iraqi security forces, they had to be turned over to civilian Iraqi government officials, not to the police or the army, because new rules prohibited CERP funds from being spent on security forces. It didn't matter that Khadasia Secondary School had absolutely no use for fifty jersey barriers and 200 meters of concertina wire. That was their problem.

The orders from the IGFC and MoI, along with the orders that had been received much earlier through US force channels, delineated the division of security responsibility for the elections. Simply put, the Americans were supposed to be postured to support, but invisible. The only US forces that were permitted to be on the street were those escorting observers from the provincial reconstruction team (PRT) and the United Nations Assistance Mission–Iraq (UNAMI, a tiny contingent of perhaps two dozen people, mostly security forces, headquartered inside the International Zone—the IZ, formerly the "Green Zone"—in Baghdad). And those forces had to be marked as UN observer vehicles. All other Americans had to be close by, ready to offer assistance in the case of mass casualty events, but not visible on the streets. We staged Alpha Battery in the Tikrit joint coordination center (JCC) at Mahmoon Palace (literally the "Birthday" Palace), Bravo Battery at the ad hoc ad Dawr JCC in the former Patrol Base (PB) Woodcock, and Headquarters and Headquarters Battery (HHB) at the IHEC warehouse inside Forward Operating Base (FOB) Danger. We had converted several of our mine-resistant armored personnel vehicles (MRAPs) to ambulances to deal with mass-casualty events and flooded the area of operations (AO) with all of our medics and our physician's assistant, Lt. Schipper. In addition to this medical assistance role, we had also been charged to escort the ballots from the qa'da (district) IHEC offices to the provincial IHEC warehouse on FOB Danger.

The IGFC and MoI orders specified that the Iraqi police would provide "inner security" in and around the polling sites, while the Iraqi army would provide "outer security" further out. The roles seemed ambiguous to the Task Force Patriot staff, but the Iraqis, who had had similar arrangements for the provincial election only a year earlier, seemed comfortable with the delineation of responsibility.

The joint US-Iraqi coordination meetings for the election, held on a semiweekly basis leading up to the election, turned out to be largely unnecessary, frequently descending into opportunities for the Iraqis to pressure Lt. Col. Bubba Cain for more barrier material or projects completely unrelated to election security. "Elections would be so much more efficient in north al Alam," Maj. Kareem, S3 (operations officer) for the Riot Dispersal Unit (RDU), suggested at one such meeting, "if only the school were renovated."

The Iraqi-only rehearsals—conducted in Tikrit, al Alam, and ad Dawr police districts—were genuinely impressive, with Iraqi army and police interoperating with fire departments and hospitals. Seeing these rehearsals in action, I was reminded of the highly publicized bioterrorism rehearsals that frequently took place in the United States.

The Americans in Salah ad Din were largely spectators for the actual elections. The majority of Task Force Patriot rolled out of Contingency Operating Base (COB) Speicher to their assigned locations the night before the elections. I rolled out with Lt. Col. Cain early the next morning, just before the moratorium on US forces on the street went into effect. We arrived at the Tikrit JCC and began to settle in for what we expected to be an uneventful day. The town was deadly silent. For the elections, all nonsecurity vehicular traffic inside the city was suspended. I sat down on the steps of the JCC and relaxed, exhausted by the week of furious activity leading up to the elections—the preparations, Operation Miami-Dade, and the aborted Operation Bright Hawk. I was happy to have the elections almost behind us.

Just as Lt. Col. Bubba Cain sat down next to me on the marble-tiled step, a thunderous boom rang out in the thick, cool morning air. We stared in disbelief at one another for several seconds before I sprang up and ran into the operations center of the JCC, remanned after over a month of dormancy since the closing of the Tikrit JCC. Smoke George Havel ("Smoke" was an honorific given to a sergeant first class who had served as a howitzer platoon sergeant) was in the operation center screaming out directions to Americans and Iraqis alike.

Within half an hour, after the obligatory inaccurate reports that always followed such an event, we finally had the full story on the explosion. Early in the morning, a vehicle full of propaganda from Jaysh Rijal al Tariqa al Naqshabandiyah (JRTN, literally "Army of the Men of the Order of Naqshabandi," the armed wing of the New Ba'ath Party) had been discovered in Owja. It was dragged inside Forward Operating Base (FOB) Danger for further investigation. At precisely 7 a.m., a bomb placed in its trunk exploded, as it had been timed to do. The bomb was much too small to do any real damage and no one was injured, but in the quiet, motionless election morning, the sound of the bomb reverberated across the city, almost certainly frightening many away from the polls until much later in the day. Without hurting anyone, the bomb had accomplished its maker's intent, to suppress voter turnout.

A few hours later, just as voters were beginning to regain their nerve, the Iraqi police explosive ordnance disposal unit (IPEOD) spooked them again. They exploded an improvised explosive device (IED) on the Tikrit bypass on Highway 1 (the main artery through northern Iraq that US forces called Main Supply Route, MSR, Tampa), northwest of the city out beyond the Tikrit JCC. They had found the IED and rendered it harmless the day before. The task could have easily been delayed until after the polls closed. Another thunderous boom rang out across the city, and many voters waited into the afternoon before coming to the polls.

Despite these setbacks, the mood was upbeat among Americans and Iraqis alike. A few American soldiers threw a ball in the broad, concrete parade route through the Tikrit JCC and delighted as S.Sgt. Jack, the military working dog that had been attached to Alpha Battery, ran after it and brought it back. The Alpha platoon sergeants broke out a grill and grilled hot dogs, hamburgers, and steaks for their soldiers. It was a brief respite of normalcy in a year of violence and anxiety.

Lt. Col. Bubba Cain and I, as was military tradition, waited impatiently until all of the soldiers had a chance to eat. Just as it seemed it might be our turn and there might be a steak left for each of us, Sheikh Sabah Muntasir Diab al Shimiri arrived with a steaming platter of goat and rice that he insisted we share with him in the Iraqi style, with our bare hands around the single plate of food.

As we reluctantly followed him into the office of the new JCC director, S.Col. Muhaymid, Lt. Col. Bubba Cain looked at me and said, "Come on, S3. You got us into this," a reference to my enthusiastic advocacy of the rural ad Dawr coalition.

While we ate with Sheikh Sabah and S.Col. Muhaymid, police commanders dropped by to pay their respects to Patriot 6. S.Lt. Col. Khalil, the commander of Emergency Response Unit (ERU) 3, was thrilled to see so many Iraqis out voting. The RDU's S2 (intelligence officer), Cpt. Fayez, and a shady civilian intelligence operative, Muzahim, came bearing claims that Samarra was cheating in the elections, allowing males to vote for the women in their families, an express violation of the election law. Sheikh Sabah, no doubt wary of the questions this might cast in our minds about those members of the rural ad Dawr coalition with closer ties to Samarra, made a very public call to an al Shimiri relative in Samarra and assured us, based on this spurious survey with a sample size of one person, that no such cheating was occurring. In the bright mood of the day, the answer seemed to satisfy everyone in the room.

The operation went well into the night and into the early hours of the morning. We watched breathlessly from aerial surveillance full-motion video, following the path of the UNAMI and PRT observers we were escorting around the battlefield, hoping they would not see anything that dismayed them. Later we watched equally breathlessly as our patrols escorted the last ballots from the most populous areas of Tikrit back to the IHEC warehouse. In the end, the Tikritis, and for that matter, all Sunni Arab Iraqis, had every reason to be proud of the day. The Salah ad Din province had an incredible 70 percent voter turnout, with al Alam boasting 80 percent. Sunni Arab Iraqis had gone to the polls and demanded a voice in their government.

Moreover, they were not voting for a Sunni. Despite the presence on the ballot of Sunni separatists like ad Dawr qa'da council chairman

Sheikh Mahsood al Duri, Sunni Arab Iraqis (with the notable exception of Samarra qa'da) overwhelmingly supported al Iraqiya and the bid of the secular Shi'a former prime minister Iyad Alawi to return to office.

As I returned with Lt. Col. Bubba Cain and his personal security detachment (PSD) from the Tikrit JCC, more than a full day after we had departed, I arrived back in the Task Force Patriot tactical operations center (TOC) to find Maj. Tim Blackwell, the battalion's tireless sentry, still on TOC watch for his twenty-fifth straight hour. At my insistence, and with my assurance that I had stolen a few hours of rest at the JCC, he reluctantly went to bed.

This was Blackwell's final battle. He would be departing Iraq with that same sick feeling I had felt when I got on the plane to go on rest and relaxation (R&R) leave. But for him the feeling would be worse. He was leaving for good, to take a post as professor of military science at Bowie State University.

His replacement, Maj. Matt Payne, was a veteran of the Dragon Brigade (4th Brigade, 1st Infantry Division), having joined as the brigade fire support officer immediately after the brigade returned from the surge in 2008. He was short, with a singular wit and a disarmingly friendly Virginia accent. Combined with his full moustache (an affectation frowned upon among army officers) and his devotion as a converted Catholic, he invited ready comparisons to Ned Flanders, the perpetually upbeat evangelical from *The Simpsons*, among the officers and soldiers of the brigade. Whereas some might be offended by the comparison, Matt wore it as a badge of honor, literally. When anyone brought up the comparison, he produced a Dragon Brigade security badge bearing his name but a portrait of the *Simpsons* character.

As soon as one got to know Sheikh Sabah Muntasir Diab al Shimiri, it became clear that he had suffered some tragic fall. He was prince of an empire of dust. While the al Shimiri tribe in Iraq stretched as far north as Sharqat and as far south as Basra, Sheikh Sabah's immediate domain, al Nammah and al Hamerine (a region al Shimiris referred to as al Aith), had been laid waste by the ravages of the war in Iraq. The region had once been a lush agricultural area. However, in 2004, "terrorists" (more likely Tuz residents unhappy sharing their electricity) had demolished the electric line that carried electricity from the power plants north of Tuz, over the Hamerine Mountains, and into al Hamerine. Without electricity to irrigate their fields, the al Shimiris of al Aith watched help-lessly as their crops died. After their crops died, the al Aith al Shimiris ate their livestock. When they ran out of livestock, they migrated to hastily constructed mud huts in the area known as Mud Town (the refugee city that had sprung up between the Khadasia neighborhood of Tikrit and the south wall of Tikrit University). The migration of his people away from al Aith was a point of intense anger and frustration, very much tied to his identity as a sheikh. "They live like insects, like pigs in the mud," he frequently said, their condition a silent indictment of his inability to provide for his people.

Sheikh Sabah had a simple concrete house in the farthest reaches of the al Jalaam ad Dawr (literally "the desert east of ad Dawr") where he of-ten stayed. However, Sheikh Sabah also had another home in downtown Tikrit, across the street from FOB Danger. He called it his "office," but one soon gathered that more than work went on there. The compound featured high T-walls (the ubiquitous concrete blast barriers that now dominated most Iraqi cities) and a concrete watchtower. Through the day, Sheikh Sabah welcomed members of his tribe living in Mud Town who could not make the long journey to his compound in al Hamerine. Once one got to know him, he would confide that he enjoyed scotch but would only partake in his Tikrit home, where "his people" could not see him. He would also joke with Americans about his Russian "secretary," though no one had ever actually seen her. The evening parties that occasionally took place there were legendary.

The two worlds of Sheikh Sabah Muntasir Diab al Shimiri very much mirrored the man himself. He was a man who comfortably bore the mantle of social leader, yet he held close to his heart the vices and passions that threatened to destroy him.

Sheikh Sabah had had an unusually long run of bad luck, but to be fair, he occasionally created his own misfortune. His healthy libido and periodic temper had landed him afoul of the other tribes of the province on many occasions since the beginning of the war. One story tells of his infatuation with the sister of Sheikh Neda, the caretaker sheikh of Saddam Hussein's tribe, the albu Nasiri, in Owja, south of Tikrit. Ap-parently, Sheikh Neda had repeatedly rejected Sheikh Sabah al Shimiri's requests for his sister's hand in marriage. As the story goes, Sheikh Sabah got drunk in his home in Tikrit one evening and decided to force the is-sue with Sheikh Neda. He arrived at Sheikh Neda's massive tribal home on the high western bank of the Tigris, armed, angry, and ready to force Sheikh Neda to relent. The situation was explosive. Sheikh Sabah was a real sheikh; Neda was not. Sheikh Sabah had no right to make such a demand. Yet, had Neda shot Sabah, it would have plunged the entire region into tribal warfare. The situation was finally resolved by Lt. Col. Ahmed al Fahal al Jibouri and the RDU, who showed up, broke up the fight, and hauled Sheikh Sabah off to jail to sober up. The whole incident—Sheikh Sabah's public drunkenness, his unreasonable demand, and his indiscretion—permanently damaged his social standing in Sunni Arab Iraq.

However, Sheikh Sabah Muntasir Diab al Shimiri's most unconventional feature was not his passions, but his vision. Most Iraqis, conditioned by thirty years of survival under the brutal regime of Saddam Hussein, only saw the world the way it was at the time. They were incapable of seeing beyond the possible dangers that a proposed action entailed, to its opportunities. In this regard, Sheikh Sabah was unique among Iraqis. He had a keen political mind that allowed him to understand both the future that was possible and the interests of the person describing that future to him. In both, he could immediately grasp not just the dangers of action but the opportunities that action created.

On this day, in mid-March, it was a battle to appeal to his vision to overcome his passions. We had gathered from the meeting between Sheikh Sabah Muntasir Diab al Duri and Brig. Gen. (ret.) Abdullah Hussein al Jebarra al Jibouri that Sabah had some issue with Abdullah, if not the entire al Jibouri tribe. However, if Task Force Patriot was going to get his ambitious electricity project off the ground, we were going to need the contracting expertise of the best al Jibouri contractor.

That meant Mohammed Ibrahim Hamid al Jibouri. Contractor Mohammed was a dark, thin man, whose proportions made him seem taller than he actually was. Energetic and engaging, within the first half hour of meeting him, one knew his life story. Mohammed began working for the Americans as a janitor, sweeping up in the halls of FOB Danger when it was still under the control of the 4th Infantry Division, before it was returned to Iraqi police control in late 2005. He taught himself to speak English by engaging soldiers in conversation around the base. When his English was strong enough, he began working as a category 1 (local national) interpreter for the Americans. After working long enough, Mohammed was granted a US visa. But Mohammed could not stand the thought of leaving his family, so he decided against going to America.

Instead, he quit his job as an interpreter and became a contractor, competing for CERP projects.

As a contractor, he had prospered. His deep understanding of Americans and how the US military thought and operated, gained from years of working with them and traveling with them on patrols, had given him a leg up on all the competition. If a unit told him they wanted to do a project, he would return a few days later with a complete packet with three project proposals (ostensibly from three different contractors in order to meet the CERP three-bid requirement) and signed letters from both the relevant qa'da council and the Salah ad Din provincial council authorizing the project. No other contractor in Salah ad Din could put this package together as quickly or as completely.

He was not as rich as Lt. Col. Ahmed al Fahal's former client, contractor Mithaq al Fahal, but he was hungrier. He worked faster and harder to get the job done. Moreover, he had a near-supernatural ability to anticipate the onerous requirements of the US Army contracting process and to produce just the right documents to get CERP projects through. If Task Force Patriot was going to get the electric line from Tuz to al Hamerine to al Othaim fixed, we were going to need contractor Mohammed.

When Mohammed arrived, I took him straight to my office. "I have a huge project, the most important project we will do in our year in Iraq, and I want you to do it." I let the statement sink in before I continued. "You have done a lot of work for the coalition and for us, and it has all been top quality and done fast. I have not talked to anyone about this except you." I paused again.

"Sir, I will not let you down. I have always worked closely with coalition forces. Since the beginning I have always worked with you. I think of myself as one of you, and I want you to succeed." Mohammed's enthusiasm had gotten the better of him, and he stopped to catch his breath.

"This is not just a project. This is about building up a man, a village, and a tribe." I paused before deciding on frankness. "This is my second time in Iraq and I know how projects work. There is the money you have to spend to build the project and there is the money you have to spend to make everyone happy." This may have been something he had not heard an American say before. Everyone lied to themselves and to each other about CERP "corruption." Many Americans even believed the lies, or wanted to believe them. "This project is for Sheikh Sabah and the al Shimiris in al Hamerine. Sheikh Sabah has to be happy. That is the point of the project. We want him to do something for us, and we have to make him happy or he won't do it."

Mohammed started slightly when I said the name. He tried hard to make it imperceptible, but I noticed. "I have worked with sheikhs and tribes before. I know how to work with them. He will be very happy with the work I do for him and his tribe."

As I described the project to him, poring over the same maps that Brig. Gen. (ret.) Abdullah Jebarra and Salah ad Din province director general (DG) of electricity Sabhan had pored over only days before with Lt. Col. Bubba Cain, an insistent knock came at my door. It was 1st Lt. Jay Urban, now the executive officer (XO) for Bravo Battery. "Sir, Sheikh Sabah is in the conference room. He is pissed!" I had had Cpt. Simon Welte, the Bravo Battery commander, invite Sheikh Sabah on the pretext of signing a CERP contract to purchase water trucks for his village with the ulterior motive of putting Mohammed and Sabah together in a room.

Contractor Mohammed politely excused himself to the back porch of the TOC to share a cigarette with Lt. Col. Bubba Cain while I went to speak to Sabah.

I had Mike Samander, a new category 2 (secret clearance) interpreter working in our TOC, come with me. Samander was an older man. Bald and dark, he once joked he looked like an Arab Kojak (from the 1970s police drama). He was a naturalized Palestinian immigrant to the United States. He had run a wildly successful contracting business in Connecticut before he fell on hard times. To put his daughters through college, he came to Iraq as an interpreter, first in Kirkuk and then with us, in Salah ad Din province.

When I entered the conference room, the fatigue on Cpt. Simon Welte's face was clearly visible. Normally he was upright, his athletic build and his chiseled, faintly Asian features pressed into a confident sternness. Now his head hung low and his shoulders drooped forward as he pressed himself up from the table for the traditional greetings as I entered the room.

Sheikh Sabah Muntasir Diab al Shimiri was curt as he gathered up his flowing *dishdasha* (robe) and *abaya* (cloak) beyond his wrists to greet us. He greeted with only a single kiss to the cheek rather than his normally warm and welcoming three kisses. Sheikh Shakur albu Issa mimicked his patron's cold response.

As we sat down, there was no small talk. Sheikh Sabah got right to the point. "Why have you brought in this *kabeeth*?" There was no English translation for the slur. The closest American equivalent, I was once told by Lt. Col. Bubba Cain's interpreter, Simone, was "rat bastard." Sheikh Sabah was only getting started. "This is another thief from al Alam." He meant another al Jibouri. "He will steal whatever you pay, and we will be left with nothing."

We didn't have time for this. Task Force Patriot was going to take over the AO Rangers from Task Force Rangers (2nd Battalion, 16th Infantry) in two months. A month later, we were going to take over AO Wolverines from Task Force Wolverine (4-1 Brigade Special Troops Battalion). Soon we were going to be stretched too thin to concentrate on building the rural ad Dawr coalition. We needed to move fast.

But we needed Sheikh Sabah. Whatever his faults, he had the legitimacy to pull together all of the tribes of the al Jalaam ad Dawr and al Jalaam as Samarra (literally "the desert east of Samarra"). He was a real sheikh. That was no small thing. If you spent more than a week on the ground in Iraq, you would meet at least a half dozen people who called themselves "sheikh." Some of these men (like Sheikh Mahsood al Duri of the ad Dawr qa'da council or Sheikh Wanus al Jibouri of the al Alam Sons of Iraq) were brothers or close cousins of sheikhs. Others were subtribe sheikhs, like Sheikh Kaseeb al Duri or Sheikh Khemis al Jibouri, heads of a collection of families but not of a bona fide tribe. But most, like Sheikh Khaldoun al Duri of Wynot, had simply bought a *dishdasha* and *shemagh* and *agal* and started calling themselves sheikhs. None of them were actually sheikhs.

There were only seven real sheikhs (those who could trace their nobility back to the Nejd and Hejaz, the ancestral Arab homeland on the Arabian Peninsula near modern-day Yemen), and Sheikh Sabah was one of them. All of the other sheikhs of rural ad Dawr knew and respected that. While it is not clear what happened to Sheikh Sabah's father, Sheikh Sabah readily admitted on multiple occasions that he was certified as sheikh of the al Shimiri in Iraq by Saddam Hussein before his fall.

I employed some theater to get Sabah's attention. "We Americans, we are like a winter rain. We come through for a short time, sprinkle over the desert, and make the land green for a while. But then we go away and all is dry and barren again." Sheikh Sabah was now completely rapt; I had made an admission of weakness. "You are the sheikh of the al Shimiris. You and your sons will be in the land forever. Who am I to tell you what to do?" Now I was complementing him. He wanted to know where I was going. "This is my second time in this country and I have learned something I would like to share with you, if I may."

Sabah gestured for me to proceed.

"When we came to Iraq, we tried to build democracy. But Iraq is Iraq, and you can't change a country in a few years. In America, all you need to get elected is the love of the people," I continued. "In Iraq, now, you also need the love of the people. But, as has always been the case in Iraq, you also need money and guns."

Sabah nodded deeply, agreeing with the statement.

"First you need money to get the right to run, and then you have to pay people not to steal the election away from you," I explained. "And the guns are to keep someone from taking the office away from you after you are elected."

I completed the thought, "Sheikh Sabah, the Americans want to take ad Dawr qa'da away from the al Duris. They are bloody with Naqshabandiyah [what Iraqis called JRTN] and they steal from the people. We want to give ad Dawr qa'da to you, Sheikh Sabah, and Sheikh Shakur and the other sheikhs of the al Jalaam ad Dawr and the al Jalaam as Samarra."

"Sheikh Sabah," I concluded, "you have the love of the people; you are their sheikh." (The truth was more complicated, of course; he was in a struggle with Sheikh Ali for the love of his people.) "You also have the guns; you are an al Sawah ["Awakening" movement] sheikh. But you don't have any money. If I could just give you two million dollars right now to do what I need you to do, I would. But I can't. There are rules, and I have to follow those rules."

I paused for him to speak, but he said nothing. He was thinking, calculating as I spoke.

"The al Jibouris in al Alam are rich. Do you know why they are rich?" I didn't wait for him to answer. "They are rich because they know exactly how to get the Americans to give them money. They know how to build contracts and get them approved. They control all of the people who give the signatures to get projects approved." I could see his passion, his anger threatening to return, so I quickly continued. "We need to get an al Jibouri to work for you if we are going to get you your money. Mohammed is the best contractor there is at getting projects. We need Mohammed."

Sabah was going to protest, but his vision was beginning to win over his passions. He paused instead, waiting to hear more.

"As you know, I was just talking to Mohammed. I explained your electric project to him. I told him to build the whole project packet for us to submit." I rapidly continued, again before he could protest, "But I also told him that he would only get the project if he made you happy and you were happy with him."

With Sheikh Shakur sitting in the room, Sabah had to protest. "I want nothing for myself. I only care about my people. I want them to have electricity so they can come back to their farms and feed their families."

"Of course, Sheikh Sabah," I offered apologetically. "I meant that you must be happy with the work and that he should not charge more than the cost and that he should not bring outsiders to provide security in an area where you can guarantee his safety."

Sheikh Sabah had understood loud and clear and was willing to entertain the possibility, the opportunity. His vision had prevailed over his passionate hatred of the al Jibouris. "I will talk to this man. But, by Allah, if he offers me a bribe I will cast him away back to al Alam and the other thieves."

With the elections out of the way, the drawdown of US forces was the imperative that began to drive operations across Iraq. President Obama had repeatedly promised to reduce US force levels from the 95,000 currently in Iraq to 50,000 by the "end of combat operations," mandated by the US-Iraqi security agreement to be August 2010. Task Force Patriot had already closed its two bases and begun to turn in unused equipment in anticipation of this drawdown. However, 45,000 troops couldn't leave Iraq all at once; there were only so many aircraft that could move them and so many airfields from which they could move. US Forces–Iraq (USF-I, formerly two headquarters, Multi-National Force–Iraq and Multi-National Corps–Iraq, before the last foreign forces left and these two headquarters consolidated into one, under Gen. Ray Odierno) mandated an ambitious timetable.

The Dragon Brigade and the other brigades of US Division–North (USD-North, the 3rd Infantry Division, formerly Multi-National Division–North) would begin a process the division dubbed "thinning the lines," redeploying some battalions and allowing others to expand to fill and assume responsibility for the empty areas. While in the abstract the process sounded like a simple fluid motion, in reality it was a hugely complicated endeavor. There were more bases to close and more pieces of

The US base at the Bayji Oil Refinery.

equipment to be turned in. There were people to be moved from base to base or redeployed out of Iraq. There were relationships with Iraqi leaders to hand from departing to remaining units.

In Salah ad Din province, two battalions—Task Force Patriot and Task Force Black Lions (1st Battalion, 28th Infantry)—would assume responsibility for the entire brigade's area of operations, previously covered by four separate battalions. Two battalions could only do half as many patrols as four battalions, so by necessity the remaining battalions would not be able to do as much in each qa'da.

Beyond that, the Task Force Patriot staff wasn't sure what it was going to do with the new, larger AO Proud Americans it was about to inherit. What we did know was that we did not know enough. The staff began an effort to learn about these areas of Salah ad Din with which we had very little experience. The battalion's first trip would be to Bayji to talk to the Task Force Rangers staff and visit the Bayji Oil Refinery, the most important economic engine in Sunni Arab Iraq.

Before the invasion of Iraq, when Saddam Hussein still ruled the country, he gave the al Qaysi tribe in Bayji qa'da control of the lucrative Bayji Oil Refinery, a facility that produced over a third of Iraq's gasoline and a large percentage of the petroleum products used across Iraq. Since the invasion, the al Qaysis had leveraged this control to build a lucrative economic empire in both the legitimate trucking and the smuggling and black market sale of gasoline. They had, in turn, parlayed this economic power into political and military power by securing key positions in both the qa'da government and police force. They were even able to use their control of the refinery to gain influence over the 48th Iraqi Army Brigade, with responsibility for the qa'da, until the brigade's corruption became so overt that the brigade was swapped with the 14th Iraqi Army Brigade, with responsibility for Tikrit qa'da.

The refinery itself was a huge, complex maze of pipes, tubes, and storage tanks. The air was thick with the smell of petrol, and one's skin felt oily after only a few minutes outdoors in the facility. Trucks lined Highway 1 for kilometers in both directions leading into the facility, and one was immediately struck by the enormous task of moving 2 million liters of gasoline out of the refinery each day to sites across Iraq, a process ripe for economic exploitation. Of course the United States, always obsessed by the quest to reduce corruption, had hatched a number of schemes to move fuel out of the refinery more efficiently, including pipelines and railroads. However, each of these schemes seemed to immediately fall prey to "terrorists," and the trucking industry was once again going strong. The refinery system, actually a complex of several different types of refineries, was also capable of making vegetable oil, fertilizer, detergent, and other products. But these facilities were always in disrepair. All anyone cared about was gas.

While the al Qaysis controlled the Bayji qa'da and extracted money from the smuggling of fuel out of the refinery and the theft of oil going into the refinery, inside the facility, Dr. Ali al Obeidi was king. Through the protection of Col. Adel, commander of the Oil Protection Force (OPF) in the Bayji Oil Refinery, and Dr. Obeidi's close relationship with the company of American soldiers living on the refinery grounds, he was able to maintain absolute control of movement inside the refinery.

Maintaining the security of Dr. Obeidi and the refinery was a priority that ran all the way to the top of USF-I; Task Force Patriot would be mandated to retain a US presence on the base after Task Force Rangers left. To help us meet that requirement, the Dragon Brigade agreed to take one company from Task Force Rangers, the Alpha Company "Outlaws," commanded by Cpt. Will Sitze, and attach them to Task Force Patriot to maintain security on the base.

At the same time Task Force Rangers was helping us understand Bayji and Sharqat, Task Force Wolverine was providing us with information about Tuz. Whereas the vast majority of Salah ad Din province was nearly uniformly Sunni Arab, Tuz was nearly evenly split between Sunni Arabs, Turkomen (the distant descendents of the Seljuk Turks who once controlled much of what is now Iraq as part of the Seljuk Empire), and Iraqi Kurds. In addition to its ethnic differences from the rest of Salah ad Din province, it was also physically separated. It was a tiny appendage hanging off the end of the province, beyond even distant al Hamerine, separated from the rest of the province by the Hamerine mountain range. In fact, in the late 1980s, Tuz qa'da had been part of Kirkuk province but was sliced off and given to a dominant Sunni province in an effort to weaken the Iraqi Kurds.

Inside the qa'da were two nahiyas (subdistricts that, in reality, were independent, answering directly to the provincial council), the Turkomen-dominated Amerlie nahiya and the Sunni Arab-dominated Sulayman Bak nahiya. The qa'da council had representation from each ethnic group but was clearly dominated by the Kurds. The intelligence agency of the Kurdish Regional Government (KRG), the Asayish, operated like secret police in the qa'da, and the KRG's constitutionally protected military force, the Peshmerga, had bases on the eastern frontier of the qa'da. The 16th Iraqi Army Brigade, with its headquarters on FOB Bernstein, colocated with Task Force Wolverine, had forces both in Tuz and in the easternmost reaches of ad Dawr qa'da, in al Hamerine and al Othaim. The brigade was a former Peshmerga brigade, overwhelmingly Kurdish.

During his meeting with Lt. Col. Bubba Cain, Lt. Col. Eric Moore, Wolverine 6, always unabashedly optimistic, repeatedly insisted that there was no sectarian or ethnic divide in Tuz qa'da. Yet all of the evidence indicated that Tuz was the front line of the war between Sunni and Kurdish separatists. The qa'da was constantly beset by IEDs, sniper attacks, and car bombs, Kurdish Ansar al Sunna against Sunni Arabs or Sunni Arab JRTN against Kurds. The very presence of the nahiyas, virtually autonomous regions within the qa'da, was a testament to the inability of the three groups within Tuz to reconcile their differences. It was a problem that could consume entire battalions for years (in fact it already had).

However, after Task Force Rangers and Task Force Wolverine departed, Task Force Patriot could not even afford to dedicate a battery solely to Tuz qa'da, and we only had it for two months. It became clear to the staff that it was time to reexamine our priorities and decide what we could realistically do with the rest of our time in Iraq.

In addition to saying good-bye to Cpt. Scott Steele, former Bravo Battery commander, Cpt. Skip Turner, former Headquarters and Headquarters Battery (HHB) commander, and Maj. Tim Blackwell, former Task Force Patriot XO, the battalion also said good-bye to its satellite PRT (the individual PRT representative for our AO), Michael Boyle. Boyle had worked hard to maintain a collegial relationship with the battalion, and his willingness to focus on points of common agreement, combined with his pleasant demeanor and silent, remarkable courage, had endeared him to the battalion.

Task Force Patriot's relationship with his replacement, John Bauer, was less positive. John Bauer had replaced Michael Boyle in Sharqat qa'da after the injury that cost Boyle his arm, months before. When the Sharqat JCC closed, Bauer moved with the Charlie Company of Task Force Rangers to Contingency Operating Site (COS) Summerall, their sprawling base outside Bayji. Now that Summerall was closing and Task Force Rangers was redeploying, he was reassigned to Tikrit and ad Dawr qa'da.

Bauer was an older man, in his fifties. He had been a city planner for years before coming to Iraq to ply his trade in Iraqi cities. He had a no-nonsense approach to local government problems that clashed horribly with the Iraqi penchant for working in the margins and exploiting ambiguity. Iraqis had tolerated his belligerence in Bayji and Sharqat because Task Force Rangers had given him considerable power over their CERP projects. But he immediately ran into problems in AO Proud Americans, where our battalion had developed a more political method of targeting CERP funds.

Bauer managed to get himself permanently barred from patrols with Lt. Col. Bubba Cain on his very first outing. The two had traveled to see Imam Mohammed Khuthair al Jibouri, a close US ally who was part of the tectonic shift of the al Alam al Jibouris toward the Americans in 2004. In the critical days of early 2004, when the al Alam al Jibouris, under the leadership of Sheikh Naji Hussein al Jebarra al Jibouri, made the decision to align their tribe with coalition forces, the senior imam of the al Alam mosque, Imam Mohammed Khuthair al Jibouri, was a key player, the first olive branch held out to the Americans.

Imam Mohammed had just survived a suicide vest attack in al Alam and, so close to the death of Lt. Col. Ahmed al Fahal, with such similar means, the Task Force Patriot staff could not help but suspect the Iraqi Islamic Party (IIP), Governor Mutashar, and the al Samarra'i tribes. The Task Force Patriot staff thought it might be a good idea to pay our respects and perhaps gather more information.

When they arrived to meet Imam Mohammed, Lt. Col. Bubba Cain's patrol found Sheikh Wanus Naji al Jibouri, Sheikh Khemis' younger brother and al Alam Sons of Iraq leader, staked out at the engagement, waiting to petition Cain for CERP projects. John Bauer immediately inserted himself into the conversation and began to belittle the important, if junior, al Jibouri leader. "Come on," Bauer told him, "You guys aren't stupid. You can figure these things out without help from us."

When the patrol returned, Lt. Col. Cain cornered me in my office at the back of the TOC and closed the door. "Keep that jackass away from me," Cain told me. "He doesn't know shit about Iraqis."

In our delicate CERP projects with the rural ad Dawr coalition sheikhs, Bauer wanted to renegotiate, rebid, and outsource projects in order to save money. Try as we might, we could not bridge the gap in understanding; Task Force Patriot was trying to enrich these sheikhs to make them more economically powerful. Things finally came to a head over a project to rebuild the Mohammed bin al Qasim School, a demolished school building in front of Sheikh Sabah's desert compound. John Bauer refused to sign the CERP packet because he believed he could get someone else to do the work for less money. Both the battalion commander and I had separate, closed-door discussions with Bauer about who the "commander" in charge of the Commander's Emergency Response Program was before he would relent. He still included a lengthy, handwritten dissent below his signature on the CERP packet.

Bauer was eventually able to find a niche for himself. Cpt. Steve Ackerson, our new Alpha Battery commander, had come to us from Task Force Rangers, where, as the fires and effects coordinator, he had worked closely with Bauer on projects. He turned his CERP planning over to Bauer and used the old city planner to train the Tikrit qa'da and al Alam nahiya councils to prioritize, gather bids for, and manage projects. But there was friction here as well. Lt. Col. Bubba Cain used projects as a means to maintain leverage and influence with provincial leaders, the most important of whom lived in al Alam. Bauer chafed against what he perceived as a trespass in his area of responsibility.

However, all of these cultural differences could have been overcome. The incident that finally alienated Bauer from Task Force Patriot was not a philosophical difference but a violation of trust. As had been the case with Michael Boyle before him, we always invited John Bauer to sit in on our weekly planning meetings to determine what operations Task Force Patriot would execute over the next week. On one occasion, as the assumption of Bayji qa'da approached, the staff thought it might be a good idea to talk to abu Mazen (Ahmed Abdullah abd Khalaf al Jibouri, the provincial council chairman) about whom he thought we should meet to better understand Bayji and Sharqat. After all, Lt. Col. Bubba Cain already had a relationship with him, and abu Mazen was from Bayji; he obviously knew the area better than we did. Even if we decided not to take his recommendations, it would give us insights into the Bayji al Jibouris' allies inside the Bayji and Sharqat qa'das.

As soon as the subject of abu Mazen was broached, Bauer interjected, "That is the PRT leader's KLE [key leader engagement]. You should let them talk to him."

The sentiment itself was a valid one. We did risk further desynchronizing the PRT's already disastrous foray into the provincial political deadlock between the governor and the provincial council. We decided that we should share anything we learned from abu Mazen on that topic with the PRT and continued with the other business of the meeting.

Within forty-eight hours, the PRT leadership exploded with accusations, claiming we were stepping into their business and trying to usurp what they believed was their exclusive right to engage government leaders. The Dragon Brigade was in an impossible position. David Stewart, director of the Salah ad Din PRT, and Barbara Yoder, the PRT governance lead, had aired their grievances with Maj. Gen. Tony Cuccolo, the USD-North commander, and demanded redress. We spent a week explaining that we had intentionally stayed out of the war between the provincial council and the governor and had no intention of entering it four months before we left Iraq. We were simply looking for insights into our expanding AO. In the end, Col. Hank Arnold saw the logic of the operation and permitted it to continue. However, our relationship with John Bauer, who had violated our trust, was irrevocably damaged.

Once we set the al Hamerine electric project—and the rural ad Dawr coalition—in motion under the auspices of Sheikh Sabah al Shimiri, with contractor Mohammed as the economic driver, things began to move very rapidly. Sheikh Sabah's unique vision and Mohammed's energy created unstoppable momentum.

Only a week after we had put the two together, they had hammered out an agreement and a proposal for the project. At contractor Mohammed's invitation, I accompanied Patriot 6 on his weekly pilgrimage to al Alam so I could visit Mohammed at his home. There waiting for us was Sheikh Sabah. After exchanging warm greetings, he joked that he felt like he was behind enemy lines, an obvious reference to his dislike of the al Alam al Jibouris. I again resolved to get to the bottom of the feud between him and Brig. Gen. (ret.) Abdullah Jebarra.

After dinner, Mohammed handed me a project packet, complete with the required three bids and all of the provincial government paperwork and stamps, ready to be submitted. Sheikh Sabah sat next to me on one of Mohammed's huge couches, while Mohammed stood in front of us. I was leafing through the packet looking for the price. Mohammed knew what I was looking for and finally reluctantly answered my unspoken question. "Sir, the price will be one million five hundred thousand dollars."

I couldn't suppress my disappointment. The cost would be a problem. It was well below the $20 million or more that Brig. Gen. (ret.) Abdullah had estimated for the project, but it could just as well have been $300 million. We would never get it approved. The rules for CERP required that the USF-I commander, Gen. Ray Odierno, approve any project over $500,000. Moreover, the convoluted rules in the ironically named pseudo-regulation on CERP, *Money as a Weapon System*, prohibited "project splitting" (i.e., dividing one project into little projects to get it approved). Contractor Mohammed Ibrahim al Jibouri, the king of the al Alam CERP industry, of course knew this.

"OK, Mohammed," I said. "We both know this isn't going to fly. We have to make this three separate projects. They have to serve three separate areas, or we will be accused of project splitting."

Sheikh Sabah sat next to us. We were speaking English, which he did not understand. But he, of course, knew what we were talking about. He was probably there because Mohammed had warned him this would be a problem. He was keeping an eye on his paycheck.

I thought for a moment and then continued. "One of these projects, costing $499,999, is the 'al Othaim electric project.' The next one, costing $499,999, is the 'al Hamerine electric project.' Now all you have to do is go out there and find one more village between al Hamerine and Tuz, and that will be your third electric project. You know what it will cost?"

"$499,999," Mohammed answered.

"Of course you are going to have to make the prices a little different, but still under $500,000," I warned, "or it will be too obvious."

He seemed about to protest that I was asking him to lower the price. "You can make it up on one of your other projects."

At this, contractor Mohammed felt compelled to explain the situation to Sheikh Sabah. They were not going to get the whole $1.5 million for the electric project. The two had no doubt brokered some deal for Sheikh Sabah's cut, and Mohammed didn't want to get stuck with the loss.

Sheikh Sabah asked, through Mohammed, "We can do other projects?"

"Hell yes!" I exclaimed. Sheikh Sabah was taken aback by my energetic response, but he didn't need a translation. "You have electric, but you are going to need an electric grid to get it to the farms for irrigation, right? You tell me what else you need. We need to get your farms up and running so your people can come back and vote for you for the qa'da council, right?"

Sheikh Sabah al Shimiri stood, and I instinctively did the same. Sabah took my hand and pulled me close, embracing me with his other arm and touching his bristly cheek to mine. "You are truly my brother!"

Brig. Gen. (ret.) Abdullah's electric project for al Hamerine seemed to suddenly be moving along as well. On 22 March 2010, as promised, Lt. Col. Bubba Cain took Brig. Gen. (ret.) Abdullah Hussein al Jebarra al Jibouri and DG of electricity Sabhan for a helicopter ride over ad Dawr qa'da to survey their proposed power line, through the middle of the Salt Flats and, coincidentally, past DG Sabhan's home village. After that, they also traced alternate routes, from the city of ad Dawr to al Hamerine, and from al Alam to al Hamerine.

In the end, it was this last path, from al Alam to al Hamerine, that would get funded by the government of Iraq. Of course Brig. Gen. (ret.) Abdullah Jebarra had an angle on this project, much as he did on everything that went on in Salah ad Din. When we met with him a week after his helicopter ride, he told us that the government had agreed to fund some of the project, if the United States funded some as well. The US share of the project would conveniently cost just under $500,000. He again told us that a new electric substation was being built in Samarra and added that, when the new station was done, the old one would be moved to al Alam, to power the new al Hamerine line.

I could not help but smile as he told us. In one project, he had managed to bilk the United States for half a million dollars, get an electric substation for his hometown, and take something away from his rivals in Samarra. He was a master.

If Brig. Gen. (ret.) Abdullah's fortunes were rising, provincial council chairman abu Mazen's were in freefall. As a result of his epic battle with the governor, the 4th Iraqi Army Division had briefly been ordered to surround the governor's office in Tikrit and bar him or anyone else from entering the building. However, once the charges of forging his high school diploma were leveled against abu Mazen, Maj. Gen. Salah and his division were instead ordered to surround the provincial council building, prevent anyone from entering, and arrest abu Mazen on sight.

During the same meeting in which we discussed Brig. Gen. (ret.) Abdullah's electric line scheme, he also told us that "they" (he never specified who) had offered him either the governorship or the position of provincial council chairman if he agreed to give the other billet to a member of Governor Mutashar's Iraqi Islamic Party. Abdullah had indignantly refused, and the stalemate continued.

Abu Mazen was too busy to notice. He was constantly on the road, between Salah ad Din and Baghdad, alternately looking for allies in Baghdad to legitimize the council's replacement for Governor Mutashar Hussein al Aliwi, engineer Khalid, and trying to shore up waning support in the provincial council for continuing the battle.

With not one but two electric projects now under way, Task Force Patriot could get on with the business of building the rural ad Dawr coalition. The first step was building up Sheikh Sabah Muntasir Diab al Shimiri as an important figure in Salah ad Din politics. And we were afforded an opportunity to do that by the US Department of Agriculture (USDA).

Tom Pick and Sainey Ceesay, two USDA representatives with the Salah ad Din PRT, came to me for a favor. Pick was a soft-spoken high-country farmer; Ceesay was an African immigrant. Both were a treasure trove of agricultural knowledge, knowledge that Task Force Patriot desperately lacked and needed if it was going to bolster the economy of rural ad Dawr qa'da. The two wanted us to escort them, along with the senior USDA representative in Iraq, Mr. Ron Verdonk, to see the al Alam food distribution center, a kind of soup kitchen of fresh produce and grains for the large number of unemployed in the qa'da.

I immediately thought of the publicity potential for Sheikh Sabah. "We would be happy to," I told the two men, "but we need to take Mr. Verdonk someplace else, first."

A few weeks later, the arrangements were all made, and we set out with Ron Verdonk, Tom Pick, and Sainey Ceesay for Sheikh Sabah's home in al Hamerine. We first met Sheikh Sabah at a storehouse near the home of a subtribe sheikh, adorned with an impressive collection of waist-high red flowers that filled the front yard, at the intersection of the al Alam–Tuz road (what US forces called Route Pepper) and Sheikh Mohammed Road (what US forces called Route Grape). As had been prearranged, a Salah ad Din Television reporter and camera were present, ready to record the event. Sheikh Sabah brought Mr. Verdonk and the TV crew to the tribal storehouse that held the communal food stores to feed the hungry of the region. The building was perpetually empty, and Sheikh Sabah made sure Verdonk (and the TV camera) saw that the roof was a thin thatch, through which both sunlight and rainwater easily streamed.

While the men talked in front of the camera, US soldiers began to unload "humanitarian aid": hundreds of pounds of rice, sugar, and tea that we had purchased through CERP for the storehouse. A poor farmer arrived, right on cue, to thank both US forces and Sheikh Sabah for the food to feed his family.

From there, we drove a short distance to a tiny patch of green in the desert. The camera captured Mr. Verdonk and Sheikh Sabah as they walked together through the tiny field. As the reporter drew near, Sheikh Sabah shifted masterfully into campaign mode, speaking both to Verdonk and to the people of rural ad Dawr. "Once this whole land was lush and green. We had electricity to water our fields, and our farms prospered. By the grace of Allah, we could feed our families. But now the city of

The visit of the senior US Department of Agriculture (USDA) representative from Baghdad provides an opportunity to build Sheikh Sabah's legitimacy as leader of the rural ad Dawr coalition. From left to right: Sheikh Sabah al Shimiri (back turned), Ron Verdonk (senior USDA representative), Sainey Ceesay (USDA, Salah ad Din PRT), and Salah ad Din Television reporter.

ad Dawr has electricity and water and food, while our crops die and our people starve."

"What are you going to do?" the TV reporter asked, having lost himself, now as rapt by the presentation as the people of ad Dawr would be that evening.

Sheikh Sabah knew exactly what to say. "I am done waiting for the ad Dawr qa'da council to do their job. I am going to work with the Americans and I am going to work with the provincial council and I am going to save my people myself." He couldn't have done better if we had written the speech for him.

From there we traveled to Sheikh Sabah al Shimiri's home. Sheikh Sabah lived in a nondescript compound at the foot of the Hamerine Mountains in the ill-defined region of the al Jalaam ad Dawr called al

Hamerine. While the residents seemed to have a clear understanding of what was and was not within the bounds of this region, to the outsider, it was only identifiable by a slightly higher density of homes and the intersection of the al Alam–Tuz road and Sheikh Mohammed Road that led southeast, paralleling the Hamerine Mountains toward another ill-defined region called al Othaim, on the north bank of the al Othaim River.

Sheikh Sabah's compound was seemingly intentionally unadorned and modest. In front of his compound stood a pile of rubble that—as Sheikh Sabah would frequently remind anyone who would listen—used to be a school before it was destroyed by "terrorists." It stood just outside the three-foot-high berm that surrounded Sabah's home. The only entry through the berm was a checkpoint manned by disheveled "Sons of Iraq" invariably dressed in a hodgepodge of old, US army woodland camouflage and civilian clothing. The gate itself was a simple iron bar with a counterweight that allowed the guard to lift it just high enough to allow each huge MRAP to gingerly pass.

Inside the compound were two modest buildings. The first was his family home, where his wife and children resided, never seen by outsiders. The other, larger building was the *diwan*. It was the tribal meeting hall, living room, and dining room for the al Shimiri tribe. Dirty green seat cushions, periodically interrupted by rectangular armrest pillows, circled the floor of the hall. The floor was covered in dirty Persian-style rugs. When lunch was served, long, decorative plastic tablecloths were stretched over the carpet, and great communal plates of food were set out at intervals along the length of the room on each side. Two great pillars held the three-meter-high ceiling in place. The light green walls were broken by tall floor-to-ceiling windows draped with dirty white curtains. The three wall-unit air conditioners were insufficient for the task of cooling the open, twenty-meter-long room against the brutal desert heat.

On the wall of Sheikh Sabah's *diwan*, near the door and opposite his place of honor, were pictures of Sheikh Sabah with prominent coalition figures like Gen. David Petraeus and Ambassador Ryan Crocker in front of the Presidential Palace in Baghdad. But one could imagine that ten years ago, before the arrival of coalition forces, where these pictures now hung were pictures of Sheikh Sabah with Saddam Hussein or some other prominent Ba'ath figures, maybe even Izzat Ibrahim al Duri. Sabah was not a Ba'athist, but he certainly understood the value of association with power.

Sheikh Sabah Muntasir Diab al Shimiri's *diwan* in al Hamerine in early 2010. From left to right: Mike Samander (interpreter), Maj. Pat Proctor (Task Force Patriot operations officer), and Sheikh Sabah (al Shimiri sheikh).

As we sat in his *diwan* after dinner, chatting and sipping *chai*, Sheikh Sabah leaned over to me and said, "I saw a helicopter fly over my home a few days ago. Inside, I could have sworn I saw Lieutenant Colonel Cain, Abdullah Jebarra, and DG Sabhan." Of course, he had been told this event had occurred. It is improbable that he picked out three faces from a helicopter moving at full speed, thousands of feet in the air. But I did notice that he did not call the al Alam provincial council chairman a brigadier general. It was the first time I had ever heard an Iraqi omit his title.

"Let Abdullah Jebarra take his helicopter ride, Sheikh Sabah." I mimicked his disrespect. "While they talk about getting electricity for al Hamerine, you and I will do it."

While the quest to politically and economically empower rural ad Dawr was proceeding at breakneck pace, it was beginning to create dissention in the Task Force Patriot staff. In fact, just about everything the task force was doing seemed to be creating dissention.

One of the true strengths of Lt. Col. Bubba Cain as a battalion commander was the environment he created in his battalion; he set a goal and then empowered his subordinates to achieve that goal. In fact, he often said that he was successful if he became "obsolete," meaning the staff and commanders understood his intent and were able to achieve it without constant guidance. I tried to mirror this approach within the staff by creating a collegial atmosphere in planning sessions where everyone felt empowered to offer suggestions and input, regardless of rank; after all, while rank indicates experience, it does not necessarily indicate superior intelligence or ideas.

However, that freedom proved to be a liability in the last months of the deployment. Much of the core staff that had written the original campaign plan and then taken the journey from Task Force Patriot's initial counterinsurgency approach to its current approach—isolating the city of ad Dawr and empowering the rural leaders—had left the staff. Our S7 (information operations officer), 1st Lt. Caleb Riggs, and our S9 (civil affairs officer), 1st Lt. Chad Hunara, had left to lead platoons. Perhaps the most painful loss was that of Cpt. Simon Welte, the most senior and respected captain in the staff; he had left to take command of Bravo Battery. In their stead, the Task Force Patriot staff received a number of former platoon leaders, like the former PSD platoon leader, 1st Lt. Matt Balach, and the 1st Platoon, Alpha Battery, platoon leader, 1st Lt. Jamie Sanjuan. The staff also began to receive new officers from the United States, including Cpt. Matthew Wilden. Without the context of the eight months of learning the battalion staff had done, and with their perspectives shaped by their own experiences, either in their small part of AO Proud Americans or, in the case of officers like Cpt. Wilden, their previous deployments, it was difficult for them to understand how the battalion had ended up where it was.

At first this manifested itself in grumbling in the weekly targeting meetings. Lt. Col. Cain was spending too much time in al Alam. Sheikh Sabah was "shady" or "a terrorist." We should be dealing with this local *shurta* (policeman) or that. However, when the staff gathered to begin revising its campaign plan to encompass the new areas the battalion would be assuming from Task Force Rangers and Task Force Wolverine, this dissatisfaction erupted into a full-scale insurgency.

The discussions began innocently enough. After we had gathered all of the facts about the two new areas, the staff began to discuss the problems and try to identify which we wanted to tackle and which were simply too big or too impractical or not important enough to deal with. I drew a big map of our projected larger AO on the whiteboard in our conference room and, next to it, listed all of the problems Task Force Rangers and Task Force Wolverine had identified in their respective problem statements, as well as those in Task Force Patriot's current problem statement. It was a huge list, so we discussed which problems would not be issues once US forces departed and eliminated them from the list.

The first shot of the insurgency was not fired by one of our new staff officers. It came from our most senior remaining captain, Cpt. Dan Peck, the fires and effects coordinator. "The biggest problem in our AO isn't up there. It's corruption. Contractors are robbing us blind. Everyone is taking a cut. The police, the government, everybody. And we are helping them do it."

It had apparently been a topic of conversation before the meeting, because, at the very mention of the word "corruption," the room exploded as all of the young idealistic officers began to rattle off their tales of graft or the names of the most corrupt qa'da council members in their previous areas of AO Proud Americans. It wasn't just CERP corruption, either. They were raging over the corrupt justice system that had released all of our Operation Patriot Raptor prisoners.

They were also raging against corrupt police who extorted money from Iraqis. Someone mentioned the alleged kidnapping and fencing ring between Lt. Col. Ahmed al Fahal and provincial council chairman abu Mazen, and the room suddenly fell silent; it was a sentiment that had not been spoken out loud in a meeting since his death. It was like a barrier had been broken. Suddenly officers were screaming at one another and slamming their fists on the table. The meeting descended into an angry mob. It took a full half hour for Maj. Matt Payne, the battalion XO, and I to get the meeting back under control.

Maj. Payne and I both knew that trying to stop corruption was a fool's errand. It was like trying to stop speeding at the Indianapolis 500. Nepotism and official corruption were cultural fixtures in the Arab world long before the Iraq war. And now the Americans were here, in Iraq, and they had barrels of cash to spend. The Iraqis wanted that money and had nothing but time to think up ways to circumvent the system to get it.

Moreover, it was not always bad that they got more than the project was worth. Creating large profit margins gave us huge leverage with the Iraqis. In some places, that just kept them from shooting at us. In other places, it helped us persuade them to do things they didn't want to do. In ad Dawr qa'da, it was helping us tip the balance of power from the al Duris to our rural ad Dawr coalition.

Besides, Lt. Col. Bubba Cain was the commander, and he had, on dozens of occasions, said we were not going to waste our time fighting corruption. In his opinion, we had better things to do than tilt at windmills.

This line of thinking was a cancer. If I just shut it down and said no, the staff would cease to support the whole operation, or worse, begin to sneak anticorruption tasks into our orders to our subordinate units. If I let anticorruption take over the operation, it would destroy all of our influence and bring to a halt everything we were doing in AO Proud Americans. Maj. Payne and I had tried for half an hour, without success, to persuade the younger officers of the folly of the idea. The only remaining option was to try to guide them toward the realization that it was a futile effort.

I decided on a mechanism to dilute the weight of the anticorruption cabal that had suddenly exposed itself. First, I listed corruption on our list of problems as three separate problems—CERP corruption, police and justice corruption, and government corruption. Then I went around the room, allowing each member present, perhaps a dozen people, to pick the three problems of the over twenty listed that they most strongly felt we should spend the rest of our time in Iraq trying to solve. S.Sgt. Oliver, the S4 NCOIC (logistics noncommissioned officer in charge) abstained, feeling he did not know enough about any of the topics to choose. Maj. Matt Payne and I voted last.

As we went around the room, nearly half of the room voted for some form of corruption, but CERP and police and justice corruption took the most votes. The collapse of the Iraqi media after the disappearance of US dollars also gave a strong showing. Inefficiency in the Iraqi oil and fuel processing and transportation system (which I had narrowly steered away from becoming "oil corruption") also garnered a number of votes. However, as we reached the end of the voting, with only my vote remaining, no one had voted for defeating JRTN through the rural ad Dawr coalition.

"Really?" I asked. "Everyone in this room thinks we have been doing the wrong thing for the past six months?" No one would say anything.

I needed to impress upon them the weight of this issue before I made my move. I had no choice but to resort to theatrics, and I felt disgusted with myself as I did it.

"Jamie," I asked, looking right at 1st Lt. Sanjuan, "You don't care about beating the guys who killed Carrasco? Really?" 1st Lt. Jamie Sanjuan's brother, 1st Lt. Javier Sanjuan, had been Cpl. Tony Carrasco's platoon leader on that horrible day in November.

Sanjuan sunk his head and would not look me in the eye. I looked around the room. No one would meet my gaze. It was time to make my move.

"I am putting all three of my votes, plus Staff Sergeant Oliver's three votes, on the rural ad Dawr coalition and defeating JRTN." While my back was turned, a few haranguing protests went up, but as I shot around, looking at all of them, the protests fell silent.

With the voting done, I began to assign tasks. Two or three officers were assigned to each of the five top problems. All the other problems were removed from consideration. I broke the staff down into teams, each charged with studying one of the problems, presenting a detailed description of that problem as it existed in our area, giving a history of what had been done in the past to address the problem, and suggesting an approach that would potentially fix the problem.

I didn't assign a team to the rural ad Dawr and JRTN problem, ostensibly because it was a known quantity; we had worked on it for six months. However, I also did not want the anticorruption insurgency mounting a counterattack by using a study of the problem to further undermine it as part of our strategy. Besides, I was the only one who voted for it.

As the staff broke up and the meeting adjourned, officers huddled together in circles, talking in hushed voices. People were taking sides in the war.

With the conference room empty, Maj. Payne walked up to me and asked in his disarming Virginian style, "You want me to put the kibosh on all this corruption nonsense?"

I sighed. "No. I am sending them on a voyage of discovery. Hopefully they will return having figured out for themselves how pointless it is." I was not entirely confident that was true, but I had at least bought a few more days for the current strategy.

As the battalion began to make progress in moving economic opportunity and political power outside of the city of ad Dawr, JRTN responded with gradually increasing levels of violence. At the end of March, a patrol from our 363rd Military Police (MP) Company was attacked by an RKG-3 (a hand-thrown antiarmor grenade) on the Tikrit bridge while returning from the village of albu Qodal, east of the former PB Woodcock. A few days later, on the first day of April, the battalion commander's PSD was forced by the continuing 4th Iraqi Army Division cordon around the provincial council building to turn off of Business 1, the branch of Highway 1 that goes through the middle of Tikrit, and take narrow, congested 40th Street through the middle of Tikrit. A few hundred meters after they turned onto the road, two teenage boys emerged from an alley and threw RKG-3s at the two trail armored high-mobility multiwheeled vehicles (HMMWVs, or "hum-vees"). One struck the back corner of the trail vehicle; the other struck the road. Neither attack injured US soldiers, but the second attack wounded a young man and his son, innocent bystanders on the street. The sniper attacks in southern Tikrit, south of the provincial council building, also escalated. A civilian contractor was killed during a stop at the Tikrit IPEOD building, shot through the head while standing on the balcony just above the building's T-wall protection.

This uptick in violence was the impetus for Task Force Patriot's next big kinetic operation, Operation Vigilant Patriot. All four police battalions—ERUs 1, 2, and 3 and the RDU—along with the 2nd Battalion, 48th Iraqi Army Brigade, would both cordon southwest Tikrit and find and capture targeted individuals inside the cordon. Task Force Patriot would provide a mobile tactical operations center (TAC) to link the police to aerial observation and OH-58D Kiowa attack helicopter scout weapons teams (SWTs). We would also provide another platoon as a quick reaction force (QRF) at the former Tikrit JCC at Mahmoon Palace.

The first joint planning meeting with the Iraqis went as well as any we had yet had. I unrolled the map after we arrived at S.Lt. Col. Khalil's office in the ERU 3 headquarters inside FOB Danger and started to run through the operation, but Khalil interrupted and started briefing the operation himself. I was happy to step aside and let the Iraqis take over.

The police battalions were particularly concerned about the shantytown on the southwest edge of town, south of the Mahmoon Palace. At a break, ERU 3 commander S.Lt. Col. Khalil told us that there were a large number of internally displaced people living in this area, and, according to informants, there were many insurgents hiding among them. This was in the vicinity of the car bomb that had detonated only days before the death of Lt. Col. Ahmed al Fahal, so we were eager to do the operation.

As the American contingent of the operation prepared to roll out to the Tikrit JCC for Operation Vigilant Patriot, we received a call at the Task Force Patriot TOC from S.Lt. Col. Khalil. One of his *shurta* had been shot in the head while executing an Iraqi-only operation in as Siniyah, west of Bayji and just outside COS Summerall, the headquarters of the 14th Iraqi Army Brigade and former base of operations for Task Force Rangers before the base was given over to sole Iraqi control. Khalil was asking to bring the Iraqi to the US combat support hospital (CSH, pronounced "cash") for medical attention.

Both the CSH commander and the USD-North division surgeon refused the request. According to their new medical rules of engagement (ROE), designed to "wean" Iraqis off of US support, even Iraqi police injured fighting insurgents would be denied aid if they were not fighting alongside Americans. However, when the *shurta* showed up at the front gate of COB Speicher, the CSH found it more difficult to justify the esoteric point. The Iraqi was let onto COB Speicher but died of his wounds, Alpha Battery soldiers standing at his bedside.

The three platoons of Task Force Patriot, two platoons from Alpha Battery (one to secure the Mahmoon Palace compound and one to stand by as the QRF) and the battalion commander's PSD (to act as the TAC) departed from COB Speicher just as the wounded ERU 3 *shurta* entered the base. We also brought Michael Gisick, an embedded reporter from *Stars and Stripes*, who happened to be with the battalion while the operation was taking shape.

The American contingent arrived at the palace to find it swarming with police, waiting for fuel, ultraviolet chem-lights, and all the other goodies US soldiers brought to a fight. Right on time, at all the other Iraqi police and army staging areas around the city, vehicles started up and police began to leave for their assigned areas. We watched the action from our aerial surveillance aircraft and waited for the prisoners to come in. One by one, police vehicles returned loaded up with prisoners that were placed in a makeshift holding pen Alpha Battery soldiers had constructed from concertina wire on the far side of the broad concrete parade route through the middle of the palace compound.

Several of the police battalion commanders, including S.Lt. Col. Khalil of ERU 3 and Lt. Col. Khalid of ERU 2, stopped by the TAC throughout the night and became entranced by the full-motion video of their *shurta* moving through Tikrit. At one point, S.Lt. Col. Khalil recognized one of his patrols loitering and smoking on a street corner where it should have been pulling guard and began yelling at them on the radio. He smiled in delight as they snapped to attention on the TV screen and resumed their vigilance, looking about for their unseen commander.

While the patrols continued into the early morning, our security platoon cataloged, photographed, and fingerprinted detainees, and our human intelligence (HUMINT) collection team (HCT) questioned them. One of our HCT members asked a thin but healthy-looking Iraqi man, "Do you know why you were detained?"

"No," the man replied. "The Iraqi police apologized when they arrested me, but said the Americans had my name on a list."

He was not an American target. We were still trying to ascertain his identity.

"Why do you think the Americans wanted you?" the HCT soldier asked.

Rather than answer the question, the man said, "They always detain me. My father is the Mukhtar of al Zohair neighborhood, and he is rich."

I felt a sickening feeling in the pit of my stomach. I pulled the HCT sergeant to the side and asked him what the other detainees were saying. They were all saying similar things. Only two of our prisoners actually had warrants, previous US Special Forces operational detachment alpha (ODA) targets. Most of the thirty-two detainees the police captured that night were construction workers for the same wealthy construction contractor, living in Tikrit while working on his project. The contractor would no doubt be forced to pay for the release of the workers. Task Force Patriot had just been an unwitting accomplice in thirty counts of kidnapping.

A few weeks later, the Tikrit sniper struck again. An Alpha Battery patrol came under attack while the platoon was stopped, awaiting the return of the platoon leader and his ground team from inside a building. A single armor-piercing sniper shot pierced the turret armor of the MRAP and struck the armor on the other side, only inches from the gunner's face. Operation Vigilant Patriot had done nothing to disrupt JRTN.

We might not have defeated JRTN, but the anticorruption insurgency within the Task Force Patriot staff did come to an end. When the staff reconvened to discuss the five problems we had settled on at the previous, rancorous meeting—CERP corruption, police and justice corruption, health of the Iraqi media system, inefficiency in transportation and refinement at the Bayji Oil Refinery, and JRTN and al Duri domination of ad Dawr qa'da—corruption failed to gain the traction it needed to survive.

Cpt. Josh Jeffress, our soon-to-depart S2 (intelligence officer) who had recently been promoted, delivered the first death blow with his group's brief on CERP corruption. His "brief" was several paragraphs cut and pasted onto PowerPoint slides from a cursory, Wikipedia-deep survey of the Internet about government corruption that neither specifically addressed corruption in our area nor suggested a way to stop it. He concluded the brief with a stirring speech. "We can't fix it. They are all crooks. We should just say 'Fuck the Iraqis' and wait for redeployment." Cpt. Dan Peck made a halfhearted attempt to salvage the subject as a problem for our campaign plan, but the dismal presentation had killed the topic.

The remaining insurgents, the four-man team arguing for the inclusion of police and justice corruption as a problem for the battalion, would be more difficult to defeat. Rather than building a single brief, each officer had built his own brief. They made their pitches in rapid succession. Most were simply a chronology of the issues we had had with the Iraqi police and judges in our AO. 1st Lt. Jaime Sanjuan's argument was the most compelling. He began by attacking the battalion commander's constant presence in al Alam with the al Fahal family, especially "Lt. Col. Ahmed's mom." He had certainly hit a raw nerve. Many in the staff saw the commander's close attachment to the family as a drain on his time, time that could better be spent doing other things. The idealistic young lieutenant very effectively painted the whole business in al Alam as something more sinister.

I was beginning to worry that I might have to unilaterally shut down discussion of corruption, but then Sanjuan made a critical error. He was trying to make the case that we, as a battalion, should instead be focusing on "good cops." However, as an example, he cited the Tikrit 911 commander, Brig. Gen. Muhammad. It was a mistake borne of too little staff experience. He simply had not done his homework.

One of the first things we had learned from Task Force Steel (3rd Battalion, 7th Field Artillery) and confirmed through our own operations was that Brig. Gen. Muhammad most definitely was *not* a "good cop." He actively avoided speaking to US forces, and whenever Task Force Steel had called his forces for the mandated Iraqi police escort, those patrols that Tikrit 911 escorted were consistently attacked by insurgents.

Moreover, only a few days before, Lt. Col. Bubba Cain had had an altercation with the Tikrit 911 commander. Lt. Col. Cain was chastising all of the police and justice officials at the weekly Tikrit security meeting for not being more aggressive in helping us get warrants for the four Jadir brothers, captured in ad Dawr and suspected of having been involved in multiple attacks on Bravo Battery, including the shooting that killed Cpl. Carrasco. Brig. Gen. Muhammad said glibly, "We lose *shurta* all the time. Why should I be worried about one dead American? What's the big deal?"

Cain was infuriated. "Wipe that smile off your face," Lt. Col. Bubba Cain told the smug Iraqi, "or I will come across this table and slap the shit out of you!" The Tikrit 911 commander stopped smiling. S.Lt. Col. Khalil, the ERU 3 commander, had to step between the two to keep them from exchanging blows.

Everyone else in the staff already knew about the Tikrit 911 commander. But 1st Lt. Sanjuan, oblivious to his error, compounded it by showing a slide presentation, candid shots of himself and the smiling Iraqi at 911 headquarters. Cpt. Dan Peck buried his head in his hands. The argument was over, as was the anticorruption insurgency.

In the end, the Task Force Patriot staff settled on three problems:

1. JRTN and the New Ba'ath Party dominates the ad Dawr qa'da government, and the appeal of the New Ba'ath Party message and JRTN intimidation has made the Salah ad Din justice system unwilling to fight JRTN.
2. Temporary US money and presence props up the Salah ad Din economy, and lagging qa'da governments in Bayji and Tikrit are incapable of managing services and projects for their communities.
3. As Task Force Patriot's AO (including government and security partners) and its list of brigade-specified tasks grows, it will become increasingly difficult to maintain key relationships and situational awareness, especially in the outlying areas of AO Proud Americans.

We were already well on our way in executing a strategy to address the first problem.

1. Use CERP and engagements to maintain pressure on the Salah ad Din justice system to prosecute JRTN and get Iraqi security forces to conduct security operations to disrupt JRTN. Use engagements and targeted CERP in ad Dawr qa'da to build economic engines in rural ad Dawr that would continue to increase rural leaders' power after US forces depart. Build a coalition of rural ad Dawr sheiks that would run a unity slate for the qa'da elections in late 2010.

The approach to the second problem was, first, an acknowledgement of the importance of the Bayji Oil Refinery as an economic engine. Second, it was an acknowledgement that our satellite PRT, John Bauer, could still play a role with the qa'da governments in Tikrit and Bayji qa'das. (Bauer had himself concluded that Sharqat's qa'da government was ready to stand on its own.)

2. Increase the efficiency of the Bayji Oil Refinery by using engagements and targeted CERP to rebuild aging infrastructure; get Sons of Iraq hired as Oil Protection Forces to increase the refinery's capability and employ Sons of Iraq. Use engagements and CERP to train Bayji and Tikrit qa'da governments to manage essential services, projects, and private development for their communities.

Since the Task Force Patriot staff wasn't going to stop Patriot 6 from focusing on al Alam, we decided to simply incorporate it into the approach to the third problem.

3. Use CERP and engagements in Al Alam to maintain influence with key provincial security and political leaders and conduct periodic combined patrols of satellite PRT, our stability transition team (STT) member, and Task Force Patriot elements to qa'da capitals across AO Proud Americans (excluding ad Dawr qa'da) in order to maintain relationships with security and government leaders at the qa'da level.

Our effort to marginalize the al Duris and shift the economic and political center of power out of the city, into rural ad Dawr, had survived, at least for now.

In fact, Task Force Patriot's effort to starve JRTN and the New Ba'ath Party in ad Dawr of legitimate political power hadn't just survived; it was thriving. The rural ad Dawr coalition was finally expanding into the al Jalaam as Samarra.

Sheikh Sabah Muntasir Diab al Shimiri brought the most important sheikhs of southwest ad Dawr qa'da to COB Speicher for a meeting. Sheikh Mohammed al Bazi and Hajji Hamid al Abbasi attended, as did Abu Awf (abd al Rahman Hamid, from a village near the salt factory at the edge of the Salt Flats, deep in the al Jalaam as Samarra). Sheikh Farris also attended, from a tiny village in a region called Sheikh Mohammed Village, west of Sheikh Shakur albu Issa's much more prosperous area, al Othaim. Of course, Sheikh Sabah and Sheikh Shakur were also present, the former to officiate the meeting.

The first task was convincing the new sheikhs that they actually were from ad Dawr qa'da. Lt. Col. Bubba Cain opened the meeting, explaining that we wanted them to work together to build a party or coalition for the next qa'da elections, which we believed would be in December 2010. They protested that ad Dawr was not their qa'da. Their polling sites and their al Sawah base were both just off Highway 2 (what US forces called Alternate Supply Route, ASR, Dover) at the extreme southwestern edge of the ad Dawr qa'da boundary with Samarra qa'da. Many of the leaders shared tribal affiliations with the people of Samarra, and many of their Sons of Iraq manned checkpoints in and around Samarra. The arguing went on for thirty minutes before Lt. Col. Cain had to leave to meet with Brig. Gen. Patrick Donahue II, the deputy commanding general for maneuver (DCG-M) of USD-North.

I pressed on with the group. Their people, I insisted, were inside the ad Dawr qa'da. "Twenty-some years ago, Izzat Ibrahim al Duri and his al Duri kinsmen drew a line in the sand that cut you off from your tribe in Samarra. Now you can use that against them and take their qa'da away from them."

They still seemed incredulous.

"There are more people outside the city of ad Dawr than there are inside the city. If you all vote together, as one bloc on one list, you will take the qa'da government away from them."

The idea didn't seem to be getting through.

I tried to put it in the basest terms. "You won't have to go to Samarra to ask for money and electricity and water and schools. You will have your own qa'da and you can decide where the money and the electricity and water and schools go."

They were hooked, but they would need our help to convince their subtribe leaders and families. They invited us to their Sons of Iraq compound, just northwest of Samarra, to make the pitch.

Our effort to move the political and economic center of ad Dawr qa'da out of the city and into the rural areas still had setbacks. Among the worst did not come from intransigent sheikhs or JRTN insurgents; it came from the US State Department. In late March, the Task Force Patriot staff discovered that, at the same time the battalion had been trying to starve ad Dawr of resources, the US Agency for International Development (USAID) had spent over $200,000 dollars on them.

Cpt. Simon Welte, on a patrol through the city, noticed a new, freshly painted and renovated marketplace. A little investigation with the local leaders, like Sheikh Ali Nwaf Diab al Shimiri and Cpt. Muntasim, the al Duri commander of the ad Dawr concerned local citizens (CLCs), revealed that the money had come from a USAID initiative called Community Action Program (CAP) III. The program assembled a group of local leaders, a community action group (CAG), to nominate and execute projects of up to $100,000 each. A bit more investigation found that the ad Dawr CAG included Sheikh Ali and engineer Dhaif al Duri (director of the Salah ad Din Company, on the grounds of the former PB Woodcock), among others.

With the help of Tom Pick, the USDA rep with whom we had worked to help Sheikh Sabah, we were able to meet with Greg Adams, the USAID representative for Salah ad Din province, who worked as part of the Salah ad Din PRT at their headquarters, "PRT Main," on COB Speicher. We tried to get him, first, to stop spending money on the city of ad Dawr and, second, to assemble an alternate CAG consisting of the rural ad Dawr coalition we were forming. He was noncommittal and evasive, and it soon became clear that he had no ability to alter the program.

Meanwhile, USAID continued to pour money into the al Duri and JRTN coffers.

When Task Force Patriot finally got the opportunity to meet all of the sheikhs of the al Jalaam as Samarra, we were determined to make a good case, so we decided we shouldn't come empty-handed. Bravo Battery had already submitted and gotten approval for dozens of microgrants (small grants of around $5,000 each, nominally to help small businesses expand, but frequently with a healthy kickback to the sheikh, *shurta*, or government official who had helped procure it). We brought all of that money, over $100,000 in Iraqi dinars, with us to hand out at the meeting. This would both guarantee the broadest attendance and give us more credibility when we made promises.

The meeting itself was at a Sons of Iraq compound inside Samarra qa'da, northeast of the city. It was an old Ba'ath Party headquarters in a corrugated tin building with wooden interior walls and doors. A broad concrete lot, once a military motor pool, would act as the landing zone for Lt. Col. Bubba Cain's helicopter when it arrived. I traveled with the Bravo Battery commander and one of his platoons to secure the site ahead of time and begin the meeting. The whole compound was surrounded by a dirt berm perhaps a meter and a half high.

Sheikh Sabah and contractor Mohammed, traveling in a long, white car that might have been a 1970s-era Cadillac, met the Bravo Battery patrol with which I traveled at the exit to COB Speicher and led us the entire distance to the meeting. Instead of going through Tikrit, we went through the northwest corner of Samarra, skirting the city before turning back to the north. As we did, we passed the famous Samarra spiral minaret, al Malweyya, part of the sprawling mosque complex that also included the al Askari Mosque, visible on the skyline behind us as we departed the city. It was covered in a maze of scaffolding, still not completely rebuilt after its destruction by al Qaeda in Iraq in 2006.

When we arrived at the Sons of Iraq base, we were welcomed and briskly walked to a meeting room in the Sons of Iraq headquarters. The small room had tacky wood paneling and was lined on each wall with dirty green furniture that sagged and strained as we sat down on it. Hajji Hamed sat, officiating the gathering, behind an old metal army desk. I sat next to Sheikh Sabah, opposite the door, at the place of honor. But it was not I who was being honored; it was Sheikh Sabah.

While we talked inside, a small celebration ensued outside as 1st Lt. Jay Urban, the XO for Bravo Battery, dispersed the thousands of dollars we had brought with us. Every few moments, a lesser family member would come in and whisper to one of the subtribe sheikhs, telling him their take. The sheikh would raise his *chai* glass to me, saying, "Shukran jazeeran." Thank you very much.

I would gesture back, my right hand over my heart. "Af wan, sheikh." You are welcome.

By the time the commotion had passed, the sheikhs were happy enough to buy whatever we were selling. It was time to close the deal. But then Cpt. Simon Welte came to the door. As I looked up, he signaled first by whirling his index finger horizontally in the air and then by dragging a flat palm across his throat. The helicopter carrying Lt. Col. Bubba Cain was not coming. I was going to have to make the pitch myself.

I nodded to Mike Samander, my interpreter, sitting to my right. He leaned forward, straining in the sagging couch, ready to translate. "Gentlemen, we have come to talk to you today about the future of Iraq, and also about your future." I paused longer than the translation took, to make sure their attention was focused before I continued.

At this, Sheikh Sabah motioned with a hand gently on my left forearm. "Habibi" (Dear friend). He was signaling for me to let him speak.

"Iraq is suffering from two diseases," Sabah began. "It will die of these illnesses if we do not act. The first illness is the corrupt politicians who think only of themselves. They take and they take while regular people starve. The other illness is Naqshabandiyah [JRTN]. They are terrorists and they kill regular people. These diseases are why I have come to you. You are all sheikhs. You know how to take care of your people. You would not be a sheikh if you did not take care of your people."

Of course they weren't sheikhs, and Sabah knew it. But, as he later told me, the title was like a drug to them. When he said it, they became proud and happy and wanted to do whatever he said just to hear him call them sheikhs again.

"You are also al Sawah. You have fought and bled and died to kill the terrorists and protect your people," he continued. "I know you all to be men of courage, and now I need you to fight at my side again. It will be the most difficult battle you have fought since our time of trouble began. The time for guns is coming to an end. We are entering the time when fighting will be done at the ballot box. But the stakes are just as great. If the wrong men are put in charge, the people will starve and terrorism will continue."

"You all have family in Samarra," Sabah said, "and you have Sons of Iraq protecting Samarra, but your families and your tribes live in ad Dawr qa'da because some *kabeeth* [roughly "rat bastard"] drew the line in the wrong place."

Everyone laughed. They knew which *kabeeth* he was talking about—Izzat Ibrahim al Duri, former vice president of Iraq.

"Right now your qa'da, ad Dawr qa'da, is suffering from both diseases. The al Duris steal from all of us and sleep with the Naqshabandiyah in their houses every night." In Arabic, the phrase was particularly poetic, since *ad Dawr* means, literally, "the houses."

"There are more of us *bedu* [Bedouins] in ad Dawr qa'da than there are al Duris in the city," Sabah concluded. "Together, we will take the qa'da away from them and feed the people and starve Naqshabandiyah."

Everyone looked at Hajji Hamed, the senior member of the gathering. "We all recognize Sheikh Sabah as our al Sawah leader. We will follow him and we will fight this battle and we will win and he will be the leader of our qa'da." The room began to ripple with increasingly enthusiastic agreement.

"La, la, la," Sabah loudly interrupted. No, no, no. "If I come here and my good friend, Maj. Proctor, brings you money and I ask you to vote for me, I am no better than the al Duris."

I instinctively leaned away, looking at Sheikh Sabah. I didn't know where he was going with this.

"I am not asking you for your vote. I am asking you to save our country. I will submit names for a list, and you will submit names for a list. We will pick good men whom we can trust to be good and honest. We will all vote for this list. It will be the 'ad Dawr al Sawah list.' My name will not be on it."

The move was masterful. The sheikhs all nodded to one another. The rural ad Dawr coalition was born.

A few weeks later, Sheikh Sabah's three electric projects—which would progressively extend power along the damaged power line from Tuz, through al Hamerine, to al Othaim—were finally approved, at a total price of $1.5 million.

When Brig. Gen. (ret.) Abdullah Hussein al Jebarra al Jibouri told Lt. Col. Bubba Cain about the government-funded electric project to take electricity from al Alam to al Hamerine, he also invited Cain to come inspect the project with him. He quipped that he knew the perfect spot to inspect, which also happened to be thick with quail.

As soon as he made the suggestion, the Task Force Patriot staff saw an opportunity. If the battalion brought Sheikh Sabah Muntasir Diab al

Shimiri to the inspection, as well as cameras from Salah ad Din Television, it could be an opportunity to tell the people of the al Jalaam ad Dawr that Sheikh Sabah was fighting to get them electricity.

I was wary about bringing the idea up to Sheikh Sabah. While we had still not gotten to the bottom of why, we knew that he definitely did not like Brig. Gen. (ret.) Abdullah Jebarra, or, for that matter, the al Alam al Jibouris. I decided to first broach the idea when he was in a good mood. The day he and contractor Mohammed Ibrahim al Jibouri came to sign the Tuz–al Hamerine–al Othaim electric project contracts seemed the perfect opportunity.

"Your habibi, Abdullah Jebarra," I began—he laughed instinctively at the suggestion he was friends with the powerful al Jibouri—"has invited us to inspect his new electric project. We both know how much he likes cameras. Why don't we bring some? You can join us and tell al Jalaam ad Dawr who is really getting them electricity."

The idea appealed to his desire to outwit his al Jibouri nemesis. He loved the idea and agreed to come to the event.

After the signing was complete, we ate a lunch of kebabs and rice that contractor Mohammed had brought for the occasion. While we ate, talk turned back to Brig. Gen. (ret.) Abdullah Jebarra, and Sheikh Sabah told us a story. Sabah told us that Lt. Col. Ahmed, when he was still a major, conducted an operation in which Izzat Ibrahim al Duri was captured. As the story went, then-Major Ahmed al Fahal brought Izzat to his patron, Brig. Gen. (ret.) Abdullah Jebarra. After a long night of negotiation, Izzat Ibrahim al Duri was supposedly released in exchange for $1 million.

When I heard the story, all the other suspicious reports I had heard about the al Jibouris—Sheikh Wanus' and Sheikh Khemis' gunrunning chief among them—rushed back to me. Yet again, I dismissed the suspicion this report cast on the al Alam al Jibouris. First, we knew Sabah harbored deep animus toward Abdullah; perhaps he was just trying to create suspicion. Second, even if the report were true, releasing the powerful New Ba'ath Party and JRTN leader for a substantial sum of money did not necessarily equate to complicity in his Sunni separatist ambitions; money is, after all, money. We would hear the story repeated by other Iraqis, with variation in the details, multiple times over subsequent months, but I continued to dismiss the story as myth.

On the day of the inspection of Brig. Gen. (ret.) Abdullah Jebarra's al Alam–al Hamerine electric project, Sheikh Sabah's dislike for Abdullah turned out not to be a problem; neither Abdullah Jebarra nor the DG Sabhan showed up for the event. In their stead, a woman from the DG's office, engineer Hadijah, arrived.

She had apparently not been told why she was being sent to the location. When she arrived and saw American soldiers, Sheikh Sabah Muntasir Diab al Shimiri, and cameras from Salah ad Din Television, she immediately concluded that there was some problem with the project and she had been set up to take the fall for the director general. It took several minutes to convince her we were not upset over the project, and several more to convince her to speak on camera about the project, but eventually we got her in front of the camera— the new electric towers stretching off into infinity behind her—answering the reporter's questions about the project. A hot wind was blowing. She fought with her 1960s-style flower-patterned *hijab* as it blew in the wind, struggling to uncover her face as she talked.

"How long will the project take to finish?" the reporter asked.

Engineer Hadijah answered, "Perhaps sixty days."

The reporter continued, "How much did the project cost?"

She responded that the project cost $1 million in Iraqi dinars, all of which had been appropriated for the province in the budget from Baghdad.

If the money was already appropriated, I wondered, why did Brig. Gen. (ret.) Abdullah Hussein al Jebarra al Jibouri need $500,000 from US forces? But before I could investigate, it was our turn in front of the camera. I stood in the middle, my Kevlar helmet under my arm. Sheikh Sabah stood on my right, and my interpreter, Mike Samander, stood on my left.

"Sheikh Sabah," the reporter asked, "what do you think of this electric project?"

"I am so happy that, after five long years, electricity is finally coming back to al Hamerine," Sabah said. "I want to thank the government of Iraq and US forces for making this possible."

The reporter turned to me and asked a question in Arabic.

Mike Samander was flustered, unaccustomed to being on camera. He repeated what the man had said to me, but said it in Arabic. "Thanks, Mike," I joked, trying to put him at ease. "Now what does that mean?"

Samander seemed puzzled for a moment and then realized his mistake. "He would like to know why the Americans chose to do this project."

The reporter had teed up our pitch perfectly. "I would like to take credit for this project," I said. "But I can't. Everything you see here," I waved my hand out toward the electric poles stretching out behind us toward the horizon, "is because of Sheikh Sabah."

I waited for Mike Samander to catch up and then continued. "Sheikh Sabah al Shimiri was determined to help the people of al Hamerine and al Othaim and al Jalaam as Samarra. He would not take no for an answer. He demanded that the provincial council and US forces help his people. This project would not have happened without him."

· 6 ·

Task Force Wolfhounds

$\mathscr{P}$erhaps Brig. Gen. (ret.) Abdullah Hussein al Jebarra al Jibouri, the powerful former deputy governor and provincial council member from al Alam, saw and was angered by our news story giving Sheikh Sabah credit for Abdullah's al Alam–al Hamerine electric project. Or maybe he was simply enraged when he found out about our unilateral Tuz–al Hamerine–al Othaim electric project. Whatever the reason, on the morning of 4 May 2010, police from S.Lt. Col. Khalil's ERU 3 went to contractor Mohammed Ibrahim al Jibouri's work site in the western foothills of the Hamerine Mountains and ordered them to stop working.

The first frantic calls came from contractor Mohammed. His call was followed by a call from Sheikh Sabah Muntasir Diab al Shimiri. Sabah was angry and kept repeating, "That *kabeeth* [roughly "rat bastard"] is doing it to me again." He was talking about Brig. Gen. (ret.) Abdullah Jebarra, but it was not clear what Abdullah had done before to elicit this particular reaction.

Mohammed spent most of the day talking to the Salah ad Din province director general (DG) of electricity Sabhan and Brig. Gen. (ret.) Abdullah but was not able to reach an agreement.

At 8 p.m. that night, Mohammed called the cellular phone in the Task Force Patriot (2nd Battalion, 32nd Field Artillery) tactical operations center (TOC) to tell me that he had found out from other sources that Brig. Gen. (ret.) Abdullah had already gotten all of the money to build his electric line and paid for all of the materials. He intended to pocket the $500,000 he was pressing us to provide for the project. Further, when contractor Mohammed talked to Abdullah, the powerful al Jibouri insisted that our Tuz–al Othaim project be stopped and that all of the materials Mohammed had bought for the project be given to Brig. Gen. (ret.) Abdullah, presumably so he could use them for other government-funded electric projects and pocket the government money for those as well.

We were running out of time. Soon a new unit would be on the ground. They might not carry on the rural ad Dawr coalition, our approach to defeating Jaysh Rijal al Tariqa al Naqshabandiyah (JRTN, literally "Army of the Men of the Order of Naqshabandi," the armed wing of the New Ba'ath Party). Task Force Patriot's electric project would restart Sheikh Sabah's farms in al Hamerine and Sheikh Shakur albu Issa's farms in al Othaim. Over time, the economy in both areas would grow stronger and stronger, tipping the balance of power in ad Dawr qa'da (district) from the city of ad Dawr to the al Jalaam ad Dawr (literally "the desert east of ad Dawr") regardless of what the next unit did.

We needed this electric project completed soon. We needed to engage Brig. Gen. (ret.) Abdullah and get this problem resolved quickly. The only problem was that Lt. Col. Bubba Cain was confined to his quarters, sidelined by cripplingly painful kidney stones.

I brought Lt. Col. Bubba Cain's interpreter, Spc. Ortega, to the TOC. I had him call Abdullah using the battalion commander's phone. "Tell him you are calling for the battalion commander and he is really pissed off," I instructed him. "Either we do our electric project, or there will be no money for anyone. We will not pay for Brig. Gen. (ret.) Abdullah's contract and we will take the electric poles we have already bought and store them on COB [contingency operating base] Speicher and no one will have them."

Spc. Ortega negotiated masterfully. Brig. Gen. (ret.) Abdullah began by trying to exert his authority as a provincial council member, a tactic that had made him a very wealthy man. Ortega seemed to be genuinely enjoying telling the Abdullah that wasn't going to work this time. "Lieutenant Colonel Cain is pissed," he said in English, before reverting to Arabic. "I have never seen him this mad."

Next, Abdullah tried to confuse the issue with technical jargon about incompatible wattages and voltages that he understood no better than we did. But Ortega had been armed for that tactic, as well. "Contractor Mohammed took Mohammed Halawi with him to approve the project." Brig. Gen. (ret.) Abdullah had to acknowledge that he knew the man, an engineer for the DG of electricity who went by abu A'aisha, and that he was very competent. He was the same engineer who had designed Abdullah's al Alam–al Hamerine project.

"I only want what is best for the province," Abdullah insisted. "This is not for my own benefit."

Ortega was definitely ready for that argument. We heard very little else from Iraqis everywhere we went. "General Abdullah," Spc. Ortega said in English, "Lieutenant Colonel Cain is serious. Either Salah ad Din will have two electric projects, or it will not have any."

"OK, OK," I heard Brig. Gen. (ret.) Abdullah say back in English. "Let me talk to Sabhan."

The next day, when contractor Mohammed went back to talk to DG Sabhan, however, he was as adamant as ever that the Tuz project would not be restarted. We had to gamble. The Task Force Patriot commander, Lt. Col. Cain, Patriot 6, wasn't going anywhere. He had not left his trailer all day. But we still called both DG Sabhan and Brig. Gen. (ret.) Abdullah and set a meeting for 10:30 a.m. on 6 May.

I had Spc. Ortega make the phone calls and emphasize how upset Cain was. Ortega added his own brilliant embellishment. "I don't know what he is going to do, General Abdullah," he said in English. "He was storming around the TOC talking about arresting both of you for corruption."

That night we received a call from contractor Mohammed. "Sir, I have good news. DG Sabhan has allowed us to go back to work. We start again tomorrow."

That call was followed a half hour later by one from Brig. Gen. (ret.) Abdullah, canceling our meeting for the next day, saying he had to go out of town unexpectedly.

We held our breath the whole next morning until, at 10 a.m., we received a call from contractor Mohammed. He was at the work site and they were back at work, erecting electric towers.

A few weeks later, I got the opportunity to ask contractor Mohammed what he had had to do to get the project working. He told me that Brig. Gen. (ret.) Abdullah had insisted that Mohammed build a home for the widows of Lt. Col. Ahmed al Fahal adjacent to the home of Ahmed's mother and father.

"That's interesting," I said, "because contractor Mithaq al Fahal already promised Lieutenant Colonel Cain he would use the profits from the al Alam girls' school we are renovating to build Lieutenant Colonel Ahmed's widows a house." Both of us knew where that money would now be going.

One of the smaller projects we had submitted for Sheikh Sabah Muntasir Diab al Shimiri was for four water trucks. The trucks were allegedly so he could provide free drinking water to make living in the desert more affordable, so his people could come back to their family homes from Mud Town, the small makeshift village that had sprung up between the Khadasia neighborhood of Tikrit and Tikrit University. The project would cost $140,000, with Sabah purchasing the trucks and the US Army reimbursing him.

There were, of course, a dozen ways Sabah could increase the profit margin on this project. He could just rent the trucks, get a fake bill of sale, and then return the trucks after he had his money. He could get older trucks, give them a fresh coat of paint, and try to palm them off as the newer trucks he had agreed to buy in the contract. I was not so naive as to think he would not try one of these tricks, or some other way to skim from the contract. In the end, I was more interested in him getting the money anyway. If he was going to get a party list established and a slate of candidates elected, he was going to have to spread a lot of money around the province.

On the day of the project inspection, we discovered that Sabah had both rented the trucks and chosen older trucks. To shave even more money off of the project, he didn't even bother to paint them. It was an error borne of inexperience with the Commander's Emergency Response Program (CERP); he didn't understand that not everyone in the US Army was in on the joke. He had to at least go through the motions.

When conscientious, idealistic 1st Lt. Jared Carpenter arrived with a Bravo Battery patrol to inspect the water trucks, he was indignant. Carpenter was an older lieutenant, nearly thirty. He had worked for years as a carpet installer before joining the Army, completing his degree, and being commissioned as a lieutenant. He was a worrier; his round plump face would flush when he was stressed by the demands around him, and he was now bright red.

The trucks were clearly from the 1980s, rather than the current decade as the contract had stipulated. Moreover, the bill of sale had been so shoddily forged that the vehicle identification numbers did not even match the receipt. When Carpenter investigated, he cornered Mohammed into admitting that he had fronted the money for the purchase and the trucks had only cost $90,000. (More likely, the trucks had required a $90,000 deposit, $80,000 of which they would recover when they returned the trucks.) Sheikh Sabah had already used the other $50,000 to buy a new SUV—complete with DVD player and rear bumper camera—which he had driven to the site of the inspection.

When 1st Lt. Carpenter returned, he was beside himself over the whole matter. During the CERP pay agent classes, the instructors had filled his head with horror stories of Americans going to jail over malfeasance surrounding CERP. The truth was that the only process more inefficient than the process to request and get CERP projects approved was the process to investigate alleged CERP abuses. The very few cases in which Americans went to jail over CERP involved US Army officers or American interpreters who were taking kickbacks or bribes or were outright stealing CERP money. In the end, the only people who ever held Iraqis accountable to contracts were people like 1st Lt. Jared Carpenter, outraged by the audacity of Iraqi greed.

The only officer in Task Force Patriot more outraged by Sheikh Sabah's "corruption" than 1st Lt. Carpenter was Cpt. Dan Peck, the talented young fires and effects coordinator who had led the anticorruption insurgency that had threatened to derail our campaign planning only a few weeks before. The situation was perfectly calibrated to trigger a virulently emotional response in him. It had all of the elements that he had decried only weeks before.

Try as we might, neither Maj. Payne nor I could convince the two younger officers to relent. The harder we pressed, the more indignant they became. Maj. Payne tried to couch the question in terms of the effects we were trying to achieve. I tried to appeal to Peck's better nature; by winning this battle politically, rather than by mounting large, "kinetic" (violent) operations, we were saving both Iraqi and American lives. He wouldn't budge. He would not authorize paying more than $90,000 for the trucks. I told him he was sticking contractor Mohammed with the bill, that Sabah wouldn't miss a dime. He was still unmoved.

We invited Sheikh Sabah Muntasir Diab al Shimiri and contractor Mohammed Ibrahim al Jibouri to COB Speicher to break the news. Contractor Mohammed brought us lunch, making me feel even worse about what I was about to tell him.

In mid 2010, I have to break the news to Sheikh Sabah al Shimiri (in Army garb) and contractor Mohammed Ibrahim al Jibouri (on the right on the same sofa) that they will not be getting full price for the water trucks they have purchased. Left of Sheikh Sabah al Shimiri is Cpt. Dan Peck. Right of contractor Mohammed is 1st Lt. Jamie Sanjuan. We are meeting in the morale, welfare, and recreation (MWR) building in the Task Force Patriot life support area at COB Speicher.

I tried to use the rules as an excuse for breaking my promise to them. I was suddenly very glad I had Mike Samander there; he had a gift for putting the best possible tone to the worst possible news, in Arabic or English. "You know, Sheikh Sabah, if I could, I would just write you a check right now. But I'm not able to do this. There are rules I must follow."

"I do not need money, habibi," Sabah said. "Your friendship and the friendship of Lieutenant Colonel Cain is enough." He might not understand CERP, but he understood being a sheikh. Real sheikhs were supposed to be above money. "I am just worried about our brother, Mohammed. He deserves to be paid for what he has done for my people, these water trucks he has brought us."

I directed my attention to contractor Mohammed. "Our division has rules about how much they will spend on this truck or that. For the trucks you bought, I can only give you $100,000." (At the eleventh hour, I had gotten Peck and Carpenter to relent to an additional $10,000 by pointing out that CERP rules permitted the contractor to make a 10 percent profit.)

Contractor Mohammed knew CERP better than I did. It had been his life for four years. He knew my explanation was nonsense. But he knew the script we were following, and he graciously accepted the explanation. His graciousness made me feel even worse.

11 May 2010 was another busy day for Task Force Patriot. Lt. Col. Bubba Cain was in al Alam, opening the notorious al Alam girls' school. I would travel to al Hamerine to see Sheikh Sabah Muntasir Diab al Shimiri.

Cpt. Simon Welte was in Tuz qa'da with Task Force Wolverine. The handover of Bayji and Sharqat qa'das a few weeks before had been relatively simple; Task Force Rangers (2nd Battalion, 16th Infantry) had left an infantry company, their Alpha Company "Outlaws," to assume responsibility for both qa'das from the US compound inside the Bayji Oil Refinery. Task Force Wolverine (4-1 Brigade Support Battalion), on the other hand, would be departing from Iraq and handing the single US base in Tuz qa'da, Forward Operating Base (FOB) Bernstein, over to the 16th Iraqi Army Brigade. We had only a few weeks for Cpt. Welte and his Bravo Battery to become familiar with the distant qa'da before the Wolverines departed.

My patrol's first task in al Hamerine was to deliver humanitarian aid (tons of rice, sugar, and coffee) to the al Shimiri storehouse to bolster Sabah's credibility with the people of al Nammah and al Hamerine and further marginalize his cousin and rival, Sheikh Ali Nwaf Diab al Shimiri. We met Sheikh Sabah at the same storehouse we had shown to senior US Department of Agriculture (USDA) representative Mr. Verdonk a few months earlier and delivered the truckload of rice, sugar, and coffee without incident.

For the trip to Sheikh Sabah's home, he insisted we take his new SUV. During the short trip to his compound, we watched a DVD of the Salah ad Din Television news story about the al Alam–al Hamerine electric project we had taped several weeks before. Even Mike Samander laughed as we watched him struggle to translate under the pressure of the television camera.

From there it was on to Sheikh Sabah's *diwan*, where we were met by Sheikh Ibrahim albu Qodal. Sheikh Ibrahim was the newest addition to the rural coalition. At the height of the Sunni insurgency, he had been an al Qaeda in Iraq facilitator. In fact, Sheikh Sabah al Shimiri and his Sons of Iraq had once captured Sheikh Ibrahim and taken him to detention at High Crimes in FOB Danger. After his release, Sheikh Ibrahim albu Qodal fled to Syria. Now he was back and ready to put the past behind him and join the new Iraq. Our pitch to unseat the al Duris was particularly appealing to him; his village of albu Qodal, about ten kilometers southeast of the city of ad Dawr, was virtually an occupied territory, dominated by the local police station run by a Col. Farhan al Duri.

While we ate lunch, 2nd Lt. Jesse Hall, the platoon leader for the Bravo Battery platoon that had brought us to al Hamerine, came in. "Captain Welte just got RKG'd [attacked with an RKG-3, a hand-thrown antiarmor grenade] in Tuz!" Even the Iraqis in the room started, alarmed by the soldier's tone.

Cpt. Welte's patrol had just left the Tuz qa'da council, where irate council members had berated both the captain and Lt. Col. Eric Moore, Wolverine 6, for the insult of handing the qa'da off from a lieutenant colonel to a captain. They were also incensed by Task Force Wolverine's failure to deliver the dozens of projects they had promised but not yet completed. Welte's patrol was at the outskirts of Sulayman Bak, the Sunni enclave and nahiya (subdistrict) capital in southeast Tuz qa'da, when their patrol was attacked by two RKG-3s. Their vehicle was damaged, but no one was injured. The JRTN insurgents got away.

After dinner we completed the remainder of our business in al Hamerine. 1st Lt. Jared Carpenter, our diligent young battalion S9 (civil affairs officer), along with his Iraqi-American category 1 interpreter, Larissa, completed a survey of Sheikh Sabah's well in preparation for a CERP project proposal to provide the area with a massive, solar-powered water purifier. "After all," Sheikh Sabah had quipped at our last meeting, "what good are our new water trucks without a water source?" He might have been new to the CERP game, but Sabah was catching on fast.

With our business completed, we said our good-byes, loaded up, and departed for COB Speicher. On our way back, on the al Alam–al Hamerine road (what US forces called Route Pepper) about one kilometer south of the Tikrit–Kirkuk road (what US forces called Alternate Supply Route, ASR, Clemson), at the northwest corner of the village of abu

Ajil, our convoy was attacked by an improvised explosive device (IED). From my vantage point in the second-to-the-last vehicle, I watched as the instantaneous plume of gray-black smoke engulfed the rear MRAP in which 1st Lt. Carpenter and Larissa were riding. Mike Samander, in my MRAP, was so violently startled awake by the sound of the explosion that he nearly broke his nose on the opposite bulkhead.

After a cursory inspection, we determined that the damage had been superficial and returned to COB Speicher without any more excitement. But the attack really rattled 1st Lt. Jared Carpenter. It had been his first time under fire, and he didn't care for it. "I know it was Sheikh Sabah," he insisted. "He is trying to kill me over the water trucks." His broad round face was uncharacteristically pale as he recounted the event.

I tried to be supportive as I explained, first, that the relatively small IED was meant more to make good footage for JRTN Internet videos than to cause injury and, second, that insurgents usually lacked the precision to attack a particular person with an IED. "Besides," I said, "why would Sheikh Sabah want to kill you? You're his new paycheck!"

1st Lt. Carpenter would not be consoled.

After all of the major operations we had done across Area of Operations (AO) Proud Americans since we arrived in Iraq, we only still had two detainees in jail, two of the four Jadir brothers—Jamal and Ali Jadir Ali al Duri—confirmed JRTN operatives captured during Operation Miami-Dade. Bravo Battery soldiers had identified Jamal as present at the shooting of Cpl. Tony Carrasco. This in and of itself was not enough to keep him in jail. However, he was found with a cell phone that contained video child pornography. It was on those grounds that he was still in jail. Bravo Battery soldiers had identified the other brother, Ali Jadir al Duri, as the man who threw an RKG-3 at their convoy as it traveled down the military bypass on the southeast corner of ad Dawr. The other two brothers, and all of the over one hundred other prisoners we had captured since we arrived in Iraq, had been released.

Ever since we had captured the Jadir brothers, the Salah ad Din justice system had been trying to let them go. They were first released only hours after their capture; the aborted Operation Patriot Hawk forced the Riot Dispersal Unit (RDU) to return to ad Dawr and recapture them. Next, Judge Faisal, the senior judge in Salah ad Din, threatened to let them go. Once we finally pinned the elusive judge down to hear the testimony, Bravo Battery soldiers testified under oath in Faisal's office about the two brothers. This worked for a while. But then the judge ruled that the testimony of infidels was not valid in Iraqi courts. Next, Bravo Battery found an al Duri witness who had fled to Samarra after overhearing the Jadir brothers talking about shooting Cpl. Carrasco in November 2009. After a great deal of negotiation and several aborted attempts, we were finally able to get this secret witness and Judge Faisal into the same room and keep the two remaining Jadir brothers in jail for a few more weeks.

In the latest episode of the continuing saga of the Jadir brothers, the two had been moved to the ad Dawr city jail. Of course the Task Force Patriot staff was terribly suspicious of the move, suspecting that the al Duris would let the JRTN operatives wander about their city freely, only securing them when we showed up to confirm their continued detention. We wanted to get them moved back to Tikrit or, even better, to Baghdad. To accomplish this, Task Force Patriot enlisted the help of Cpt. Farmer, the Dragon Brigade's female trial counsel (the Brigade judge advocate—senior lawyer—Maj. Wade Faulkner, had already redeployed as part of the responsible drawdown of forces).

Farmer met every week with Judge Faisal and in our first meeting with her relayed his view on the matter. "The only evidence you have against Jamal Jadir is the telephone with child porn," she said. "Because it was in the custody of Americans, he says there is suspicion you planted it to keep Jamal in jail. You have the uncorroborated testimony of one secret witness about crimes the Jadir brothers aren't charged with. The testimony of your soldiers against Jamal and Ali is not valid because they are not Iraqis." She avoided the word Judge Faisal had used, *infidels.* "Without evidence, they are going to be released."

The two Bravo Battery officers in the meeting, Cpt. Simon Welte and 1st Lt. Jay Urban, were about to object, but I stopped them.

"So you need the testimony of another Iraqi," I asked.

"That would be helpful," Cpt. Farmer replied.

"Fine," I replied. "I have $200,000 worth of CERP projects in the queue for Lieutenant Colonel Uday [commander of the 2nd Battalion, 48th Iraqi Army Brigade]. He captured them. I will ask him to testify that he found the camera with the porn and both brothers confessed to shooting Carrasco."

Farmer visibly recoiled at the suggestion that I ask the Iraqi to lie. "We are trying to build the Iraqi justice system," Farmer began in a slightly condescending tone.

"Stop," I interrupted. "This is a war. These people are trying to kill us—they did kill Carrasco. Then, when we catch them, they use this facade of a justice system we have built for them to get out of jail. Don't talk to me about the integrity of the justice system. I have two sons of bitches on film laying an IED in Owja and then being warned by an IP [Iraqi policeman] and helped by another guy to escape. All four of them are out on the street, scot-free. We are all soldiers. Our job is to take the enemy off the battlefield, and that is what we are going to do."

There were no further protests. A week later, S.Lt. Col. Uday met privately with Judge Faisal. It is not clear what they talked about, but the Jadir brothers moved back to the High Crimes jail in Tikrit.

In mid-May, Lt. Col. Bubba Cain was preparing to return home for his own long-awaited rest and relaxation (R&R) leave. He had timed his return to watch his son graduate from high school near Fort Hood, Texas, where his family had remained while he went to Fort Riley, Kansas, to take command of the Proud Americans battalion (2nd Battalion, 32nd Field Artillery).

As he prepared to leave, he told Maj. Matt Payne, the battalion XO, "You have assumption of command orders" (temporary command of the battalion as was commensurate with his role as second in command). Then he turned to me, "You have assumption of goat-eating orders." Since I was more familiar with the operational details of Task Force Patriot's mission in Salah ad Din, I would take over all of his engagements with Iraqis during his absence.

Sheikh Sabah Muntasir Diab al Shimiri called just before Cain departed, insisting on seeing the commander before he left. "I have a gift for him before he goes," he told us.

Lt. Col. Cain, Patriot 6, was not enthusiastic about the engagement. Over the course of the deployment, largely because of the dramatic events surrounding the death of Lt. Col. Ahmed Subhi al Fahal al Jibouri, he had gravitated toward al Alam and the al Jibouris. Because of his closeness to the al Jibouris; his frequent engagements in Tikrit with Iraqi police commanders, judges, and political officials; and the extreme distances required to travel to al Hamerine, al Othaim, and the other important locations in rural ad Dawr, he had largely left maintenance and expansion of the rural ad Dawr coalition to me. As a result, he did not know Sabah as well as I did. Under pressure, Cain finally agreed to the meeting.

Sheikh Sabah arrived with a modest meal, kabobs and chicken over rice. While we were, as usual, compelled to eat with our hands around a communal plate, as was the Arab custom, both Cain and I were secretly glad that, for a change, it wasn't goat. As the meal concluded, Lt. Col. Bubba Cain was becoming impatient, wanting to get to business so he could finish packing for his leave.

Sheikh Sabah Muntasir Diab al Shimiri stood and presented a flat garment box to Lt. Col. Cain. Patriot 6 opened it and found inside a plush brown *abaya* (a traditional Arab cloak). He was gracious as he accepted it, but he had received nearly half a dozen since he arrived in Iraq.

Eager to move the meeting along and if possible hand it off to me, Lt. Col. Cain said, "Major Proctor is in command while I am gone. He has my complete confidence. Please treat him as well as you treat me."

Lt. Col. Bubba Cain was about to say his good-byes and depart when Sheikh Sabah reached into his own *abaya* and withdrew an envelope. "Then this gift I will give to my dear brother, Major Proctor."

Cain looked puzzled as he handed the envelope to me. I opened it and found a small piece of paper inside, stationery from the al Rashid Hotel in Baghdad. On it was Arabic writing. I handed it to Mike Samander, seated next to me on my side of the conference room table. Cain instinctively leaned forward, as curious as I was to hear what was on the paper.

"The following four men laid the IED near abu Ajil that attacked Major Proctor and his men." Samander read off the names one by one. They were all abu Ajilis. The paper also included directions to their home.

"There is more on the back," Sheikh Sabah said, satisfied.

"The name of the Tikrit sniper," Mike read, "is Suttar Jummah al Jibouri, from Kirkuk province. He comes to Tikrit once a month to conduct attacks." The note concluded with directions to his apartment in Tikrit.

I couldn't conceal my delight with the information. The name he had given us for the Tikrit sniper, as well as his pattern of movement, exactly coincided with our own independent analysis, making the rest of the information he was providing much more credible.

Lt. Col. Bubba Cain was stunned and surprised as Sheikh Sabah excused himself, sensitive to Cain's desire to be off to America. Patriot 6's farewell was genuinely warm.

Our elation abated dramatically as we actually tried to make good on the information. After Patriot 6 departed, I assumed his normal engagements in Tikrit and tried to get the Iraqi police to follow up on the information. None of the Salah ad Din police would investigate. My first stop was S.Lt. Col. Khalil, our closest ally in the Iraqi police and the "top cop" in the province after the death of Lt. Col. Ahmed al Fahal. I readily accepted his invitation to lunch after the weekly Tikrit security meeting at the Tikrit joint coordination center (JCC) in the Mahmoon ("Birthday") Palace in northwest Tikrit.

He readily accepted the information on the abu Ajili insurgents and promised to arrest them the same day, but as the days wore on, it became clear he had no intention of prosecuting the targets. The next day, when we called him, he pretended not to know what targets we were talking about. We gave him the information again and two days later queried him on his progress. He claimed he was not able to get warrants. "I can't arrest them without warrants."

That didn't seem to slow you down, I thought to myself, when you were rounding up people for ransom in southwest Tikrit during Operation Vigilant Patriot.

Sheikh Sabah was able to use his connections in Baghdad and Sulaymaniyah in Iraqi Kurdistan to get us warrants, which we presented to S.Lt. Col. Khalil at our next meeting, along with the information, one more time, on where the insurgents lived. "Would you like us to send a patrol with you for security?" I asked.

"La, la, la." No, no, no, he insisted. "We can handle this."

That was unusual. Iraqis were usually thrilled to get the assistance of US forces, if for no other reason than the free gas and goodies they received.

Two more days later, we asked him about his progress. "We went to the location, but they weren't home," he claimed.

We decided to widen the net, to try to find some other police agency that would prosecute the targets. We also tried to get Khalil and others to stake out and capture the Tikrit sniper. But we got the same reaction from all of the police battalions in our area of operations.

No one wanted to round up real JRTN insurgents.

Our first efforts to stop the US Agency for International Development (USAID) from spending money in the city of ad Dawr, going through USAID channels, had failed. No one we had contacted in Community Action Program (CAP) III seemed to have the authority to change the course of the program once it was set. We decided to try appealing to the provincial reconstruction team (PRT) leadership for help. With the help of Maj. Mark Chandler, the Dragon Brigade's S9 (civil affairs officer)—attached to the PRT headquarters, "PRT Main," to act as liaison—Maj. Matt Payne and I were able to get a meeting with Barbara Yoder, the governance lead, and Katherine Dennison, a young nutritionist whom the PRT had hired to be the senior health advisor for Salah ad Din province. We tried to convince the two to intervene on our behalf, but all they wanted to talk about was getting us to take them to the Bayji Oil Refinery to do an assessment of the environmental impact of the pollution the facility was causing. Even after we agreed to take them to do the assessment, we were unable to get them to help us with the USAID program.

After trying futilely to get the PRT leadership to help us end the CAP III program that was pouring money into ad Dawr or give us any information about the program's leaders, we finally resorted to asking Sheikh Ali al Shimiri—Sheikh Mahsood al Duri's vassal and Sheikh Sabah al Shimiri's cousin and rival—to give us the name and number for the American he dealt with in the program. Not knowing our purpose, he was initially reluctant but finally gave us the information. He also offered that, while there was a community action group (CAG) on paper, Sheikh Mahsood made the real decisions about where the money went. He also boasted that the program had now spent $240,000 in the city of ad Dawr.

The name and number we received was for the regional director of CAP III in Kirkuk. We reached Suzanne Saulniers but she, too, was unhelpful. She did not have enough money to start a new CAG for rural ad Dawr and had no authority to cut off the flow of money to the JRTN-dominated city of ad Dawr. She suggested we talk to USAID at the US embassy in Baghdad but couldn't tell us with whom we should speak.

Our next stop was Col. Guthrie, the new deputy director for the PRT. With his help, we tracked down a USAID representative in Baghdad who knew something about the project. By this time, nearly two months after we had discovered the program, we had accumulated a mountain of evidence for canceling the program. We had assembled secret information implicating most of the members of the CAG in insurgent activity. We could also show that USAID had paid for three projects, two markets and a water control unit, that had already been paid for with CERP money by Task Force Cacti (2nd Battalion, 35th Infantry), Task Force Steel (3rd Battalion, 7th Field Artillery), or other units that had had responsibility for the city of ad Dawr in the past. We sent all of this evidence to the contact in Baghdad before we called.

We spent an hour on the phone, at PRT Main, with Col. Guthrie and Salah ad Din USAID representative Greg Adams. At the end of the conference call, we had accomplished nothing. The only good news was that the CAP III program had run out of money, meaning no more money would be spent under the program on the city of ad Dawr.

"Don't worry," Greg Adams said without a hint of sarcasm as the meeting broke up. "There may be a CAP IV!"

The results of the Iraqi national election had both complicated issues for Iraq and simplified issues in Salah ad Din. Sunni Arab Iraqis voted in such strong numbers for al Iraqiya and its leader, former prime minister Iyad Alawi, that the coalition had taken the greatest number of parliamentary seats of any coalition in the election, even beating out Prime Minister Nuri al Maliki's State of Law coalition. Unfortunately, it had not captured enough votes to constitute an outright majority, and a months-long stalemate began, in which Alawi and Maliki struggled to form coalitions big enough to constitute a majority in the Council of Representatives and win the right to form the next government.

In Salah ad Din, however, as the Task Force Patriot staff had hoped when we chose to stay out of the struggle between provincial council and the governor, Governor Mutashar al Aliwi had been elected to the Council of Representatives. This solved the problem of the provincial council's insistence that Governor Mutashar leave office, but one issue remained. The provincial council had voted to install provincial council member engineer Khalid to be the provincial governor, but the current Iraqi government refused to certify his selection for the governorship.

Thus began a new round of shuttle diplomacy, with abu Mazen on the road between Baghdad and Salah ad Din, sometimes alone, sometimes with other members of the provincial council, to get someone, anyone, in the national government to certify engineer Khalid as governor of Salah ad Din.

It was on one of these trips that abu Mazen fell prey to the Iraqi Islamic Party's (IIP's) allies in the Shi'a-led government. While in Baghdad, abu Mazen was arrested, tried in a lightning-fast trial, and convicted of forging his high school diploma so he could run for the provincial council. He was sentenced to four and a half years in prison, which he began serving immediately. The news hit the Iraqi airwaves like a thunderclap, and Salah ad Din held its breath, bracing for a clash between the al Alam and Bayji al Jibouris and the al Samarra'i tribes.

Through a bit of political wrangling (and no doubt a substantial exchange of cash), abu Mazen got his confinement moved to plush quarters in FOB Danger, overlooking RDU Island. It was not long before Task Force Patriot started hearing stories of wild, two-day-long parties taking place in the compound.

If abu Mazen was making the best of a bad situation, Brig. Gen. (ret.) Abdullah was doing even better. With abu Mazen incarcerated, he got the siege of the provincial council building by the 4th Iraqi Army Division lifted and had himself instated as the temporary provincial council chairman. Many in the Task Force Patriot staff wondered aloud if this had not been the whole point of the destructive conflict between the provincial council and the governor in the first place.

By the end of May, it had been a long time since anyone in the Task Force Patriot staff had spoken to the leadership of the al Duri tribe. Bravo Battery had continued to meet with them, keeping, as they say, our enemies closer. I had met with some of the lesser figures in the tribe, like engineer Dhaif al Duri (director of the Salah ad Din Company at the site of the former Patrol Base, PB, Woodcock); Imam Dia al Duri (imam of the mosque in Mujamma, the housing complex immediately south of the Salah ad Din Company); and Sheikh Ali Fayzee al Duri (leader of the concerned local citizens, or CLC—the al Duri version of the Sons of Iraq—in abu Dalef). But the battalion leadership had not met with the senior tribal leadership, Sheikh Mahsood al Duri or Sheikh Kaseeb al Duri, since just after the death of Cpl. Carrasco in November 2009.

At the request of ad Dawr qa'da council chairman Sheikh Mahsood, that silence ended in late May, when Sheikh Mahsood al Duri and ad Dawr mayor Uthman al Duri came to COB Speicher to see me. They had come to petition Task Force Patriot to restart CERP projects in the city of ad Dawr. All projects had ended in the town after the death of

Carrasco, when the battalion had arrived at its present strategy, empowering rural ad Dawr sheikhs to shift the balance of economic and political power out of the city, away from the al Duris, the New Ba'ath Party, and JRTN.

Sheikh Mahsood portrayed the city's leaders as innocent victims of the insurgency and insisted that we were punishing the civilians for the inadequacies of the police. I let him go on for a very long time until he finally exhausted his argument and fell silent, waiting for me to speak.

"Every time we go to ad Dawr we get attacked. We get shot at or we get RKG'd [attacked with RKG-3s]. My own convoy has been attacked within one hundred meters of a police checkpoint, and your kinsmen stood by and did nothing." I paused for a moment and then concluded. "Naqshabandiyah [JRTN] runs ad Dawr, not you."

Sheikh Mahsood al Duri lost himself for a moment, insulted not by the suggestion that their town was run by insurgents, but that we had misidentified them. "Ad Dawr does not have Naqshabandiyah. Naqshabandiyah are religious fools. Ad Dawr has the Ba'ath Party. The town is run by the Ba'ath Party. Ad Dawr is the birthplace of Iraqi Ba'athism. Ad Dawr is where the Ba'ath Party began."

Mahsood stopped, realizing what he had said, and tried to repair the error. "We are not Ba'athists, of course. But there are Ba'athists in our town. There are terrorists in our town, and the police will not fight them. This is not our fault." He indicated himself and Mayor Uthman sitting silently to his right.

I had found a pressure point. They didn't like being called JRTN. JRTN was just a marketing ploy to attract former al Qaeda in Iraq insurgents. At their heart, the al Duris were Ba'athists. To keep them off balance I ignored their correction. "And these Naqshabandiyah terrorists that are operating in your town, they are from somewhere else? They couldn't possibly be al Duris, right?"

Mahsood dipped his eyes slightly, avoiding eye contact with me. "They are al Duris. They are young and they have been led astray. Young people do not listen to their elders anymore. They do whatever they want."

I had no intention of spending CERP money in ad Dawr or believing their denials, but I was hoping to corner them into divulging some new piece of information to help us better understand the dynamics of their town and the New Ba'ath Party and JRTN across Salah ad Din and Sunni Arab Iraq. I kept moving, trying to keep them off balance. "Sheikh

Mahsood, you *are* a sheikh. Your brother is Sheikh Kaseeb, sheikh of the al Mua'shit tribe, right? Mayor Uthman," I spoke directly to the junior al Duri at the table. "You are a sheikh, too; your father is Sheikh abd al Kareem al Mumdalal, right?"

Both men nodded. "Nom." Yes. They knew they were being backed into a trap, but they didn't know how.

"These young men are from your tribes. If you wanted them to stop, you could tell us who they are and where they live. We would stop them from hurting themselves and others. We could help protect your city." I wasn't asking them to help; I was explaining why, even if everything they said was true (which of course it wasn't), they were still complicit.

It was time to push Mahsood to see how far he was willing to carry this pretense. "You could help us find the Naqshabandiyah from your tribe," I said, looking Sheikh Mahsood in the eye. "You could help me find terrorists like Ahmed Shahab Ahmed al Duri." Ahmed al Duri was Izzat Ibrahim al Duri's closest advisor and confidant in Iraq. He was also Sheikh Mahsood's brother. (He was, in fact, captured just a month after this conversation, ferrying money into ad Dawr from the New Ba'ath Party in Syria.)

Mahsood smiled and chuckled slightly as he leaned back away from me, both hands flat on the long wooden conference table. The veil had been lifted from his face. We understood him, and he understood us. There would be no détente between US forces and ad Dawr. There would be no accommodation between Task Force Patriot and the New Ba'ath Party.

The conversation turned to surprisingly frank small talk. Suddenly we were two enemies meeting at the center of a battlefield at a pause in the battle before resuming hostilities. Mayor Uthman seemed confused as we talked, surprised at Mahsood's frankness.

As the meeting concluded and we all stood up to say our good-byes before the men left, Mahsood smiled and took my hand. "You know you won't stop the Ba'ath Party," Mahsood said. "It is everywhere in Salah ad Din, in every government office and in every police station."

"I don't have to stop you," I replied. "When the people of Salah ad Din are given a choice between living in the past or getting on with the future, they will choose to follow those who will lead them into the future."

Sheikh Mahsood laughed hardily. I had never heard him really laugh before. It stunned me. Then he said, "You mean men like your good friend Sheikh Abdullah Jebarra? He is the biggest Ba'athist of them all! He is the head of the snake!"

My heart pounded as the sheikh departed. Mahsood was incontrovertibly tied to the New Ba'ath Party; on this evening of frank talk, he had nothing to lose and no particular reason to lie. He had used Abdullah Jebarra's tribal title, sheikh, to indicate not just Abdullah Jebarra personally but his entire tribe. Mahsood had just told me that the al Alam al Jibouris—the tribe closest to US forces in all of Sunni Arab Iraq—were aligned with the New Ba'ath Party and, by extension, JRTN.

All of the reports I had dismissed out of hand suddenly rushed back into my mind—the report from the Tikrit operational detachment alpha (ODA) that Sheikh Wanus al Jibouri was a gunrunner, the reports of Sheikh Khemis al Jibouri and his younger brother buying hundreds of thousands of dollars worth of weapons for the "New Iraqi Resistance," and the story about then-Major Ahmed and Brig. Gen. (ret.) Abdullah letting Izzat Ibrahim al Duri go after capturing him.

I felt sick as I left the conference room, recounting all of the money we had poured into al Alam al Jibouri coffers since we arrived in Iraq. We had been so worried about the $240,000 that USAID had given the New Ba'ath Party in ad Dawr. If what Sheikh Mahsood had said was true, we had given the New Ba'ath Party in al Alam nearly $10 million.

With the departure of Task Force Wolverine, in addition to responsibility for Tuz qa'da, Task Force Patriot also inherited Billy Hall, their "satellite PRT" (an individual representative of the Salah ad Din PRT assigned to a single geographic region). Hall was a tall, thin, bespectacled Tennessean with a large family. His measured speech and tentative word choice reminded one of James Rebhorn playing the unlikeable secretary of defense in the summer blockbuster *Independence Day*. He had a PRT-instilled sense of superiority to the military units with which he was forced to work; just as US Forces–Iraq (USF-I) claimed to be in support of the US embassy in Baghdad, he believed, Task Force Patriot should subordinate itself to him.

At our first meeting, at the PRT headquarters on COB Speicher, Billy Hall gave Cpt. Simon Welte, the Bravo Battery commander, and me a briefing about Tuz qa'da and its nahiyas (subdistricts). Maj. James Lockridge, the Task Force Wolverine S3 (operations officer), was there but spoke little. The brief had been advertised as an information brief, but as he spoke, Hall enumerated the authorities he expected to have bequeathed to him.

"The Sheikhs' Council meets once a month at the Tuz qa'da council building." Hall proclaimed, "That is my meeting. Only I attend that." He went on to list all of the other qa'da and nahiya meetings he expected to be his exclusive domain.

After the meeting, I asked Maj. Lockridge if Hall had really enjoyed that level of authority in Tuz qa'da. "We tried to give him what he wanted," Lockridge said. "Wolverine 6 worked around him where he could."

His forcefulness with Task Force Wolverine, jawboning himself into a coequal or even superior position with Lt. Col. Eric Moore, had earned him the favor of the PRT leadership at COB Speicher. John Bauer's inability as a satellite PRT to force similar concessions from us had earned him a ticket back to the United States, along with Terry Elmore—the satellite PRT we had briefly inherited from Task Force Rangers (2nd Battalion, 16th Infantry) after their departure—who stubbornly refused to live at the Bayji Oil Refinery despite our warnings that it was the only way he was ever going to get to see the Bayji or Sharqat qa'da councils. Hall was now our only satellite PRT, ostensibly responsible for Sharqat, Bayji, Tikrit, ad Dawr, and Tuz qa'das.

At the same time we were receiving pressure from the PRT to relinquish control of our operations and our CERP contracts to Billy Hall, we were receiving pressure from the Dragon Brigade to abdicate our role in qa'da and nahiya governments. In most instances, we were happy to comply; John Bauer had long had a leading role in shaping our relationship with the Tikrit qa'da and al Alam nahiya councils. Effectively partnering with the distant Sharqat qa'da council was difficult for anyone, but if Terry Elmore had been willing to suffer the indignity of living on a base full of soldiers, we would have been happy to give him a leading role in partnering with the Bayji qa'da and Siniyah nahiya government. We tried to offer Bill Hall similar authority in partnering with the Tuz qa'da and Amerlie and Sulayman Bak nahiya councils. Once the other satellite PRTs left, we were ready to help him partner with all of those qa'das as well. Our only red line was the ad Dawr qa'da council, which we were trying to replace through the rural ad Dawr coalition.

This was not enough for Hall. His interpretation of the direction we had received from the Dragon Brigade was that we would dedicate forces to him to unilaterally partner with everyone who did not wear a police or army uniform. His expectation was that Task Force Patriot leaders would not accompany him or speak to civilian leaders, period. It was an impractical expectation. He was one man, and there were five qa'da and five nahiya governments in AO Proud Americans. We had dozens of ongoing CERP projects across the AO that, because of the intricate patronage networks that had developed to extract money from US forces, required interaction with qa'da and provincial government officials to complete. Moreover, US forces were ultimately responsible for security in the province. If a year in Salah ad Din had taught us anything, it was that it was impossible to understand the dynamics of the insurgent threat in the AO without knowing and understanding the political figures in the AO. This was access that, if Billy Hall had his way, we would be denied.

Moreover, it was Billy Hall's expectation that he would have absolute control over the expenditure of CERP throughout AO Proud Americans. We would, in his estimation, be reduced to executors of his will, processing paperwork as his staff and making payments and project checks on his behalf. All authority for CERP would fall to him. This was, of course, anathema to Task Force Patriot's approach in AO Proud Americans, using CERP both to maintain influence with key political, security, and judicial figures and to change the economic balance of power in ad Dawr qa'da.

It was CERP that sparked Task Force Patriot's first clash with Billy Hall. Task Force Wolverine executed a surge of CERP project submissions just before they departed, leaving us with over a dozen submitted projects and ninety-one proposed microgrants (small $5,000 grants, ostensibly to small businesses to spur growth). It was unrealistic to expect us to execute so many projects in a single qa'da, as many as in the rest of AO Proud Americans combined. But when we sat down to finalize the decision in a meeting with Billy Hall, he objected.

"We need to do these projects," Hall insisted. "These microgrants will spur economic growth in the Hellaywa and Yangesia areas."

"The commander does projects for three reasons," I explained, trying to be diplomatic. "He does them to empower people we want empowered, to create security, or to gain influence. The only reason we would have to go to either place is to pay out these microgrants. Is there some reason we need to empower these people? Do we need these people to do something for us?"

They were honest questions, but Hall clearly took them as an assault on his PRT-given authority over us.

At points where we could have worked toward common goals, he stubbornly refused to help. In early June, as the Tuz–al Hamerine–al Othaim electric project neared completion, the Tuz qa'da council chairman, Qadir Ali Saleh, stubbornly declared that he would not send any electricity down the line to ad Dawr qa'da. This impasse would have been a great opportunity for Hall to build bonds with Task Force Patriot and at the same time expand his credibility with the Tuz qa'da council. He knew the qa'da council better than we did and could have easily negotiated on our behalf to break the deadlock. Frankly, we were so desperate to get the issue resolved that, if Hall had pressed, we would have probably given way on the CERP project argument he had just lost.

Instead, he stubbornly refused to get involved, unwilling to work on any priority that was not his priority.

In the end, we had to turn to Brig. Gen. (ret.) Abdullah Jebarra to intervene. We also had to stop payment on all of the CERP projects in Tuz until the qa'da council relented. The approach both increased Abdullah's power and forced Task Force Wolfhounds—the battalion that would soon replace us—into a position where it would have to continue to do CERP projects in Tuz to keep the electricity flowing to al Hamerine and al Othaim. All of these negative repercussions could have been avoided had our satellite PRT simply chosen to help.

CERP became an issue again a few weeks later, when a huge car bomb exploded in a Turkoman neighborhood of the city of Tuz, narrowly missing Niyazi Muhammad Mahdi Qambar, a Turkoman provincial council member. Six people were killed, twenty more wounded. Three houses were destroyed.

Hall insisted that we must give the qa'da council humanitarian aid. I was genuinely confused by the request. "Why? Did the VBIED [vehicle-borne improvised explosive device, a car bomb] damage some infrastructure? An electric line or water line or something?"

"No," Hall said. He was trying to sound diplomatic, but it came out sounding patronizing. "We always give humanitarian aid to the qa'da council whenever something like this happens."

I was flooded with potential responses. We didn't give humanitarian aid when a suicide vest went off in Tikrit and killed the most important *shurta* (policeman) in Sunni Arab Iraq. The qa'da council was dominated by Kurds, and this car bomb almost killed the Turkoman provincial council member; how did we know some of the qa'da council members weren't complicit? Why would I give humanitarian aid to the qa'da council and not go to the affected area and give it to the *mukhtar* (neighborhood elder)?

None of these responses would persuade him, so I settled on the least confrontational answer. "It is June. The brigade has already barred me from submitting more CERP contracts."

Hall wouldn't let the issue rest and finally repeated John Bauer's mistake. A week later, I got a call from Cpt. Pailey Eapen, the Dragon Brigade's CERP project manager. "Sir, you want to submit another project?"

"No," I answered. "What are you talking about?"

Cpt. Eapen answered, "PRT Main told me you want to submit a packet for humanitarian assistance for Tuz."

Hall had gone around me to the PRT leadership to try to pressure the battalion to process his humanitarian aid request.

"No," I told Eapen. "We don't want humanitarian aid."

With his credibility in Task Force Patriot destroyed, Hall begrudgingly accompanied Cpt. Simon Welte on semiweekly patrols to Tuz—patrols he believed he should be doing unilaterally, without military leadership present—and waited for the arrival of Task Force Wolfhounds. His only participation in the battalion's weekly meetings was to ensure that he was scheduled for time alone with the Task Force Wolfhounds leadership when they arrived, so he could plead his case directly to them.

On the afternoon of 19 June 2010, we received a dramatic call from Mohammed Ibrahim, our al Jibouri contractor working with Sheikh Sabah al Shimiri. The two had been traveling to the northern city of Irbil to purchase water trucks for Sheikh Shakur when they were stopped at a Kurdish checkpoint. According to Mohammed, when they ran Sabah's *jensiyah* (identification card), they found a list of eight charges, including terrorism, kidnapping, and, as Mohammed put it, "gay stuff." Sheikh Sabah was taken into custody. After a few days of waiting to see if he would be released, Mohammed returned to Salah ad Din.

Hot on the heels of the dispute with Brig. Gen. (ret.) Abdullah Hussein al Jebarra al Jibouri over the power lines Task Force Patriot was building from Tuz to al Othaim, the staff immediately suspected that Sheikh Sabah was being shaken down and Mohammed may have been complicit in the scheme. Perhaps he had been pressured to report on Sheikh Sabah's movements. After consulting with Lt. Col. Bubba Cain, I told 1st Lt. Carpenter to put the signing of Mohammed's next CERP contract, the Mohammed bin al Qasim School in front of Sheikh Sabah's compound, on hold until we had more information.

The next day was consumed with trying to gather information and get to the bottom of Sabah's arrest. We talked to both Judge Faisal, the senior judge in Salah ad Din, and Lt. Col. Khalil, commander of ERU 3. After looking into the charges, both called back insisting that the charges were old and had already been cleared. Later in the day, we called Sheikh Sabah's brother, Sheikh Diab Muntasir Diab al Shimiri. He told us he would go with contractor Mohammed Ibrahim later in the day to see Maj. Gen. Hamed, the PDOP, to secure Sabah's release.

The PDOP would not answer his phone, and his executive officer, Brig. Gen. Jassem, an al Alam al Jibouri and Brig. Gen. (ret.) Abdullah's "man" in the PDOP's office, seemed genuinely pleased Sabah was in jail, saying, "Good! He's a terrorist."

Contractor Mohammed Ibrahim asked if he should still buy the water trucks. I told him to wait for Sabah, an answer that didn't seem to please him. Apparently, Sheikh Sabah had insisted on going with him to Irbil in the first place to make sure Mohammed didn't skim money from the purchase at the expense of Sheikh Sabah's cut.

On the evening of 21 June, I was finally able to meet with Mohammed. He was insistent that the only side he was on was ours. He didn't want to tell us everything he knew about Sheikh Sabah because he knew Sabah was our friend. After I insisted, he finally began to open up. When he did, it could have just as easily been Brig. Gen. (ret.) Abdullah Jebarra speaking to us. Sheikh Sabah was a terrorist. When Sheikh Sabah had been head of the al Sawah council, according to Mohammed, he had led raids in which jewelry was stolen and young girls were kidnapped. When Lt. Col. Ahmed al Fahal al Jibouri's uncle was kidnapped by "terrorists" and was tortured and shot in both knees in Abu Ajil, Sheikh Sabah brokered his release, proving that Sabah was a terrorist. "He isn't New Ba'ath Party or Naqshabandiyah [JRTN]," Mohammed said, "but Sheikh Sabah is a terrorist."

The truth, as we pieced together the fragments from the meeting with Mohammed and put them together with the other information we had, was quite a bit more complicated. We also finally understood the reason for Sheikh Sabah's deep animus toward Brig. Gen. (ret.) Abdullah and possibly why Sabah had been arrested.

In addition to the other misfortune, much of it self-inflicted, that had befallen Sheikh Sabah Muntasir Diab al Shimiri since the beginning of the war, he had also run afoul of the most powerful man in Salah ad Din province, Brig. Gen. (ret.) Abdullah Hussein al Jebarra al Jibouri. It was this conflict, more than any other misfortune that had befallen him, that had forced Sheikh Sabah al Shimiri into exile at his desert residence in al Hamerine.

With agriculture in al Hamerine devastated by the war-induced drought, Sheikh Sabah al Shimiri was desperate to provide for his tribe and bring families back to his area. Around 2007, when the al Sawah movement that began in al Anbar province finally spread to Salah ad Din province, Sheikh Sabah, a man of singular vision, saw his chance. While the al Jalaam ad Dawr had seen quite a bit of al Qaeda activity, it had mostly occurred south of al Hamerine, in Sheikh Shakur albu Issa's area of al Othaim. Al Qaeda in Iraq maintained dominance in a number of safe houses on the northern bank of the al Othaim River from which they could launch attacks into neighboring Diyala province.

Sheikh Sabah had no ties to al Qaeda, nor did they hold influence in his area. He was in a great position to stand up the first Sons of Iraq units in Salah ad Din and begin collecting payment from US forces at minimal risk to himself or his kinsmen. At the same time Sheikh Muawiya Naji al Jebarra al Jibouri was standing up the al Sawah council in Salah ad Din, Sheikh Sabah Muntasir Diab al Shimiri established one of the largest Sons of Iraq units in Salah ad Din, in al Aith (the al Shimiri name for the region encompassing al Nammah and al Hamerine).

Having gotten in on the ground floor of al Sawah in Salah ad Din, Sheikh Sabah al Shimiri had a big head start on the other tribes in the province. To bring other tribes along, Sheikh Muawiya Naji al Jebarra al Jibouri made Sheikh Sabah al Shimiri his deputy. This is why Sheikh Sabah was riding in the same vehicle as Sheikh Muawiya when the latter was killed by an IED in October 2007.

As deputy, Sheikh Sabah suddenly became the head of the Salah ad Din al Sawah council, receiving payment for every Sons of Iraq unit in the province and, as was the Iraqi way, taking his cut off the top before distributing the rest to other tribes. Commensurate with his new position, Sheikh Sabah moved into a palatial new residence on FOB Danger.

But the al Jibouris, the most powerful tribe in the province, were not about to give up their lucrative al Sawah business. In late 2007, a party at Sheikh Sabah's new home on FOB Danger handed the al Jibouris the opportunity to make their move. Sabah had a drunken disagreement with a Tikrit local. As the evening wore on and Sheikh Sabah got drunker, he and several of his men roughed up the man, threw him in Sheikh Sabah's trunk, and—depending on who tells the story—either dumped him somewhere in Tikrit or took him to jail as a "terrorist." Unfortunately, this young man also worked as an interpreter for a US Special Forces ODA. The green berets were notorious for their fierce loyalty to their local national allies. When they heard of the assault, they organized a "sting" operation against Sheikh Sabah.

The Bastogne Brigade (1st Brigade, 101st Airborne Division), then in control of Salah ad Din, sent patrols down the roads Sheikh Sabah's Sons of Iraq were supposed to be guarding in civilian trucks (to avoid being detected in advance) and found many of the checkpoints deserted. Armed with this evidence, they stopped Sheikh Sabah in his vehicle and executed a search; they caught Sabah with a trunk full of Sons of Iraq pay he had skimmed from the other Sons of Iraq leaders. Sheikh Sabah was arrested for corruption. While he was in jail, al Alam al Jibouris came forward with additional charges—theft, kidnapping, and worse—allegedly perpetrated by Sheikh Sabah and his Sons of Iraq over the previous year.

While he was in jail, Sheikh Sabah was evicted from his home in FOB Danger, and leadership of the al Sawah council passed to Sheikh Hamid Ibrahim Salim al Jibouri, of the Bayji al Jibouris. Sheikh Ali Nwaf Diab al Shimiri tried to usurp him, no doubt with Brig. Gen. (ret.) Abdullah's encouragement. Moreover, it almost certainly cost Sheikh Sabah al Shimiri tens of thousands of dollars to extricate himself from jail and clear the charges. Sabah's reputation was irrevocably damaged. Sheikh Sabah receded into exile in al Hamerine.

At least this latest detention was not terribly onerous for Sheikh Sabah Muntasir Diab al Shimiri. Despite the charges or political games swirling around him, he was still sheikh of the al Shimiri, one of only seven true sheikhs in Iraq. His cell in High Crimes at FOB Danger was more like quarters, with a separate bathroom, kitchen, and bedroom, as well as satellite television. Every evening, his jailors took him out to a different restaurant in Tikrit to eat.

But this didn't make us feel any better about him remaining in jail. Task Force Wolfhounds (1st Battalion, 27th Infantry) was coming in days. If we didn't have him out of jail by then, it would destroy any credibility the Task Force Patriot staff had in getting them to embrace and continue our approach, building the rural ad Dawr coalition.

Many of the newer, younger, more idealistic staff officers in the Task Force Patriot staff, never happy with our strategy, were balking at the pressure we were placing on the Salah ad Din justice system to secure Sabah's release. Cpt. Dan Peck had already redeployed to the United States to prepare Fort Riley for our return, but another insurgency was brewing in the staff, ready to once again threaten our approach, just as we prepared to hand over our area of operations to a new unit.

"Let the law work its course," Cpt. Matt Wilden, the newest captain in Task Force Patriot, said in that week's targeting meeting. "If Sheikh Sabah is innocent, they will let him out."

"Are you kidding?" I asked, incredulous. "Nobody had any qualms about interfering with the Iraqi justice system when they let the Jadir brothers out and we were going to go back to ad Dawr to get them back."

It ended the argument, but I could feel the rumblings of another, more dangerous insurgency brewing, threatening to erupt to the surface. The staff just needed to hold together for a few more weeks to hand the operation over to Task Force Wolfhounds. We couldn't afford more dissension.

Task Force Patriot was finally able to secure the release of Sheikh Sabah through the help of Judge Taleb, the investigative judge for Tikrit. Months before we had submitted and initiated a CERP project to build a school with a sizable parking garage inside FOB Danger across the street from Judge Taleb's office. The judge enthusiastically supported the project. Thus, when the case fortuitously fell to him, he eagerly volunteered that, while the old charges had been cleared, two men—Sofian Akram Thabit from the PDOP's media office and Jamal Rabia Hafeth from ERB 4—were leveling new charges.

I had Mike Samander call the ERB 4 commander while I called Cpt. Hicks at the US Special Forces ODA team in Tikrit, the ERB 4's partnered unit, to inquire about the second individual and his complaint against Sheikh Sabah. That was all it took. Within two hours, both men were in Sheikh Sabah's quarters at High Crimes, apologizing for the misunderstanding and promising to drop the charges.

However, the next day, after Judge Taleb dismissed the case and ordered Sabah released, High Crimes dragged its feet, claiming it had no knowledge of the order. Lt. Col. Bubba Cain had had enough. Back from leave and already in Tikrit for a separate meeting, he diverted his personal security detachment (PSD) to FOB Danger, to High Crimes. As soon as he entered the famous "Horse Gate" of the compound, Sheikh Sabah was released, put in his car, and ordered to leave FOB Danger. After a brief stop at the Task Force Patriot conference room to express his gratitude, Sabah was back home in al Hamerine.

The second insurgency within the Task Force Patriot staff did finally erupt a few days later, over the topic of our relief in place (RIP) brief to Task Force Wolfhounds, which we were preparing in anticipation of their impending arrival. The center for this new insurgency was Cpt. Matt Wilden.

Wilden was a very junior captain, having joined us immediately after completing the Field Artillery Captains Career Course. He was short, with a broad neck and small features that seemed permanently affixed in a half scowl, half smirk. His outlook on warfare had been shaped entirely by his time as a platoon leader in Iraq on his previous deployment.

At heart, Wilden was a counterinsurgency and military doctrine purist. When Cpt. Wilden first came to Task Force Patriot and found us engaged in a political battle to empower rural ad Dawr sheikhs and marginalize al Duris, he recoiled; we should be addressing the al Duris' grievances and working with the legitimate qa'da government. When he participated in his first "targeting cycle" with us, more of a free-form creative discussion than a typical military planning process, he was horrified; we should be following all of the steps of the military decision-making process (MDMP) as dictated in the army field manuals. He lacked the context of a year of hard-fought experience in what worked and what didn't work in Salah ad Din province. He also lacked the introspection to know he lacked that context.

When the staff reached the portion of the RIP brief that discussed our approach in ad Dawr qa'da, Cpt. Wilden made his move. "Why are we working with these sheikhs? We should be working with the legitimate government instead of marginalizing it."

He had broken the seal. The staff erupted, with 1st Lt. Jamie Sanjuan going on about how we suspected the "good" contractor Mohammed while trusting the "terrorist" Sheikh Sabah.

1st Lt. Matt Balach added tentatively, "We are supposed to be supporting the government of Iraq, right?"

Our new satellite PRT, Billy Hall, decided to lob a grenade of his own into the room. "Even if you did want to change the qa'da government, which is not your place, you don't have the capability to change the economy of rural ad Dawr with CERP." It was a grave miscalculation; he had already managed to alienate himself from most of the staff, and his input was not welcome. Figuring that discretion was the better part of valor and unwilling to bother arguing with us so close to our departure, Hall stood up and left before the fireworks turned into mortar shells.

None of these complaints was the real threat to Task Force Patriot's strategy, however. The real threat came from Cpt. Joe Breedlove. Cpt. Breedlove, after relinquishing command of Alpha Battery to Cpt. Steve Ackerson, had taken command of Headquarters and Headquarters Battery (HHB). Soon after taking this command, Task Force Patriot began expanding and realigning its battle space, and his battery lost its small area of operations, AO Hellraisers, which had contained Owja, Wynot, and Tarabala, south of Tikrit. HHB also assumed a greater share of the tasks associated with transporting the PRT and executing prisoner releases. Relegated to the more administrative elements of Task Force Patriot's operations, Breedlove had soured on the mission, the battalion staff, and the battalion leadership.

His dissatisfaction manifested itself as an escalation of insubordinations, refusing to do missions, doing unscheduled and unapproved search missions in Tikrit, and exerting his limited power over the soldiers and noncommissioned officers (NCOs) in the staff to disrupt the battalion's operations. It was yet another insurgency that had beset Task Force Patriot late in its deployment.

Now, with the mission under assault by this new counterinsurgency insurgency, he saw his opening. "Patriot 6 doesn't want to work with Sheikh Sabah anymore," he declared. "He told me he thinks you are too close to Sabah and you can't see clearly anymore."

The room fell silent. No one said a word. A line had been crossed. Cpt. Breedlove had, without saying it outright, accused me in an open forum of siding with an Iraqi at the expense of the best interest of the battalion and, by extension, the United States. I was speechless as well. I was not shocked by the impertinence; I had no illusions about Cpt. Breedlove's sentiments toward me. I was more concerned about the mission and the threat to our approach. We were so close. Both electric lines, the one from Tuz and the one from al Alam, were almost complete. The rural ad Dawr coalition was formed. We just had to see it through and effectively hand it over to Task Force Wolfhounds.

At that critical moment, when the strategy was under its most serious threat, two men stepped in and saved Task Force Patriot's year in Iraq: Chief Warrant Officer 2 Tedd Hatcher, the battalion's targeting officer, an Iraq war veteran with an easy humor and a personable style that disarmed everyone who knew him, and Smoke Terrance Goff, the Task Force Patriot TOC enforcer and the most respected and competent noncommissioned officer in the battalion, a former Alpha Battery platoon sergeant under Breedlove who now served as the battalion operations sergeant. They launched their counteroffensive at Cpt. Wilden, but they were really talking to Cpt. Breedlove.

"You don't know what you are talking about," Chief Hatcher told the superior but less experienced officer. "You are talking about counterinsurgency and MDMP and stuff. Those are book answers. This is the real world. We need real answers to the world the way it really is."

Wilden started to protest.

"Sir," Smoke said, "you need to shut up and listen to people who know more than you."

Wilden was stunned, the rage flaring in his temples. I didn't see it because I was staring right at Cpt. Breedlove, watching his reaction, watching to see if he would strike again.

"This is a good plan," Chief Hatcher insisted. He was usually a silent observer in meetings. He had never, in a year, jumped out in front like this. I had no idea he felt so strongly about our strategy.

"We tried it your way, sir," he told Wilden, looking also to Cpt. Breedlove as he continued. "It didn't work. It got Carrasco killed. Now we are doing it this way, and we are almost there. We just have to carry it through to the end."

Wilden mumbled something unintelligible, and the counterinsurgency insurgency died as quickly as it had begun.

Our last major "kinetic" (i.e., violent) operation in AO Proud Americans took shape only weeks before the arrival of Task Force Wolfhounds from Schofield Barracks, Hawaii. The operation, dubbed Operation Patriot Falcon, began as an air assault onto islands in the Tigris River between ad Dawr and the small town of Wynot, south of Owja. However, as often happens when planning with Iraqi police and army commanders, it became much larger and more complex over time. The aircraft were scrubbed from the mission; the responsible drawdown of forces had hit combat aviation brigades as hard as maneuver brigades, leaving a dearth of transport aircraft. We were able to get an OH-58D Kiowa attack helicopter scout weapons team (SWT), though.

The final plan had 2nd Battalion, 48th Iraqi Army Brigade, forming a backstop west of ad Dawr on the east bank of the Tigris, while ERU 1 and ERU 3 scoured the west bank of the Tigris and two large islands in the river—connected by narrow footpaths to the mainland—looking for IED-making material and weapons caches. The operation would even incorporate the Salah ad Din boat patrol, with both of its small watercraft patrolling the waters between the two forces.

The actual operation was anticlimactic. The SWT did spot someone fleeing from the Iraqi police and hiding in a spider hole as they approached the shore, but the aircraft couldn't designate the correct location to the Iraqis. Even with the aid of an infrared laser and night vision goggles, the Iraqis and the US QRF dispatched to help them couldn't find the spider hole. At one point, the SWT used flares to mark the location, only to set the grass on fire for an area of one hundred meters in every direction. After the fire died, one pilot resorted to dropping a bottle of Gatorade on the spot from his aircraft. When ground forces investigated, they found nothing.

Iraqi police and Army forces returned at the end of the evening empty-handed.

Once Task Force Wolfhounds arrived in Salah ad Din province, days became a blur. There were a million questions to answer, dozens of Iraqis for each Wolfhound leader to meet, and thousands of pieces of equipment—everything from machine guns to MRAPs—to be transferred from old to new unit. As the chaos overwhelmed us, I thought to myself that we had condemned Task Force Steel and the handover they had given us unfairly. Trying to put myself in the boots of Wolfhound 6, Lt. Col. Donald Brown, a seasoned veteran about to assume huge responsibilities, I imagined he must see us in much the same way.

The process of relief in place (RIP) and transfer of authority (TOA) was complicated by the presence of five separate forces, all pulling the

Wolfhounds in different directions. The first was Patriot 6, Lt. Col. Bubba Cain. He had built a close relationship with the al Alam al Jibouris, and especially Lt. Col. Ahmed al Fahal's family. The first place he took Lt. Col. Brown, only two days after he arrived in Iraq, was to see Lt. Col. Ahmed's mother and family in al Alam.

The next place they went, a few days later, was to the provincial council building, to sit in on a provincial council meeting and meet Brig. Gen. (ret.) Abdullah Jebarra. "This guy is the most powerful guy in Salah ad Din," Cain told Brown. "Stay close to him and he will help you do whatever you need to get done."

The next faction trying to sway the course of the RIP was the core of the Task Force Patriot staff, including myself. We wanted to convince the Wolfhounds to continue building the rural ad Dawr coalition and help it on its course to economically and politically overtake the al Duri/ JRTN–dominated city of ad Dawr.

This faction struck its first major blow just after Lt. Col. Bubba Cain returned from Lt. Col. Ahmed's home in al Alam with Lt. Col. Donald Brown. The staff had put together its operations and intelligence (O&I) brief to orient the commanders and staff of Task Force Wolfhounds to their new AO. The brief had been carefully crafted, under strong protest from the dissenters within the staff, to build the case toward the rural ad Dawr coalition. It walked the Wolfhounds through our journey from our original approach in ad Dawr, through the history of the town as we learned it, and toward the building of our coalition. "We have already planted the seeds," I concluded. "All you have to do until the qa'da elections, somewhere around December [2010], is feed them with a little CERP to bolster the coalition's legitimacy and show your face to demonstrate US support. They will do the rest themselves."

The coup de grace for the staff faction was supposed to be the opening of the Tuz–al Hamerine–al Othaim electric project, which occurred at the Hamerine electric power station, only a few kilometers from Sheikh Sabah's home. When the patrol pulled up before the fenced al Hamerine substation, it found the al Shimiri subtribe sheikhs all lined up in front of a large banner, declaring erroneously in Arabic that the project was another good work of the Salah ad Din provincial council.

Inside, we found Sheikh Sabah pushed out of the limelight, sidelined by Brig. Gen. (ret.) Abdullah Jebarra, acting provincial council chairman, on hand to take credit for the whole event. He walked around, looking

Brig. Gen. (ret.) Abdullah Jebarra (right with sunglasses) and DG Sabhan (behind him) take credit for the Tuz-al Hamerine-al Othaim electric project during the transition from Task Force Patriot to Task Force Wolfhounds in July 2010. The soldier in the center with sunglasses is Lt. Col. Donald Brown (Wolfhound 6). To his right is Simone (interpreter).

official, asking questions of the power station head, playing for the Salah ad Din Television cameras. The switch was thrown and the ribbon was cut, and Abdullah was again in front of the camera, claiming credit for the project he had nearly killed a little over a month before. "The provincial council is working for the benefit of all Iraqis in Salah ad Din," he proclaimed. "I will not rest until electric power is restored in all of the areas of our province."

Next it was Lt. Col. Mike Brown in front of the camera. Lacking any context on the project, Brown compounded the damage when he responded, "We just want to continue to support the government as they provide for the people of the province."

Abdullah concluded the event by recognizing not Sheikh Sabah Muntasir Diab al Shimiri but contractor Mohammed Ibrahim al Jibouri, who was genuinely shocked by the recognition. "Contractor Mohammed is a great contractor," Abdullah told both Lt. Col. Brown and the Salah ad Din Television audience. "We will trust him for all of our projects."

At the huge tent that Sabah had erected at his home in al Hamerine, things did not go much better. Sabah sat at the head of the tent, next to Wolfhound 6, trying to be a gracious host. But on Brown's right, Brig. Gen. (ret.) Abdullah Jebarra confided quietly to him, commenting on each presentation.

The culmination of the event was to be a traditional tribute, spoken by the most respected commoner of the al Shimiri tribe, read in a loud voice, as if speaking to the whole world, the praises of the sheikh, Sheikh Sabah, for bringing good fortune to the tribe. It was a very old Arab tradition that Sabah had no doubt anticipated as the time of the project opening approached. It would be his moment of final defeat over Sheikh Ali Nwaf Diab al Shimiri, the usurper. The more junior Wolfhound officers, not understanding the significance of the event, were amused by the theatrical display. Brig. Gen. (ret.) Abdullah whispered something to Lt. Col. Brown that elicited a wry smile.

In that moment, US support for the rural ad Dawr coalition to topple the al Duri/JRTN-dominated ad Dawr qa'da government ended.

Another faction trying to direct the course of the Wolfhound RIP was the PRT. The PRT Main was amply augmented with a colonel and two lieutenant colonels, members of the Warrior Brigade (2nd Brigade, 25th Infantry Division, Task Force Wolfhounds' higher headquarters) security transition team (STT). As long as they got their three patrols a day to cart them around the battlefield, PRT Main was continent to leave Task Force Wolfhounds to satellite PRT Billy Hall.

Satellite PRT Billy Hall was adamant about getting access to Lt. Col. Brown and establishing the coequal relationship he had enjoyed with Lt. Col. Eric Moore, a relationship Lt. Col. Bubba Cain had denied him. His first opportunity to plead his case came during the PRT brief, attended by the commanders of each task force as well as the STT colonels from PRT Main.

I sat quietly as Billy Hall gave his briefing, enumerating all of the authorities that should be his. It was not an effective presentation; his tone had the same effect on the Wolfhounds' officers as it had had on the Proud Americans'.

Then he began to talk about ad Dawr, and the work he wanted to do with the qa'da government. "The government in ad Dawr has been neglected and ignored by US forces for years. Units don't like to go there because of the violence in the city, so the population suffers and the government doesn't grow."

As the meeting broke up, Hall followed Lt. Col. Donald Brown. As they retreated to Wolfhound 6's office, Billy Hall looked over his shoulder at me, a sinister smile on his face. Just as they disappeared from view, he said, loud enough for me to hear, "We need to talk about how to get US military forces out of the politics of ad Dawr."

In defense of the Wolfhounds, they were also subjected to intense pressure from the Warrior Brigade to subordinate themselves to the PRT. The STT colonel in the PRT was already beginning to exert the authority of a deputy brigade commander over Wolfhound 6. The specified tasks they received from their brigade explicitly directed them to put the PRT "in the lead" in all of their operations. It was natural that they would drift toward a subordinate role in governance.

But the final, most powerful force that guided the course of Task Force Wolfhounds as they executed the RIP was their battalion staff, led by Maj. Frank Baltazar, the battalion XO. The battalion did not have a major to act as their S3 (operations officer), meaning that Baltazar had to fill both roles. Despite his heroic efforts, he was swamped with the demands of learning and understanding the logistics of a battalion task force spread out over an area the size of New Jersey while at the same time trying to craft the battalion's campaign plan, its way forward for the next year in Iraq. All of the competing external forces trying to influence his battalion's direction were, from his perspective, an unwelcome distraction.

His crisis solution was to insulate the Wolfhound staff from the Patriot staff. They literally sequestered themselves in the morale, welfare, and recreation (MWR) building on the life support area (LSA) to complete their plan, shutting off access to their network by outside agencies. This insulation led the Wolfhound staff to suspicion of the Patriot staff, and from suspicion to disdain. That disdain was also fueled by branch prejudice (infantrymen knew more about maneuver operations than field artillerymen) and organizational prejudice (the 4th Infantry Brigade Combat Team was a "legacy" force, not as sophisticated as the network-centric 2nd Stryker Brigade Combat Team).

In the end, all of the forces acting on the Wolfhounds drove them to strike out on a different path than the Proud Americans for no other reason than that it *was* a different path.

Epilogue

$\mathcal{O}$n 31 August 2010, as President Barack Obama had promised, US forces in Iraq did draw down to 50,000 troops. The question of whether "combat operations" ended on the same date is open for debate. Task Force Wolfhounds (1st Battalion, 27th Infantry) did set out on a different course than Task Force Patriot (2nd Battalion, 32nd Field Artillery) in their approach. However, the day-to-day activities in which the Wolfhounds were engaged—combat patrols to move leaders from place to place to conduct meetings, punctuated by occasional enemy contact and occasional large-scale operations with Iraqi police and army units in the lead—were largely the same as those in which Task Force Patriot engaged before the "end of combat operations."

If US casualties are a measure of combat operations, then Task Force Wolfhound was tragically more engaged in those operations than Task Force Patriot. In September 2010, two Wolfhound soldiers were killed and nine more wounded at Forward Operating Base (FOB) Bernstein when a Kurdish soldier, an undercover Ansar al Sunna insurgent, opened fire on an unsuspecting crowd; the soldiers' body armor was stowed on their vehicles just as had been Task Force Patriot's practice inside Iraqi army or police bases. In late 2010, another Wolfhound soldier was shot in the helmet by the Tikrit sniper in northern Tikrit, but miraculously he survived because the round lodged in his helmet. Another Wolfhound soldier was not so lucky in November 2010. He was shot and killed in southern Tikrit while standing in the gunner's turret of his stationary vehicle.

For the 50,000 soldiers left in Iraq after "the end of combat operations," it certainly didn't feel like combat had ended.

The outlook for Iraq seems mixed as well. In December 2010, ten months
after the national elections, Prime Minister Nuri al Maliki's State of Law
coalition finally forged a majority that won the right to form a government. Prime Minister Nuri al Maliki returned to office with the backing
of the Office of the Martyr Sadr (OMS, the party of firebrand Shi'a cleric
Muqtada al Sadr) and the Iraqi Islamic Party (IIP, the party of former
governor Mutashar Hussein al Aliwi). However, due to opposition by
Iyad Alawi's al Iraqiya coalition (of which the al Alam al Jibouri's Iraqi
National Project Front was a part), this government was unable to form
a cabinet. As of this writing, the Iraqi government still had not chosen a
minister of defense or minister of the interior, among other critical security positions.

The great game in Salah ad Din—Samarra, the al Samarra'i tribes,
the IIP, and al Qaeda in Iraq and the Jaysh al Islami fil Iraq (literally
"Islamic Army of Iraq," IAI) versus Tikrit, the Bayji and al Alam al Jibouris, the Iraqi National Project Front, and potentially the New Ba'ath
Party and Jaysh Rijal al Tariqa al Naqshabandiyah (JRTN)—continued
to escalate after the departure of Task Force Patriot. The competition
was already turning in favor of Samarra before we left; it had claimed Lt.
Col. Ahmed Subhi al Fahal al Jibouri and very nearly Imam Mohammed
Khuthair al Jibouri. In 2011, that competition reached a tipping point.

In March 2011, as many as a dozen al Qaeda in Iraq insurgents attacked the provincial council building in Tikrit. Using mortar fire and a
car bomb and dressed in Iraqi army uniforms, they overran the compound
and seized a number of hostages. In the hours-long standoff that followed, fifty-six people were killed, including the new provincial director
of police (PDOP), Col. Emad Ofan, and three provincial council members, one being the most powerful man in Salah ad Din, Brig. Gen. (ret.)
Abdullah Hussein al Jebarra al Jibouri. They were shot in the head, and
their bodies were set on fire.

Another attack, in June, brought another crushing blow to the Tikrit
power elite. A fuel truck full of explosives was detonated in front of the al
Farouq mosque inside the heavily fortified FOB Danger. The explosion
killed sixteen, including Judge Taleb al Azzawi, senior investigative judge
in Salah ad Din. A second attack struck the Tikrit Teaching Hospital as it

struggled to deal with the casualties from the first attack. A man wearing a suicide vest entered the hospital and detonated himself, killing six more and injuring, among others, S.Lt. Col. Khalil, commander of Emergency Response Unit (ERU) 3, the "top cop" in Salah ad Din.

Governor Mutashar al Aliwi had coincidentally just left the Tikrit Teaching Hospital, where he was visiting the injured, only minutes before the attack occurred.

Fearing he was next, Brig. Gen. Jassem Hussein al Jebarra al Jibouri, director of the Salah ad Din office of the National Security Agency, Brig. Gen. (ret.) Abdullah Jebarra's brother, and the sole remaining al Alam al Jibouri in the provincial government, resigned and fled to Sharqat qa'da (district) to hide among the al Jibouris there. The IIP found him. On 23 June 2011, an unknown number of gunmen shot him and another man dead. The back of the al Alam al Jibouris and their hold on Salah ad Din province had been broken forever.

While the al Alam al Jibouris receded, the Bayji al Jibouris' star rose. Abu Mazen (Ahmed Abdullah abd Khalaf al Jibouri), who had been sentenced to four and a half years for forging his high school diploma, was cleared of all charges. Engineer Khalid, whom abu Mazen had pressed the government of Iraq so long to seat as provincial governor, held the post only briefly before convoluted legal troubles caused the provincial council to force him, too, from office. In his place, abu Mazen was appointed governor of Salah ad Din province.

The post of provincial council chairman, once held by abu Mazen, and then briefly by Brig. Gen. (ret.) Abdullah Jebarra, went to Ammar Yousef Hamoud al Samarra'i, rabid ideologue of the IIP and vassal of Sheikh (and former governor) Mutashar Hussein al Aliwi. The two men, abu Mazen and Ammar Yousef, once sworn enemies, seemed to get along just fine. The power-sharing arrangement was almost identical to the one Brig. Gen. (ret.) Abdullah Jebarra had been offered but rejected just after the national elections.

The future of the rural ad Dawr coalition was not certain either. As of this writing, the promised qa'da elections had not yet materialized, a victim of the continuing political deadlock in Baghdad. It remains to be seen whether the elections will ever occur, or if they do, whether the coalition that Task Force Patriot and Sheikh Sabah Muntasir Diab al Shimiri built will coalesce once more and unseat the al Duris as the qa'da government in ad Dawr. It also remains to be seen if economic prosperity will return to the al Jalaam ad Dawr (literally "the desert east of ad Dawr) and al Jalaam as Samarra (literally "the desert east of Samarra"). As I had once told Sheikh Sabah, US forces were like a winter rain that washed over the land for a season and then was gone. Only time will tell if that rain will cause the desert to turn green once more.

One thing is certain, Sheikh Sabah Muntasir Diab al Shimiri won the two battles that mattered most to him. He had beaten his rival and cousin, Sheikh Ali Nwaf Diab al Shimiri, and he had outlasted his nemesis, Brig. Gen. (ret.) Abdullah Hussein al Jebarra al Jibouri.

The Iraq war was over for the Dragon Brigade (4th Brigade, 1st Infantry Division) and its field artillery battalion, the Proud Americans (2nd Battalion, 32nd Field Artillery). But the global war on terrorism went on. Task Force Patriot returned to Fort Riley, Kansas, and immediately began the Army Force Generation (ARFORGEN) cycle again, in preparation for its next combat deployment. Some faces would change, and some faces would stay the same, as the Proud Americans deployed to their next battlefield to write the next chapter in their storied history.

Was it worth it? Was the uncertain future we may have built worth the blood that we shed, the millions in treasure we spent, or the time that we all spent away from our families? The question is as valid for the United States and the whole Iraq war as it is for Task Force Patriot and its year in Salah ad Din province.

In the darkest days, just before redeployment, when we began to suspect that Brig. Gen. (ret.) Abdullah Jebarra and the al Alam al Jibouris might be in league with JRTN and it became clear that Task Force Wolfhounds would not continue our work in rural ad Dawr, I wasn't sure if it had been worth it. But my consolation was that, even if JRTN survived and there was a civil war after the United States departed Iraq, it was better to have a politically driven war between Sunni separatists and the government of Iraq than it was to have a jihad between Sunni al Qaeda in Iraq and Shi'a Jaysh al Mahdi (the Mahdi Militia, the armed wing of Muqtada al Sadr's OMS). The former would be a war for discrete political ends. It could be negotiated to a conclusion. The latter would be a war of annihilation that would know no end while Shi'a Muslims lived in the land of the two rivers.

As it turned out, I had it exactly wrong. It was the IIP—and the IAI, with its shadowy links to al Qaeda in Iraq—that was cooperating with Shi'a prime minister Nuri al Maliki to eliminate the Sunni separatist New Ba'ath Party and JRTN in Salah ad Din. At least in this instance, counterintuitively, Salafist jihadists—with their mortars and car bombs and suicide vests—were the stabilizing influence, trying to hold Iraq together.

As I write this, the US military is pressing both the Obama and the al Maliki administrations to allow the US Army to maintain forces, perhaps upward of 20,000 troops, in Iraq. They are concerned with what they perceive as an al Qaeda resurgence in areas like Salah ad Din. They look at car bombs and suicide vests, and they see the ghost of abu Musab al Zarqawi (the deceased founder of al Qaeda in Iraq), threatening to pull Iraq back down into sectarian carnage. As I hope the story of Task Force Patriot has conveyed, the truth is infinitely more complex.

There are many forces remaining in Iraq, threatening to rip the country apart. There is the Sunni-on-Sunni violence between the competing tribes of Salah ad Din. There is the Sunni Arab–Kurdish dispute over the contentious provinces of Kirkuk and Ninewa. And, of course, there are the Sunni separatists seeking a future for Sunni Arab Iraq free of Shi'a domination.

But no one in the US military or national government has yet to articulate a path to relieve these tensions that will be made any smoother, easier, or less violent through the presence of 20,000 American troops. If anything, the presence of these troops will simply prolong the conflict, causing it to simmer and seethe below the surface rather than erupt into all-out warfare. But the underlying forces will remain, and like a pot on a burner, as soon as the lid of US presence is finally removed, the conflict may well boil over into warfare.

Was it worth it? We will never know the answer until we leave Iraq and let the Iraqis settle these disputes for themselves.

Index

al Abbasi, Sheikh Hajji Hamid, 155
Abdullah, S. Brig. Gen., 88, 178
abu Mazen, 74–76, 91, 137, 140, 177;
   appointed governor of Salah ad Din
   province, 201; arrest of, 178
Accidental Guerilla (Kilcullen), 20
Ackerson, Steve, 136
ACUs. *See* army combat uniforms
Adams, George, 156
Adams, Greg, 177
ADC-O. *See* assistant division
   commander for operations
administration, of US bases, 21
ADSWAT. *See* ad Dawr special
   weapons and tactics team
Afghanistan, 7, 18, 19, 20
Air-Land Battle, 1, 5, 7
al Alam, 34, 46, 154; food distribution
   center, 141–42, 169; importance of
   city of, 23–24
al Alam al Jibouri tribe, 24, 25, 34,
   45–46, 47, 49, 50, 75; losing power,
   201; New Ba'ath Party and, 181
Alawi, Iyad, 124, 177
albu Issa, Sheikh Faner Mubarrak
   Muhammad, 86
albu Issa, Sheikh Shakur Mubarrak
   Muhammad, 85–86, 103, 112–13,

128, 187; detainment/release of,
   97–99
albu Nasiri, Sheikh Hassan, 103
albu Nasiri, Sheikh Neda Mahmud
   Neda, 42, 43
albu Qodal, Sheikh Ibrahim, 170
al Aliwi, Mutashar Hussein, 136, 177,
   201; removing, as governor, 20, 76,
   78, 83, 92
Alpha Battery, 95, 120–21, 136
Alpha Company "Outlaws," 134
Alternate Supply Route (ASR): Clemson,
   23, 61, 170; Dover, 72, 90, 155
American Civil War, 17
al Anbar province, 44–45
AO. *See* area of operations
ARCENT. *See* US Army Central
   Command
area of operations (AO), 10; expansion
   of, Proud Americans, 131–35;
   understanding, Proud Americans,
   22–30
ARFORGEN. *See* Army Force
   Generation
arms trade, 60
army combat uniforms (ACUs), 15
Army Force Generation
   (ARFORGEN), 4, 201

Arnold, Henry "Hank," III, 10, 20, 31, 40, 45, 63, 64, 92, 137
Arrowhead Brigade, 19
ASR. *See* Alternate Supply Route
assistant division commander for operations (ADC-O), 31
attack, 16, 17, 26, 31, 85; deadly, on Carrasco, 62, 100, 102, 115, 148, 153, 171, 172; helicopter, 94; IED, 89, 170–71, 174; preventing, 42–44; al Qaeda, in Tikrit, 200–201; by RKG-3s, 64–65, 149, 170; sniper, 114, 134, 199; suicide vest, 78–79, 83; Tikrit sniper, 149, 151, 174
al Azzawi, Taleb, 200

Ba'ath Party, 15, 26, 35, 53, 67; ad Dawr as epicenter of, insurgency, 66; in ad Dawr city, 179. *See also* Jaysh Rijal al Tariqa al Naqshabandiyah; New Ba'ath Party
Ba'ath terrorists, 39, 40
Baghdad: in February 2007, 6, 7; government, 12, 53, 67; operations of, government, 39–41; Salah ad Din and, 55
al Bakr, Ahmad Hassan, 30
Balach, Matt, 145, 191
Baltazar, Frank, 197
bases, US: administration of, 21; closure/transfer of, 86–90, 131–32. *See also specific bases*
battalion crest, 6
battlefield, managing problems on, 8
battle tanks, M1 Abrams, 5
Bauer, John, 135–37, 154, 182
Bayji al Jibouri tribe, 75, 201
Bayji Oil Refinery, 55, 75, 88, *132*, 169, 176; increasing efficiency of, 154; al Qaeda and, 133
Bayji *qa'da*, 51, 106, 133, 137
al Bazi, Sheikh Mohammed, 155
Bettis, Brian, 87–88, 89
Birds of Paradise, 82
Blackhawk Down, 3

black market, 75
Blackwell, Tim, 13, 14, 88, 124, 135
Boyle, Michael, 57, 135
Bravo Battery, 28, 61, 94, 103, 121, 135, 156–57
Breedlove, Joe, 37, 191, 192
Bremer, Paul L., 15, 66
bribery, 34
brigade combat teams, 5–6
Bronco Brigade, 9, 10, 14, 19, 31, 32, 35
Brown, Donald, 194, 195, 196
bureaucracy, 21
Burger, Timothy J., 74
Bush, George W., 4, 12, 18

CAG. *See* community action group
Cain, Robert "Bubba," 10, 11, 22, 29, 39, 46, 49, 50, 55, 63, 64, 74, 77, 99, 153; absence of, 173; death of Ahmed Subhi al Fahal al Jabouri and, 81, 82; family of Ahmed Subhi al Fahal al Jibouri and, 84–85, 194; meeting with Sheikh Sabah, 173–75; RDU and, 83–85; strength of, 145
CALL. *See* Center for Army Lessons Learned
Cambodia, 6
camouflage, 5
Camp Buehring, Kuwait, 9
CAP. *See* Community Action Program
carbines, M4, 5
car bombs, 3, 56, 83, 184
Carpenter, Jared, 166–67, 170–71
Carrasco, Tony, Jr.: memorial for, *73*; shooting of, 62, 100, 102, 115, 148, 153, 171, 172
Casey, George, Jr., 8
casualties, US Army, 199
Ceesay, Sainey, 141
CENTCOM. *See* US Central Command
Center for Army Lessons Learned (CALL), 8
Central America, 18

CERP. *See* Commander's Emergency Response Program

CERP contracting, 16–17, 24, 25, 35, 37, 50, 72, 75, 85, 135, 170; control over, 182–85; as leverage, 136–37, 154; for power lines, 112–13, 127, 138

CGSC. *See* US Army Command and General Staff College

Chandler, Mark, 176

CLCs. *See* concerned local citizens

Coalition Provisional Authority (CPA), 15, 66

COB. *See* Contingency Operating Base

COB Speicher, 21, 22, 41, 182

COIN-SOC. *See* Counterinsurgency-Stability Operations Course

Collins, Dave, 97

COLT. *See* combat observation and lasing team

combat camera team (COMCAM), 95

combat observation and lasing team (COLT), 95

combat operations, end of, 199, 200

Combined Arms Center, 2

COMCAM. *See* combat camera team

Commander's Emergency Response Program (CERP), 15–16, 46, 120; abuse, 167; projects in ad Dawr city, 178–81; PRTs and, 20; regulations, 138; security and, projects, 29, 64, 183. *See also* CERP contracting

community action group (CAG), insurgency and, 176

Community Action Program (CAP), 156; cutting off, III, 176–77

competence, 10

concerned local citizens (CLCs), 26, 62, 101. *See also* Sons of Iraq

Congress, US, 16

Contingency Operating Base (COB), 21. *See also* COB Speicher

corruption, 17, 133, 146–48, 151–52, 158, 166–67

council: ad Dawr *qa'da*, 11, 19, 28, 48, 50, 103; governor and provincial, 45, 76, 78, 91, 92, 137, 140, 177; *qa'da*, 71, 106, 127, 134, 139; Salah ad Din province, 19, 20, 48, 49, 50, 90, 127, 194, 195, 201; Tuz *qa'da*, 182, 184. *See also* Council of Representatives

Council of Representatives, 11, 46, 54, 61, 71, 76, 92, 119, 177

counterinsurgency, 2–3, 5, 7, 14, 19, 20, 31, 69, 190; dropping, 70; post, 8; violence and, 93

Counterinsurgency-Stability Operations Course (COIN-SOC), 14, 19, 20

CPA. *See* Coalition Provisional Authority

Craft, Mike, 52

Crocker, Ryan, 1, 143

Cuccolo, Tony, 137

ad Dawr city, 52, 63–64; Ba'ath Party in, 179; CERP projects in, 178–81; cutting off money to JRTN in, 176–77; economy of, 53; as epicenter of Ba'athist insurgency, 66; government, 25–26; insurgency in, 27, 93, 98; JRTN in, 65, 71, 153–54, 179; kinetic operation in, 93–96, 99–103

ad Dawr *qa'da*, 20, 53, 61, 87; changing power balance in, 71, 85, 109, 140–44, 147, 154, 155, 179; council, 11, 19, 28–29, 48, 50, 103; disenfranchisement of, 12, 13, 30, 48, 70; sheikhs of, 155–56; unifying sheikhs of, 71–74, 99, 103–6, 109. *See also* rural ad Dawr coalition

ad Dawr special weapons and tactics team (ADSWAT), 61

disclosure, absolute, 3

Diyala province, 67

doctrinal concepts, 1, 8

Donahue, Patrick, II, 77

Dragon Brigade, 5–6, 7, 9, 31, 40, 63, 87, 97, 98, 124, 201; executing phased withdrawal, 106. *See also* Task Force Patriot

208   *Index*

al Dulaymi, Khalil, 39, 44, 82, 94, 95, 123
al Duri, Dhaif, 87, 90, 156, 178
al Duri, Guyath Sami Shoki, 52
al Duri, Imam Dia, 178
al Duri, Izzat Ibrahim, 26, 51, 53, 65, 67–68, 159
al Duri, Khatan, 74
al Duri, Sheikh Ali Fayzee, 178
al Duri, Sheikh Kaseeb, meeting with, 48, *49*, 50, 52, 63, 64, 73–74
al Duri, Sheikh Mahsood Shahab Ahmed, 28–29, 48, 52, 103–4, 106, 123, 176; meeting with, 178–81
al Duri, Uthman, 29; meeting with, 73–74, 178–81
al Duri tribe, 25–26, 30–31, 45–46, 47, 49, 50, 67; dominance of, 70–71, 86, 98; economy of, 53; in government, 66; subtribes of, 52–53

Eapen, Pailey, 185
economy, 16; of ad Dawr city, 53; of al Duri tribe, 53; growth of, 183; of Iraq, 71; of al Jalaam ad Dawr, 202; of Salah ad Din province, 153, 154
Effects-Based Operations, 2, 7
EFP. *See* explosively formed projectile
elections, 11, 40–41, 47, 87, 90, 200; explosions during, 122; provincial, 71; security during, 119–21; Sunni Arab Iraq and, 119, 123; 2010, 119; voter turnout at, 123
electricity, 126, 128, 131; CERP contracting for, 112–13, 127, 138; al Hamerine, project, 106, 110–11, 113, 127, 138–39, 159–62, 163–64, 184; Mohammed Ibrahim Hamid al Jibouri receiving credit for, project, 195–96; al Othaim, project, 106, 110–11, 127, 139, 160, 163–64, 184; project opening, 194, *195*, 196. *See also* Sabhan, Director General of Electricity
Elmore, Terry, 182
Emergency Response Battalion (ERB), 96

Emergency Response Unit (ERU), 33, 39, 47, 82, 94, 95
employment, 12, 16, 55
enemy contact, first, 48
environment: pollution of, 176; understanding Iraq, 4
EOD. *See* US Navy explosive ordnance disposal
equipment, 6, 7, 9, 22
ERB. *See* Emergency Response Battalion
ERU. *See* Emergency Response Unit
exit strategies, 1
explosively formed projectile (EFP), 6
extortion, 75

al Fahal al Jibouri, Ahmed Subhi, 33, 36, 39, 40, 41, 43, 46, 47, 50, 56, 63; Cain and death of, 81–82; Cain and family of, 84–85, 194; closeness of, to coalition forces, 34–35; concern about, 44, 65, 76–77; death of, 78–79, 81–82; investigating death of, 83–85; suicide vest attack on, 78–79
al Fahal al Jibouri, Aswad, 85
al Fahal al Jibouri, Mithaq, 46, 85
al Fahal al Jibouri, Salah, 85, 92
family: of Ahmed Subhi al Fahal al Jibouri and Cain, 84–85, 194; support for, 4, 10
family readiness group (FRG), 10
Faulkner, Wade, 98
Filed Manual (FM) 3-24, *Counterinsurgency*, 2
FOB. *See* Forward Operating Base Brassfield-Mora
Fort Riley, Kansas, 9
Forward Operating Base (FOB) Bernstein, 169, 199
Forward Operating Base (FOB) Brassfield-Mora, 28
Forward Operating Base (FOB) Danger, 41, 46, 47, 78, 85, 121, 178; Sheikh Sabah on, 125, 188
FRG. *See* family readiness group

Gadson, Greg, 6
Gandia, Gabriel, 82
Germany, 18
Gibbs, Ricky, 6, 7
Gisick, Michael, 150
Goff, Terrance, 192
Golf Company, 87
"growing the Army," 5
Gulf War, 1–2, 3, 30

al Haddad, Samir, 90, 107
Hall, Billy, 191; PRT representative,
    181–85, 196–97
Hamed, Maj. Gen., 5, 35, 40, 65
al Hamerine, 72, 98, 124, 134, 142–
    43; electric project, 106, 110–11,
    113, 127, 138–39, 159–62, 163–64,
    184; humanitarian aid to, 169;
    opening of, electric project, 194,
    195, 196
Hatcher, Tedd, 192
Havel, George, 122
Headquarters and Headquarters Battery
    (HHB), 93, 121, 135, 191
health advisor, 176
HHB. *See* Headquarters and
    Headquarters Battery
High Crimes, 85, 97, 102, 116, 117,
    173, 188
high-mobility multiwheeled vehicles
    (HMMWVs), 5, 85, 149
history, regional, 11, 194
human intelligence (HUMINT), 151
humanitarian assistance, 5, 184
HUMINT. *See* human intelligence
HUMMWVs. *See* high-mobility
    multiwheeled vehicles
Hunara, Chad, 37, 145
Hussein, Saddam, 11, 26, 46, 51, 66;
    hometown of, 31–33; as Islamic
    leader, 68; plots against, 30

IAI. *See* Jaysh al Islami fil Iraq ("Islamic
    Army of Iraq")
IEDs. *See* improvised explosive devices

IGFC. *See* Iraqi Ground Forces
    Command
IHEC. *See* Iraqi High Elections
    Commission
IIP. *See* Iraqi Islamic Party
improvised explosive devices (IEDs), 3,
    6, 26, 42, 48, 83; attack, 89, 170–71,
    174; magnetic, 55, 69
infantry fighting vehicles, M2 Bradley, 5
information exchange, 4, 8, 11, 14, 22
information operations (IO), 8
infrastructure, rebuilding, 5, 16, 52, 154
insurgency, 15, 51, 149–50; in ad Dawr
    city, 27, 93, 98; CAG and, 176; ad
    Dawr as epicenter for Ba'athist, 66;
    funding, 16–17; isolating populace
    from, 2, 31; police collusion with, 44;
    populace, 69–70
"interagency," 18
interpreters, 43, 50, 128, 170
invasion, lightning, 2
IO. *See* information operations
IPEOD. *See* Iraqi police explosive
    ordnance disposal team
IQATF. *See* Iraqi Advisor Task Force
Iraq, 44, 60; advising, security forces,
    42; civil war, 52, 70, 201; economy,
    71; justice system, 116, 171–73;
    Ministry of the Interior, 41, 45,
    120, 121; outlook for, 200; political
    leaders of, 9, 10, 14–15, 16, 19; al
    Qaeda in, 66–67, 68, 187, 200, 203;
    security forces, 12; "surge," 3, 6;
    understanding, local politics, 5, 183;
    understanding environment of, 4;
    US forces entering, in March 2003,
    1, 5; US forces exiting, 4, 12, 131,
    199; US forces maintained in, 203.
    See also Iraqi army; police; populace;
    Sons of Iraq; Sunni Arab Iraq
Iraq-FORGEN, 6–7, 10. *See also* Army
    Force Generation
Iraqi Advisor Task Force (IQATF), 75
Iraqi army, 14–15, 16, 32, 33, 41, 44,
    45; 14th, Brigade, 87, 88, 133;

48th, Brigade, 88–90, 94, 133, 149; al Jabouris in, 30; joint planning session with, 95; leadership, 23–24, 36, 53, 87
Iraqi Ground Forces Command (IGFC), 119–21
Iraqi High Elections Commission (IHEC), 47, 90
Iraqi Islamic Party (IIP), 52, 83, 136, 178, 200, 203
Iraqi National Security Agency, 25, 47
Iraqi police explosive ordnance disposal team (IPEOD), 56
al Iraqiya, 93, 124, 177, 200
irrigation, 15
Islamic Army of Iraq. *See* Jaysh al Islami fil Iraq

Jadir brothers, 115–17, 153, 171–73
al Jalaam ad Dawr, 26; economic prosperity in, 202
Japan, 18
Jaysh al Islami fil Iraq ("Islamic Army of Iraq," IAI), 52, 83, 200, 203
Jaysh Rijal al Tariqa al Naqshabandiyah (JRTN), 12, 24, 28, 53, 67, 122, 200, 203; in ad Dawr city, 65, 71, 153–54, 179; cutting off money to, in ad Dawr, 176–77; defeating, 71–74, 99, 109; New Ba'ath Party moving from al Qaeda to, 68; al Qaeda and, 66, 179; in Salah ad Din, 70; support for, 65–66; unwillingness to arrest, 175; violence, 149, 151, 170, 171; violence against Iraqis, 68–69
al Jazeera al Tikrit, 21
JBB. *See* Joint Base Balad
JCC. *See* joint coordination center
al Jebarra al Jibouri, Abdullah Hussein, 15, 24, 34–35, 36, 46, 47, 50, 81, 126, 159; meeting with, 57–61, 109–10, *111*, 112, 139–40; New Ba'ath Party and, 181; Sheikh Sabah and, 160, 186–87, 194–96; suit against, 90–91; taking credit, 194, *195*, 196; trouble from, 163–66

al Jebarra al Jibouri, Jassem Hussein, 24, 40, 201
al Jebarra al Jibouri, Sheikh Khemis Naji Hussein, 25, 57, 59
al Jebarra al Jibouri, Sheikh Muawiya Naji, 25, 187
al Jebarra al Jibouri, Sheikh Naji Hussein, 24–25, 135
al Jebarra al Jibouri, Sheikh Wanus Naji, 60
Jeffress, Josh, 82, 152
al Jibouri, Eisa, 75
al Jibouri, Mohammed Ibrahim Hamid: contractor, 126–28, 130–31, 138–39, 157, 167, *168*, 185–86; receiving credit for electricity project, 195–96
al Jibouri, Mohammed Khuthair, 135–36
al Jibouri, Sheikh Hamid Ibrahim Salim, 75, 188
al Jibouri, Uday, 89, 93–94, 114, 117
al Jibouri tribe, 23–25, 30–31, 51, 75, 187, 188; power held within, 56. *See also* al Alam al Jibouri tribe; Bayji al Jibouri tribe
Joint Base Balad (JBB), 81
joint coordination center (JCC), 28; bombing of, 52; Tikrit, 32, 33, 40, 55, 91, 94, *96*, 100, 112, 120–21, 150, 175; transfer of Tikrit, 107
Joint Strategic Assessment Team, 8
JRTN. *See* Jaysh Rijal al Tariqa al Naqshabandiyah
justice system: Iraqi, 116, 171–73; Salah ad Din province, 153, 154

Kareem, Nuamah Khalil, 100
kidnapping, 151
Kilcullen, David, 20
kinetic operations, 107–8, 114–17, 149–51, 192–93; in ad Dawr city, 93–96, 99–103. *See also specific operations*
Kirkuk province, 24, 119
KRG. *See* Kurdish Regional Government

Krulak, Charles, 5
Kurdish Regional Government (KRG), 134
Kurds, 54, 119, 134
Kuwait, 2, 9

Lawson, Mike, 6
life support area (LSA), 22, 35, 197
Lockridge, James, 181
loyalty, 10
LSA. *See* life support area

MAAWS. See Money as a Weapon System
MacArthur, Douglas, 18
Mahmoon Palace, Tikrit city, *32*, 33
Main Supply Route (MSR), Tampa, 21, 42
al Maliki, Nuri, 177, 200, 203
McMaster, H. R., 8
media, 91–92, 141–42; warfare and, 3
Menhart, Rich, 99
microgrants, 74, 109, 157, 183
military operations, departure from conventional, 8
military theory, 8
military transition team (MiTT), 12
mine-resistant armored personnel vehicles (MRAPs), 5, 27, 28, 61, 94, 101, 114, 151, 171
mission analysis, 10, 11
mission readiness exercise (MRX), 7, 20
MiTT. *See* military transition team
MNC-I. *See* Multi-National Corps-Iraq
MND-North. *See* Multi-National Division-North
MNF-I. *See* Multi-National Force-Iraq
Mogadishu, Somalia, 3
money, 17, 138; cutting off, to JRTN in ad Dawr city, 176–77; former regime, 15–16; tribes and, 50, 53. *See also* Commander's Emergency Response Program
Money as a Weapon System (*MAAWS*), 17, 138
Moore, Eric, 134, 182

MRAPs. *See* mine-resistant armored personnel vehicles
MRX. *See* mission readiness exercise
MSR. *See* Main Supply Route
al Mua'shit tribe, 52–53
Mujamma housing complex, 27, 72
Mukashifa, 83
Multi-National Corps-Iraq (MNC-I), 14, 51
Multi-National Division-North (MND-North), 14, 24, 31
Multi-National Force-Iraq (MNF-I), 3, 8, 14

al Nammah, 72, 74, 103, 106, 124, 169
National Iraqi Intelligence Agency, 44
National Training Center (NTC), 7, 9, 10, 20
nation building, 17
Native Americans, 17
New Ba'ath Party, 12, 67, 69, 153, 200; Abdullah Hussein al Jebarra al Jibouri and, 181; al Alam al Jibouri tribe and, 181; moving from al Qaeda to JRTN, 68. *See also* Jaysh Rijal al Tariqa al Naqshabandiyah
"New Iraqi Resistance," 60
NTC. *See* National Training Center
nutritionist, 176

Obama, Barack, 12, 131, 199
al Obeidi, Ali, 133, 134
ODA. *See* operational detachment alpha
Odierno, Ray, 14, 138
Ofan, Emad, 200
Office of the Martyr Sadr (OMS), 200
oil profits, 75, 133
Oil Protection Force (OPF), 133
OMS. *See* Office of the Martyr Sadr
"operational design," 8
operational detachment alpha (ODA), US Special Forces, 96–97
Operation Bright Eagle, 107–8; prisoners, 117
Operation Bright Hawk, 116–17

Operation Desert Storm, 21
Operation Miami-Dade, 114–15, 171; prisoners, 116–17
Operation Patriot Falcon, 192–93
Operation Patriot Raptor, 94, 99; execution in ad Dawr city, 101, 103; objective, 100; prisoners, 102; targets in, 95, *96*
Operation Vigilant Patriot, 149; prisoners, 150–51
OPF. *See* Oil Protection Force
Ortega, Spc., 43, 164
al Othaim, 96, 97, 107–8, 134; electric project, 106, 110–11, 127, 139, 160, 163–64, 184; opening of, electric project, 194, *195*, 196
Owja, 26, 31, 51; police, 43, 44

Patrol Base (PB) Woodcock, 27, 28, 47, 63, 85, 121; closure/transfer of, 86–90
patronage network, 16, 24, 183
Payne, Matt, 124, 146, 148, 167, 176
PB. *See* Patrol Base Woodcock
PDOP. *See* provincial director of police
PDSS. *See* predeployment site survey
peacekeeping, 5
Peck, Dan, 54, 55, 81, 146, 167
personnel, 5, 6, 7, 9; rapid turnover of, 4, 10–11. *See also* mine-resistant armored personnel vehicles
Petraeus, David, 1, 2, 3, 8, 143
Philippines, 18
Piatt, Walter, 14, 32
Pick, Tom, 141, 156
PJCC. *See* provincial joint coordination center
police, 63–64, 65; building confidence in, 114; collusion with insurgents, 44; firing Iraqi, 41; inaction of Iraqi, 69; Iraqi, 10, 12, 15, 16, 23, 24, 26, 33, 34, 35, 36, 39, 40, 42–43, 44, 47, 50, 56; non-cooperation of Salah ad Din, 65, 175; Owja, 43, 44; RDU and, authority, 73; US forces and,

99–100. *See also* provincial director of police
populace, 5; addressing grievances of, 2, 3; anger of, 15, 16, 17; as insurgents, 69–70; isolating, from insurgents, 2, 31
Pottinger, Bell, 66
Powell, Colin, 1
Powell Doctrine, 1
predeployment site survey (PDSS), 10
prisoners: Operation Bright Eagle, 117; Operation Miami-Dade, 116–17; Operation Patriot Raptor, 102; Operation Vigilant Patriot, 150–51; release of, 44, 77, 116–17, 146, 171–72
Proud Americans, 6, 7, 8, 10, 12, 14; expansion of, AO, 132–35; focus of, 54; understanding AO of, 22–30. *See also* Task Force Patriot
provincial director of police (PDOP), 65, 84, 95
provincial joint coordination center (PJCC), 46, 47, 75, 88
provincial reconstruction teams (PRTs), 51, 57, 92, 137, 176; CERP and, 20; representative Hall, 181–85, 196–97; in Salah ad Din province, 19–20; in Samarra, 52; security agreement and, 18–19; subordination to, 181–85, 197
public opinion, 3–4

qa'da (district): council, 71, 106, 127, 134, 139. *See also specific districts*
al Qaeda, 12, 25, 34, 51, 56, 82; attacks in Tikrit, 200–201; Bayji Oil Refinery and, 133; in Iraq, 66–67, 68, 187, 200, 203; JRTN and, 66, 179; New Ba'ath Party moving from, to JRTN, 68; power of, 45
al Qaysi, Majid, 88, 89
al Qaysi tribe, 75, 133
quick reaction force (QRF), 56

RDU. *See* Riot Dispersal Unit
Reagan, Ronald, 1

reconstruction, 17, 18. *See also* infrastructure; provincial reconstruction teams
redeployment, 10, 22
Red Lion Battalion, 19
relief in place (RIP), 22; brief to Task Force Wolfhounds, 190, 193–97
rest and relaxation leave (R&R), 106–7
Riggs, Caleb, 85, 145
Riot Dispersal Unit (RDU), 34–35, 39, 43, 63, 75–76; Cain and, 83–85; police authority and, 73
RIP. *See* relief in place
RKG-3s, attack by, 64–65, 149, 170
ROE. *See* rules of engagement
R&R. *See* rest and relaxation leave
rules of engagement (ROE), 102; medical, 81, 150
rural ad Dawr coalition: birth of, 159; building of, 97, 103, 105, 109, 112–13, 123, 129, 136, 138, 140, *142*, 147, 156, 189, 194; end of support for, 196

Sabhan, Director General of Electricity, meeting with, 109–12, 139–40
al Sahra, 21
Salafism, 52
Salah ad Din Company, 87
Salah ad Din province, 9, 11, 13, 15, 21, 41, 52, 132, 140, 200; abu Mazden appointed governor of, 201; airport for, 61; Baghdad and, 55; change of political power in, 201; council, 19, 20, 48, 49, 50, 90, 127, 194, 195, 201; economy of, 153, 154; JRTN in, 70; justice system, 153, 154; non-cooperation of, police, 65, 175; politics, 24–25, 50, 57, 75–76, 90–91; PRTs in, 19–20; removing governor of, 20, 76, 78, 83, 92; Task Force Patriot tasks in, 55; television, 91–92, 141–42; understanding, politics, 183; wealth in, 23
Samander, Mike, 128, 158, 168, 189

al Samarra'i tribes, 51, 136, 200
Samarra *qa'da*, 28, 51, 155, 156–59; PRTs in, 52
SAMS. *See* US Army School of Advanced Military Studies
Sanjuan, Jamie, 145
Sanjuan, Javier, 64
Saulniers, Suzanne, 176
al Sawah ("Awakening" movement), 12, 25, 44–45, 67, 97, 105, 155; Sheikh Sabah and, 130, 158, 159, 186, 187–88
Schofield Barracks, Hawaii, 9, 192
schools, 24, 46, 169, 189
Scout weapon teams (SWTs), 94
Secret Internet Protocol Router Network (SIPRNet), 9–10
security, 5, 25, 33, 47, 54, 55; advising Iraqi, forces, 42; CERP projects and, 29, 64, 183; companies, 21; during elections, 119–21; Iraqi, forces, 12; tribes and, 50, 53
security agreement, 4, 131; PRTs and, 18–19
September 11th, 68
Shar'ia, 51
Sharqat *qa'da*, 106, 137
Sheikh Naqshabandi, 68
sheikhs: of ad Dawr *qa'da*, 155–56; of al Jalaam as Samarra, 156–59; authenticity of, 129; unifying, of ad Dawr *qa'da*, 71–74, 99, 103–6, 109. *See also* rural ad Dawr coalition; *specific sheikhs*
Sheikh Sabah. *See* al Shimiri, Sheikh Sabah Muntasir Diab
Shi'a Islam, 39, 40, 43, 51, 52, 67, 178, 201
al Shimiri, Sheikh Ali Nwaf Diab, 29–30, 63, 72, 176; meeting with, 73–74, 103–5
al Shimiri, Sheikh Sabah Muntasir Diab, 72, 85–86, 123, 127, 157; Abdullah Hussein al Jebarra al Jibouri and, 160, 186–87, 194–96;

arrest of, 185–88; building up, 140–44, 159–60, 162; Cain meeting with, 173–75; compound of, 143, *144*, 170; on FOB Danger, 125, 188; meeting with, 103–6, 109–13, 128–31, 138–39, 155–56, *168*; passions of, 124–26; release of, 188–90; al Sawah and, 130, 158, 159, 186, 187–88; smaller projects with, 166–69; vision of, 126

al Shimiri tribe, 63, 103, 112, 124–25

siding with Americans, benefits of, 24

SIPRNet. *See* Secret Internet Protocol Router Network

Sitze, Will, 134

small arms fire, 26, 27

sniper: attacks, 114, 134, 199; Tikrit, attacks, 149, 151, 174

Song, Peter, 51

Sons of Iraq, 13, 45, 67, 187; employment of, 12, 55, 71, 154

South Vietnam, 4, 6

stability training team (STT), 87

Stars and Stripes, 150

State Department, US, 17, 156; turning war over to, 18–20

State of Law coalition, 177, 200

Steele, Scott, 48, 51, 61, 64, 73, 87, 98

Stewart, David, 20, 137

Stryker Brigade, 7

STT. *See* stability training team

Sufi Islam, 67

suicide vest, 3, 56; attack, 83; attack on al Fahal al Jabouri, 78–79

Sunni Arab Iraq, 11, 12, 24, 51, 55, 134, 203; elections and, 119, 123; reconciliation, 41, 44, 70; unification of, separatists, 67

SWTs. *See* Scout weapon teams

Task Force Black Lions, 6, 94, 95, 106, 132

Task Force Cacti, 11, 28

Task Force Patriot, 6, 34, 35; approach to power change in ad Dawr, 71,

85, 109, 140–44, 147, 154, 155, 179; arriving in Tikrit *qa'da*, 21–22; change in time line for, 106–7; departure of, 200; deployment of, 8, 9; dissention in, 144–48, 190–92; goals of, 12–13, 50; problem statement of, 70–71, 153–56; staff replacement in, 145; tasks in Salah ad Din, 55

Task Force Rangers, 40, 129, 132, 134, 135, 169; deployment of, 106

Task Force Steel, 10, 11, 22, 34, 35, 152

Task Force Wolfhounds, 184, 185, 189; arrival of, 193–94; casualties, 199; RIP brief to, 190, 193–97

Task Force Wolverine, 129, 135, 169; departure of, 181, 183

terrorism, 68; Ba'ath, 39, 40; war on, 4, 201

Tikrit city, 31, 39–41, 47, 51, 55; Mahmoon Palace in, *32*, 33, 107, 120, 149, 175; al Qaeda attacks in, 200–201; sniper attacks in, 149, 151, 174. *See also* joint coordination center

Tikrit *qu'da*, 10, 11, 12, 24, 51, 133; Task Force Patriot's arrival in, 21–22

Tikrit University, 32

TOP. *See* transfer of partnership training, 4, 7, 10, 87

transfer of partnership (TOP), 22, 33; ceremony, 35, *36*, 37; knowledge gap created by, 40

tribal feud, 30, 45–47, 49

tribes: as money-making/security-providing machines, 50, 53; power of, 50; reconciliation of, 30–31. *See also specific tribes*

Triple Canopy, 21

Turner, Skip, 93, 135

Tuz *qa'da*, 11, 106, 134, 181, 185; council, 182, 184

T-wall barriers, 33, 47, 87, 90

unit rotations, problems of, 4

Urban, Jay, 98, 103

US Agency for International
Development (USAID), 18, 156, 176
USAID. *See* US Agency for
International Development
US Army, 2, 7, 8, 14, 15, 201;
administration of, bases, 21;
casualties, 199; transformation of,
5; in 2009, 5, 21; Vietnam War
changing, 1, 3, 4. *See also* US forces
US Army Central Command
(ARCENT), 14
US Army Command and General Staff
College (CGSC), 2, 7
US Army National Guard, 21
US Army School of Advanced Military
Studies (SAMS), 8
US Central Command (CENTCOM),
21
USDA. *See* US Department of
Agriculture
US Department of Agriculture
(USDA), 18, 140–41
US forces: entering Iraq in March 2003,
1, 5; increased violence against, 65;
maintaining, in Iraq, 203; police and,
99–100; reduction of, in Iraq, 4, 12,
131, 199
US Navy explosive ordnance disposal
(EOD), 88

Verdonk, Ron, 141
veterans, 19
Vietnam War, 2; US Army changed by,
1, 3, 4
violence: counterinsurgency and, 93;
increased, against US forces, 65;
JRTN, 149, 151, 170, 171; JRTN,
against Iraqis, 68–69. *See also* attack

war: guerilla, 2, 3, 7; Iraq civil, 52, 70,
201; media and, 3; short, 3; small,
17–18; between Sunni and Kurdish
separatists, 134; on terrorism, 4, 201;
turning, over to State Department,
18–20. *See also specific wars*
Ware, Michael, 75
Warrior Brigade, 197
Waters, Glenn, 22, 35
Weinberger, Caspar, 1
Welte, Simon, 93, 103, 109, 128, 145,
156, 170, 185
Whitehurst, Sam, 28
Wilden, Matthew, 145, 190, 192
Word War I, 17
World War II, 17, 18; post, 2
wounded, treatment of, 81–82

Yoder, Barbara, 19, 78, 92, 137, 176
Yousef, Ammar, 201

About the Author

Pat Proctor is a US Army field artillery lieutenant colonel with over seventeen years of active service. In 2007, he served in Iraq as a member of General Petraeus' and Ambassador Crocker's Joint Strategic Assessment Team, mapping the future for postsurge Iraq. Pat returned for a second tour, in Northern Iraq, as a battalion operations officer in the 1st Infantry Division. He holds two master's degrees, a master's of military arts and sciences for strategy from the US Army Command and General Staff College and a master's of military arts and sciences for theater operations from the School of Advanced Military Studies. He is currently the chief of plans for the 1st Infantry Division and a doctoral student in history at Kansas State University. Pat's recent publications include "Message versus Perception during the Americanization of the Vietnam War" (*The Historian*, Spring 2011); "Fighting to Understand: A Practical Example of Design at the Battalion Level" (*Military Review*, March–April 2011); and "The Mythical Shi'a Crescent" (*Parameters*, Spring 2008, and *Iran International Times*, 23 May 2008).